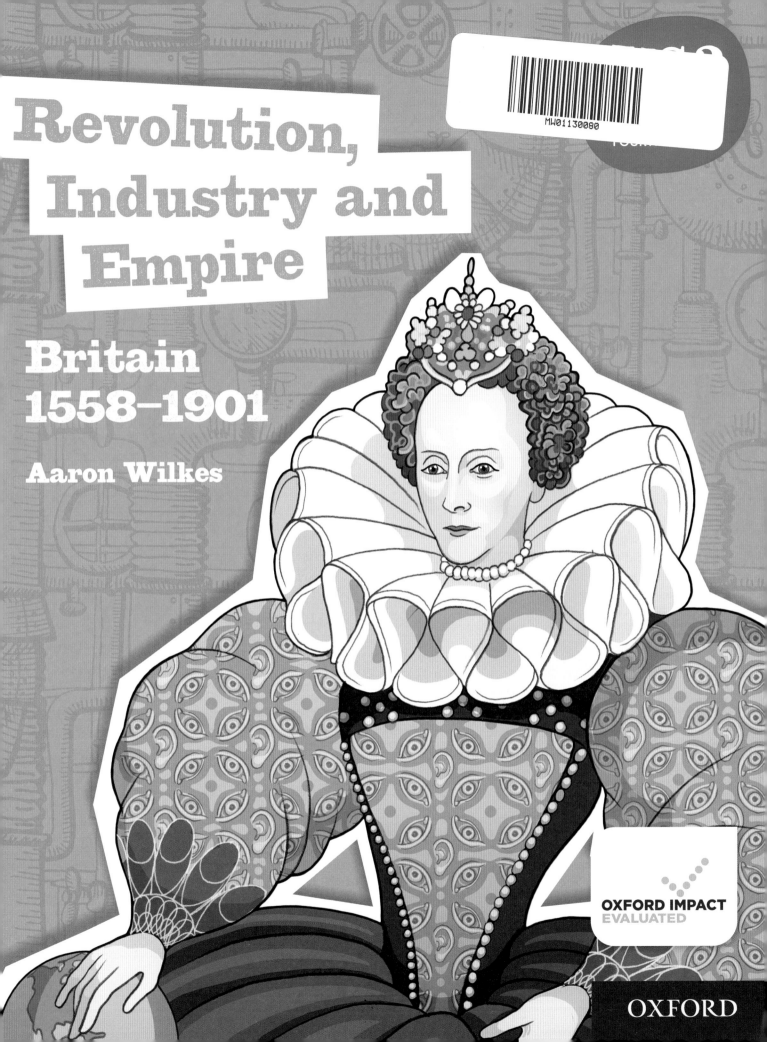

Revolution, Industry and Empire

Britain 1558–1901

Aaron Wilkes

OXFORD

Oxford Impact Evaluated

Contents

Contents

Introducing KS3 History Fourth Edition

So what is history?

History is about what happened in the past. It's about people in the past, what they did and why they did it, and what they felt. To enjoy history you need to be able to imagine what life was like long ago, or what it may have been like to be involved in past events.

How does this book fit in?

This book will get you thinking. You will be asked to look at different pieces of evidence and to try to work things out for yourself. Sometimes, two pieces of evidence about the same event won't agree with each other. You might be asked to think of reasons why that is. Your answers might not be the same as your friend's or even your teacher's. This is OK. The important thing is to give *reasons* for your thoughts and ideas.

How to use this book

Features of the Student Book are explained here and on the opposite page.

Kerboodle support

Kerboodle provides digital Lessons, Resources and Assessment for the classroom and at home. This book contains icons that highlight some of the digital resources available:

- Animation
- Film clip
- Assessment presentation
- Knowledge organiser

Key to features

Objectives All lessons in this book start by setting you objectives. These are your key aims that set out your learning targets for the work ahead.

History Skills These activities test a range of history skills, so each box has its own title. The tasks will challenge you to think a little deeper about what you have been studying. These are also important skills to develop if you are going to study GCSE History.

Over to You This is your opportunity to demonstrate your knowledge, and your understanding, of history skills. In each box the tasks become progressively more challenging.

Meanwhile... 1670 This gives you an idea of what else is going on in the world (perhaps in another country on a different continent) at the same sort of time as the period you are studying in the lesson.

Earlier on... and Later on... 1700 You will be challenged to think how the topic you are studying relates to events, people, ideas or developments that may have happened many years before... or might connect to things in the future.

Key Words These are important words and terms that are vital to help you understand the topics. You can spot them easily because they are in bold red type. Look up their meanings in the glossary at the back of the book.

Fact ✓ These are funny, fascinating and amazing little bits of history that you don't usually get to hear about! They're important because they give you insights into topics that you'll easily remember.

History Mystery These sections give you an opportunity to pull all your skills together and investigate a controversial, challenging or intriguing aspect of history, such as assessing whether the Gunpowder Plotters were framed or investigating why the police failed to catch Jack the Ripper.

Depth Study In each book, there is a depth study that focuses on an important event, person or development. This gives you the chance to extend and deepen your understanding of key moments in history.

Literacy and Numeracy

Throughout the book you will see icons like these when a task is particularly focused on your literacy or numeracy skills.

Have you been learning?

There are different types of assessments at the end of every chapter. These are opportunities for you to showcase what you have learned and to put your ability to recall key information and history skills to the test.

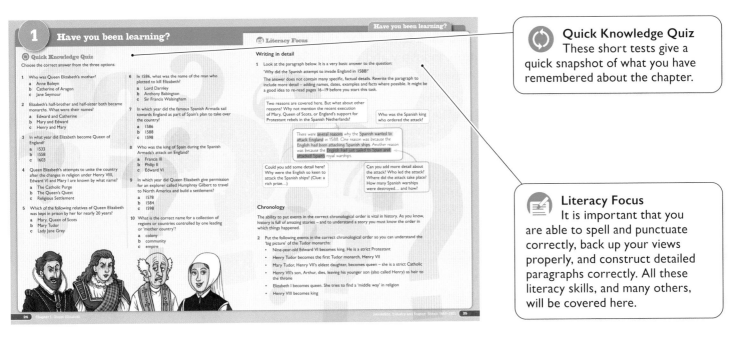

Quick Knowledge Quiz
These short tests give a quick snapshot of what you have remembered about the chapter.

Literacy Focus
It is important that you are able to spell and punctuate correctly, back up your views properly, and construct detailed paragraphs correctly. All these literacy skills, and many others, will be covered here.

History skills assessments

The assessments at the end of each chapter are designed to help you improve the way you think about history, write about history and apply your historical knowledge when you are being assessed. These step-by-step guides will help you write clear, focused answers to some challenging history questions. These concepts and skills are essential if you wish to go on to study History at a higher level, so by tackling these you are giving yourself a good foundation in history.

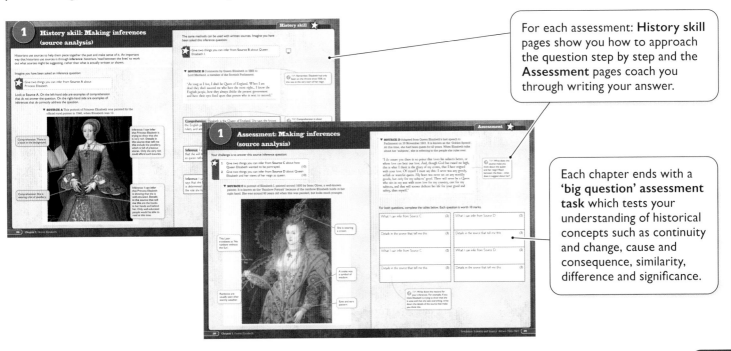

For each assessment: **History skill** pages show you how to approach the question step by step and the **Assessment** pages coach you through writing your answer.

Each chapter ends with a **'big question' assessment task** which tests your understanding of historical concepts such as continuity and change, cause and consequence, similarity, difference and significance.

Timeline from 1558 to 1901

Periods of time in History

This book covers the years 1558 to 1901 – a time famous for civil war, conspiracy, rebellion, plague, fire, revolution, industry and empire. Several periods in British history are covered:

The late Tudor period (1558–1603):
This book begins in 1558, the year Henry VIII's youngest daughter (Elizabeth) became queen. She remained queen for 44 years. This is a time when Spain tried to invade England, when Shakespeare wrote his plays, and when English explorers and traders visited distant lands and tried to establish settlements there.

The Stuart period (1603–1714):
The Stuart royal family reigned. Events such as the Gunpowder Plot, the English Civil War, the Great Plague, the Great Fire and the Glorious Revolution took place. In this period a king was executed – and for a short time, the country didn't have a monarch!

The Georgian period (1714–1830s):
A series of kings named George (and one named William!) ruled after the Stuart period. This was a time of rebellion (by the Scots) and great changes both in politics and in the way in which people lived and worked.

The Victorian era (1837–1901):
Victoria became queen in 1837 and ruled until her death in 1901. During her reign, Britain's empire grew to be the largest the world had ever known. This was a time of great political, economic, medical and social change.

1803–1815
Napoleonic Wars between France and other nations, including Britain

1796
Edward Jenner first uses vaccination

Look at the timeline on these pages carefully. It highlights some of the big events, significant people, new ideas, changes and discoveries that took place at this time.

1789
The French Revolution begins

1558
Elizabeth I begins her 44-year reign

c.1591
First performance of a Shakespeare play

1605
Guy Fawkes and the Gunpowder Plotters try to blow up Parliament

1649
Charles I is executed

1660
Restoration of the monarchy under Charles II

1588
The English defeat the Spanish Armada

1603
James VI of Scotland becomes James I of England too and unites the two kingdoms

1642
The English Civil War begins

1649–1660
Parliament, followed by Oliver Cromwell, rules instead of a monarch

1870
Elementary Education Act gives school places to all children

1832
The first Reform Act gives the vote to more men in Britain

1837
Victoria becomes queen

1901
Queen Victoria dies

1876
Telephone invented by Alexander Graham Bell

1859
Charles Darwin publishes *On the Origin of Species*

1833
Slavery ends in the British Empire

1825
First public railway journey

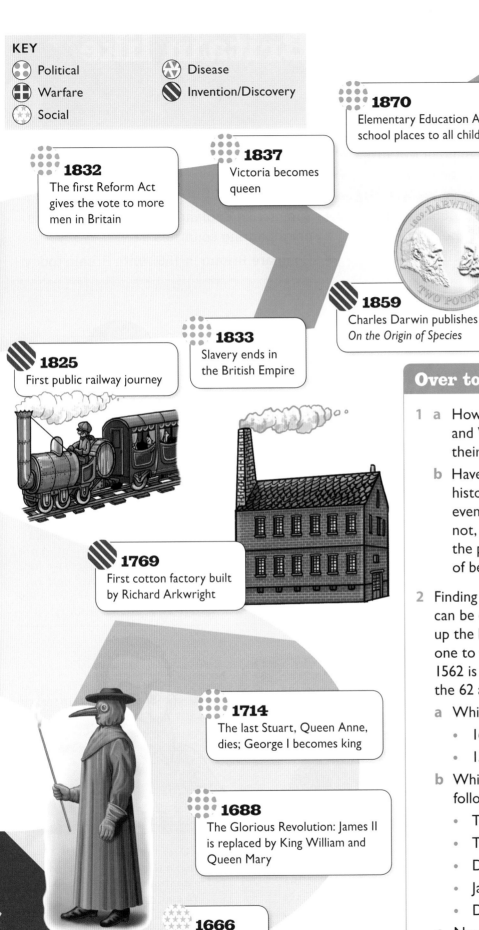

1769
First cotton factory built by Richard Arkwright

1714
The last Stuart, Queen Anne, dies; George I becomes king

1688
The Glorious Revolution: James II is replaced by King William and Queen Mary

1666
The Great Fire of London

1665
The Great Plague

Over to You ▂▄▆

1 a How do the Tudor, Stuart, Georgian and Victorian periods of history get their names?

   b Have you studied any of these periods of history before? If so, make a list of the events and people you can remember. If not, look through the timeline and list the people and events you have heard of before.

2 Finding out which year is in which century can be difficult. The easiest way is to cover up the last two numbers in the year and add one to the first two numbers. For example, 1562 is in the sixteenth century (cover up the 62 and add one to 15 to make 16).

   a Which century are the following years in?

- 1649
- 1707
- 1558
- 1837

   b Which century were each of the following events in?

- The Glorious Revolution
- The Great Fire of London
- Death of Queen Victoria
- James I/VI unites Scotland and England
- Defeat of the Spanish Armada

   c Now put the five events above in the correct chronological order (the order in which they happened, from first to last).

1.1 What was Britain like in 1558?

This book is about the people and events of Britain between 1558 and 1901, a time of great change. For you to see how important these changes were, you must first find out about Britain in 1558. Then, towards the end of this book, you will be asked to compare the Britain of 1558 with the Britain of 1901.

Objectives

- Examine what Britain was like in 1558.
- Summarise England's relationship with its neighbouring countries.
- Compare Britain in 1558 with Britain today.

Queen Elizabeth I

I am Elizabeth, the new queen. I am the youngest daughter of Henry VIII. My older sister, Mary, was queen before me. I have some major challenges ahead of me — for example, I am unmarried but my advisers want me to have a child who can rule after me. There are also major religious issues to deal with.

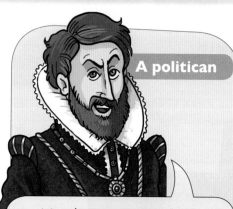

A politican

We politicians are very busy. In *Parliament*, we pass laws and collect taxes. The queen must get our agreement if she wants any tax money, so we can be quite powerful at times.

A Privy Council Member

I belong to a group of trusted advisers to the queen, known as the Privy Council. Many of us are powerful landowners and we help the queen deal with almost any issue — war, religion, and even her own personal security.

A priest

Religion is a very important part of people's lives. But in recent years this country has been in religious turmoil — it was a Catholic country during the first part of Henry VIII's reign, then it became a Protestant country, then, most recently, it has been Catholic again. Our new queen is a Protestant — will she try to end the religious conflict?

A Scottish woman

England and Scotland are separate countries. We have our own queen, Mary. The English and the Scots have fought a lot over the years, and I think of the English as the 'old enemy'. There are about half a million Scots.

An Irish chief

Over the years, English kings and queens have tried to control us but have failed to gain complete control. However, the new queen calls herself the 'Queen of Ireland' as well as England. About 800,000 people live here.

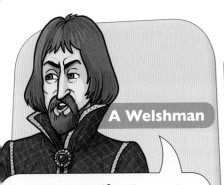

A Welshman

Henry VIII officially joined Wales with England and now Wales is controlled by government officials in England. There are about 250,000 people in Wales.

Communication: Mainly by word of mouth, but books were becoming popular

Food and drink: British people had a basic diet

Homes: The rich lived in large, impressive, brick-built homes; the poor lived in small, thatched-roof cottages

Transport: The rich travelled on horseback and by cart, while the poor walked. Roads were in very poor condition

Britain in 1558

Rulers: England and Scotland had their own monarchs – Queen Elizabeth of England, Ireland (and Wales), and Queen Mary of Scotland

Clothing: A person's clothes were a sign of their status; only the very wealthy wore expensive fabrics

The known world: North and South America, Europe, the east and west coasts of Africa, India and the east coast of China were known to Europeans

Religion: There was one common religion – Christianity – but there were two main branches. Catholics agreed that the head of the Church was the Pope, while Protestants agreed that the head of the Church was the monarch

A student

I am a student at the University of Oxford. We live in exciting times. New printed books spread ideas about art, medicine and religion. Some of the ideas of the ancient Greeks and Romans have been published too. I have heard that the new queen is very clever – I wonder if the Renaissance will continue?

Fact ✓

There were about 8 million sheep in Britain in the 1500s and only around 5 million people! Sheep were kept mainly to supply the cloth industry – Britain's most important industry. Other industries included mining for iron, tin and lead, and shipbuilding.

Over to You

1 Write out the paragraph below, choosing one answer from each pair in brackets.

   In 1558, the new Queen of England was (Elizabeth/Mary). She also controlled (Wales/Scotland) and large parts of Ireland. (Wales/Scotland) was an independent country. Some land was used for (fishing/farming) but most of it was (woodland/Disneyland). Nine out of (ten/nine) people lived in the (towns/countryside) and grew their own food. If they grew (more/less) than they needed, they might go and sell it at the local (supermarket/market).

2 Draw a bar chart to show the population of England, Scotland, Ireland and Wales in 1558. Make sure you add a title.

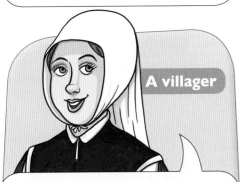

A villager

Like most of the population, we are poor and live in the countryside. Some of the land is used for growing crops or grazing sheep, but most is woodland. We live on what we grow. If we grow more than we need, we sell it at the local market in the nearest town. Most towns are still quite small but a few are growing fast. Only 10 per cent of people live in towns. There are about 3.5 million people living in England now.

Change and Continuity ⭐

1 Divide a page into two columns. Write 'Britain in 1558' at the top of one column and 'Britain today' at the top of the other. List all the ways in which Britain in 1558 was different from Britain today.

2 Explain two ways in which Britain in 1558 and Britain today are different.

1.2 Young Elizabeth: what was she like?

In 1533, King Henry's second wife, Anne Boleyn, announced she was pregnant. The king desperately wanted a son who could be king after him. He already had one daughter, Mary, but wanted a male heir to carry on the Tudor line, as a daughter's claim to the throne could be more easily challenged. On 7 September 1533, Princess Elizabeth Tudor was born. Henry was very disappointed. But he soon came to realise Elizabeth had many strengths.

Objectives

- Identify why Princess Elizabeth was such an able student.
- Examine the circumstances in which she became queen.

Elizabeth was two years old when her mother was executed. She never lived with her father, who had four wives after Anne, but was sent to live with her half-sister, Mary. The girls had three houses: Hatfield and Eltham, near London, and Hunsdon House in Hertfordshire. When they travelled between each house, they would fight over who would walk at the front of the procession. It doesn't appear to have been an easy life for young Elizabeth: a dead mother, a tough father, a half-sister and lots of stepmothers. And when her half-brother Edward was born in 1537, it didn't look like she would ever be queen!

But despite some difficulties in her life, Princess Elizabeth had one major factor in her favour – she was clever. By the time she was sixteen, she could speak five languages – English, French, Italian, Greek and Latin. So what was the secret of her success? Study the cartoons and the sources carefully.

Secret of her success No. 1: She enjoyed learning

Elizabeth had her own personal tutors and enjoyed working hard at her lessons. It was very fashionable at the time for rich young women to be highly educated and Elizabeth loved writing poems, translating foreign books and learning new languages.

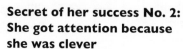

Secret of her success No. 2: She got attention because she was clever

King Henry was disappointed when Elizabeth was born but soon grew to love spending time with his clever daughter. When Henry visited Elizabeth, her half-sister was probably very jealous. Mary was often kept away in a separate room while the king and his youngest daughter chatted, swapped gifts and sang together.

Secret of her success No. 3: She was lonely

Elizabeth didn't really have any close friends. But reading books and learning new skills meant that she could talk about these things with people. People weren't going to voice their real opinions about the country to the king's daughter, but they might be honest about their views on books, music and horses.

Secret of her success No. 4: There wasn't much else to do

There was no television, radio or Internet in Tudor times. Books, music and horse riding provided entertainment for her – and she seemed to be very good at many of the things she tried.

▼ **A** Elizabeth had a very full timetable when she was being taught by one of her tutors.

Monday	Tuesday	Wednesday	Thursday	Friday
Bible study	Bible study	Bible study	Bible study	Bible study
Book translation: Greek to English	Book translation: English to Greek	Book translation: Latin to English	Book translation: English to Latin	Philosophy
Lunchtime – Food – Walking – Riding – Games				
French conversation	Italian conversation	Latin conversation	English conversation	Greek conversation
Philosophy	Book translation: Latin to English	Book translation: English to Latin	Book translation: Greek to English	Book translation: English to Greek

Elizabeth was 13 in 1547 when her father died and her younger half-brother, Edward, became king (aged 9). Although she was quite close to Edward, many people suspected she might be plotting against him during his short reign (he died aged 15, in 1533). However, nothing could ever be proved against her.

When her older half-sister, Mary, became queen in 1553, Elizabeth was again suspected of plotting against the monarch – and again nothing could be proved. To be on the safe side, Mary kept Elizabeth like a prisoner at various country houses.

Five years later, in 1558, Elizabeth received word that her sister, Queen Mary, was dead. Aged 25, Elizabeth was now Queen of England.

▼ **SOURCE B** In this portrait, painted by the official royal painter in 1546, Elizabeth was aged 13.

▼ **SOURCE C** Adapted from a letter written by one of her tutors, Robert Ascham, to a friend of his. Ascham was Elizabeth's tutor between 1548 and 1550. At this time, women were often viewed as less important than men.

'She is most eager. Her mind has no womanly weakness; her perseverance is equal to that of a man and she has a long memory. She talks French and Italian as well as English, and has often talked to me in Latin and Greek. She has beautiful handwriting and is a skilful musician.'

Over to You

1 What difficulties did Elizabeth face in her early life?

2 Look carefully at Elizabeth's timetable (**A**) on this page.

   a Explain why you think the following subjects take up so much of Elizabeth's study time:
   - Bible study
   - Conversation
   - Learning and translating foreign languages.

   b Think of three subjects that you study at school that are not on Elizabeth's timetable. Why do you think it is important that you study them?

3 Imagine you are one of Princess Elizabeth's tutors. Write a summary for King Henry about his daughter's education. It should include details about:

   a her lessons   b her strengths
   c her attitude towards learning.

Source Analysis

1 Look at **Source B**. Describe the painting in detail.

2 Give two things you can infer from **Source B** about Princess Elizabeth.

1.3 Queen Elizabeth's 'middle way'

When Elizabeth's brother (Edward VI) was king, England became a strict Protestant country. When he died, his half-sister Mary, who was a strict Catholic, became queen. England became a Catholic country once more under Mary – and she was very harsh on any Protestants who refused to become Catholics. So when Elizabeth became queen in 1558, which faith did she follow? What changes did she make? And what did her arrival on the throne mean for the way people worshipped God in England?

Objectives

- Analyse how Elizabeth tried to end religious chaos in Tudor England.

- Explain the consequences of Elizabeth's 'middle way'.

The religious settlement

Elizabeth was a Protestant – and she decided to return the country to the Protestant faith once more. However, she knew she had to find a solution to the religious chaos that had taken place during the reigns of Edward and Mary.

Elizabeth was deeply religious, but wanted to avoid some of the more extreme events that had happened during the reign of her Protestant half-brother Edward and her Catholic half-sister Mary. That way, she hoped she would please most people and keep the country peaceful. Her ideas were known as her **Religious Settlement**. It is also known as her 'middle way' – in other words, it was a course of action that avoided being totally Catholic or totally Protestant.

The middle way

1 Elizabeth made herself Governor (not Head) of the Church of England in order to please the Catholics. This meant that Catholics – if they wanted to – could still think of the Pope as Head of the Church.

2 Priests were allowed to marry to please the Protestants (this was not allowed under Catholic Queen Mary's reign) and a revised prayer book replaced the one from Edward's reign that was so hated by Catholics.

3 Catholics believed that bishops should have an important role in controlling the Church. Elizabeth kept the bishops – but they were under her control. Church services and the Bible were in English, which pleased Protestants.

4 The Catholic service from Queen Mary's reign was changed, to please Protestants. Strict Catholics, who didn't want to attend the new services, weren't severely punished. However, they had to pay a fine for staying at home (these people were known as **recusants**).

Did the 'middle way' work?

Although it pleased many people, **extremists** on both sides were left deeply unhappy by Elizabeth's ideas. Very strict Protestants, known as **Puritans**, didn't want to compromise with Catholics. They wanted to remove all trace of the Catholic faith in England. Strict Catholics believed that the Protestants were a danger to religion and 'damning the whole country to hell'. The Catholic Pope (Pius V) called Elizabeth a 'pretend' queen, and **excommunicated** her. He also ordered the people of England not to obey her. This made it very difficult for Elizabeth to trust Catholics, as any one of them could be **plotting** her death. As a result, she decided to make life a little tougher for Catholics.

The Catholic clampdown

Elizabeth's chief spy, Sir Francis Walsingham, used secret agents to keep a close eye on important Catholics. In the 1580s, new laws were passed that meant that Catholic priests could now be tried and executed. In 1581, the fine recusants had to pay was heavily increased to force them to leave the country, but instead many ran out of money and were thrown in prison. Despite the threat of execution, many Catholic priests continued to hold their Catholic services in secret. To avoid capture and punishment, some priests were hidden in 'priest holes' (see **C**) when officials came looking for them. But Elizabeth's long reign of 44 years meant that there was no Catholic comeback and the Protestant faith was firmly established. The UK still remains officially a Protestant country.

▼ **SOURCE A** From the statement read out in Parliament after Elizabeth's coronation in 1559. Queen Elizabeth was there, but this statement was read out by a member of her personal court.

> '[The Queen's aim is] to secure and unite the people of this realm in one uniform order to the glory of God and to general tranquillity'.

▼ **INTERPRETATION B**
Adapted from the Royal Greenwich museums website describing Elizabeth's aims when she became queen. The 'statement' mentioned is the one in **Source A**.

> 'The message was very clear: that they were all, including Elizabeth, members of the same team, working together for a common goal – that of a united, prosperous England. Extremes were to be avoided in order to unite, not divide. In this statement, Elizabeth very deliberately disassociated herself from the unpopularity of Mary's regime by signalling how hers would be different.'

Key Words

excommunicate   extremist
plot   Puritan   recusant
Religious Settlement

▼ **SOURCE C** This secret priest hole is in Harvington Hall, Kidderminster.

Over to You

1 Look at **Source C**.
   a What was a priest hole?
   b Why were they needed?

2 Write two lists: one headed 'Actions that pleased Catholics', the other one headed 'Actions that pleased Protestants'.

3 a Why do you think Elizabeth's actions are often called the 'middle way'?
   b Did Elizabeth's middle way work? Write a paragraph explaining your answer.

Interpretation Analysis

1 In **Interpretation B**, the author argues that uniting the country was Elizabeth's main aim. Identify and explain one way in which the author does this.

Depth Study

1.4 Why did Queen Elizabeth kill her cousin?

By 1568, Elizabeth had been queen for ten years. She hadn't married and had no children. This meant that if she died, her cousin, Mary, Queen of Scotland, would become Queen of England and Wales too.

Objectives

- Examine the threat posed by Mary, Queen of Scots.
- Discover the events surrounding the Babington Plot.

Mary in France and Scotland

Mary had been Queen of Scotland from the age of six days old, after her father (James V of Scotland) died in 1542. She was too young to rule so her mother and other important Scottish nobles ruled in her place. She was brought up as a Catholic and married several times – firstly to a French king in 1558 (who died tragically young), then to an English lord in 1565 (who was strangled to death and blown up) and then, in 1567, she married the man (Earl Bothwell) who was suspected of being involved in the murder of her second husband!

Mary in England

Many Scots were suspicious of Mary's connection to her second husband's death, and some rebelled against her. She was forced to give up the throne and her young son (James VI) was made King of Scotland. In 1568, she ran away to England, perhaps hoping that her cousin Queen Elizabeth would take pity on her.

Mary immediately caused problems for Elizabeth. For a start, she was Catholic, and made no secret of the fact that she thought she should be Queen of England if Elizabeth died. Some English Catholics agreed with Mary. Elizabeth's solution was harsh – she kept Mary a prisoner until she could decide what to do with her. Mary was imprisoned in various houses and castles for the next 19 years, and the two women never actually met. Eventually, Elizabeth was forced to take action against Mary when she discovered that Mary was involved in a plot to kill her.

The Babington Plot

In 1586, a young, rich Catholic called Anthony Babington came up with a secret plan to kill Elizabeth. He would organise six men to kill her, rescue Mary from her prison and make her the new Queen of England. However, Babington needed to know if Mary liked the idea. He needed to contact her in prison.

Secret letters

Babington managed to get Mary's servants to hide secret letters in beer barrels that were taken to her room. The letters were written in code. Mary wrote back saying she agreed to the plan (see **A**). However, Mary's servants worked for England's chief spy, Sir Francis Walsingham, who took the letters straight to Elizabeth. When the code was broken, the message was clear: Mary was supporting a plan to kill the queen. This was **treason**.

▼ **A** This is the part of Mary's letter that led to her **execution**. It was written in code, but Walsingham had the key to break it. This has been included here – can you work out what she wrote? What does she mean?

KEY

A	B	C	D	E	F	G	H	I	J	K	L	M	N	O	P	Q	R	S	T	U

V	W	X	Y	Z	AND	FOR	THAT	OF	THE	ME	REPEAT LETTER

USED TO CONFUSE:

Killing her cousin

Key Words death warrant execution treason

Despite all the evidence against Mary, Elizabeth didn't want to execute her cousin. Eventually, in February 1587, her secretary William Davison slipped the **death warrant** in among some papers she had to sign. Elizabeth pretended she didn't really know what she was signing, signed it, changed her mind, then tried to stop the execution. But she was too late. Mary, Queen of Scots, had already been executed (see **B** and **C**).

▼ **SOURCE B** A 1589 picture of the execution of Mary, Queen of Scots, in February 1587.

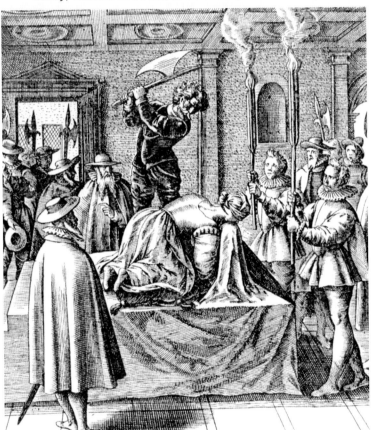

▼ **SOURCE C** Adapted from a report sent to Elizabeth's ministers by Robert Wynkfield, who witnessed the execution in 1587.

'After her prayers, the executioners asked Mary to forgive them her death. She said "I forgive you with all my heart, for I hope you shall make an end of all my troubles.'

Then, one of the women placed a cloth over the Queen of Scots' face. Mary knelt down on a cushion, without fear, and said a prayer out loud in Latin. She quietly laid down her head and stretched out her arms and cried "Into thy hands, O Lord" three or four times.

One of the executioners held her and she endured two strokes of the axe from the other executioner. She made no noise.

The executioner lifted up her head and said "God save the Queen". The wig fell off, showing that her hair was as grey as someone of 70 years old. Her lips continued to move for a quarter of an hour after her head was cut off. Then one of the executioners noticed her little dog hidden under her clothes. Afterwards, it would not leave the body and lay down between her head and her shoulders and was stained with her blood.'

Over to You

1 Create a timeline to show the main events in Mary's life.

2 Why did Elizabeth imprison Mary in England?

3 a Explain how Elizabeth found out about the Babington Plot and arranged to trap Mary.

   b Why do you think Elizabeth hesitated over her decision to have Mary executed?

4 Using the code in **A**, write out three facts about Mary's life. Make each one short and simple. Pass your coded facts to a friend and see if they can work out what you have written.

Source Analysis

1 Look at **Sources B** and **C**.
   a Describe in detail the scene shown in **Source B**.
   b Make a list of words you might use to describe Mary.

2 How useful are **Sources B** and **C** to a historian studying the execution of Mary, Queen of Scots?

1.5A Match of the day: England versus Spain

In Tudor times, Spain was the richest, most powerful country in the world. It had a huge army and Spanish ships were bringing a fortune in gold back to Spain from newly discovered lands. But in 1588, Spain's King Philip II decided to focus all his country's great power and wealth on one thing – the invasion of England. Every shipyard in Spain began building what many described as the greatest navy – or **Armada** – ever created. This massive fleet of 130 huge warships was heading for one place – England. What was Philip's invasion plan? And how successful was it?

Objectives

- Examine why the King of Spain decided to invade England in 1588.
- Compare the strengths and weaknesses of England and Spain's navies.
- Judge key reasons why the Spanish Armada failed.

Why was Philip angry with England?

On 20 April 1587, Philip received some shattering news. The most famous English explorer of the time, Sir Francis Drake, had just sailed into Cadiz harbour in southern Spain and set fire to 30 of Spain's royal warships. Philip was furious – *and* he had other reasons to be angry with the English.

- For many years, English sailors had been stealing gold and silver from Spanish ships.

- Philip (a Catholic) had heard that Mary, Queen of Scots (another Catholic) had been executed by England's queen, Elizabeth I. He thought that the people who had killed a Catholic queen should be punished. He had started to build ships that could carry soldiers to invade England – it was these ships that Drake had destroyed.

- At this time, the Spanish Netherlands (now known as Belgium and Luxembourg) were controlled by Spain. But many people who lived there didn't want this and rebelled against Spanish control. The rebels were being helped by soldiers from England.

Attack

By the summer of 1588, Philip's forces had recovered from Drake's attack on Cadiz and Philip had assembled one of the greatest fleets of warships the world had ever seen. The Spanish Armada had 130 ships, many painted red and gold, which together covered an area of

about 12km² of sea. Philip's plan for the fleet was simple: meet his soldiers at Calais on the northern coast of France, transport them over the English Channel to invade England, and remove Elizabeth from the throne. Philip would then become King of Spain *and* England.

But England had a navy too, and despite the fact that King Philip had the support of some English Catholics, Queen Elizabeth knew that most people were prepared to fight to the death to defend the country against the Spanish invaders. Read the information on these pages carefully and judge how the two sides might match up against each other.

▼ **INTERPRETATION A** A British stamp issued in 1988 to commemorate the four hundredth anniversary of the Armada. It shows a Spanish ship on its way to invade England.

ARMADA · LIZARD · 19 JULY 1588

Key Words   armada   galleon   musket

> The English have a strong navy – about 130 ships – but only 60 or so are fit to fight. The Spanish galleons are about 50m long, and the English ones are about half that length, so they are much quicker. They have two other advantages: first, they have some of the most accurate long-range guns ever built, and second, most of them use the same standard size cannonballs. Spanish ships have guns of different sizes and types, and finding the right size of cannonball for each gun during the heat of battle must be tricky!

> The Spanish have a fantastic fleet and they're confident that they'll beat the English. They even call themselves the 'invincible Armada'. They do have a problem, though. Their commander, the Duke of Medina Sidonia, suffers from seasickness. Can you believe that? A seasick sea captain!

ENGLAND

NO. OF SHIPS:	5/10
LENGTH OF SHIPS:	5/10
MOBILITY:	7/10
NO. OF SAILORS:	8/10
WEAPONS:	9/10

ABILITY OF COMMANDERS (LORD HOWARD AND SIR FRANCIS DRAKE): 8.5/10

The English are 'speedy smashers'. Their experienced sailors should be able to steer their ships to avoid the Spanish getting alongside. Instead, they will hope to position their ships about 150m away and use their superior guns to fire huge solid 20kg cannonballs through the side of the enemy ships. Then the smaller cannons known as 'man killers' will fire 8kg balls at the sailors. When the Spanish ships are floating wrecks packed with battered and tired soldiers, the English will hop on board and finish them off.

The ideal battle position for the English – with the English galleon (right) at a distance from the enemy.

SPAIN

NUMBER OF SHIPS:	7.5/10
LENGTH OF SHIPS:	9/10
MOBILITY:	3/10
NO. OF SAILORS:	8.5/10
WEAPONS:	6/10
ABILITY OF COMMANDER (THE DUKE OF MEDINA SIDONIA):	3.5/10

The Spanish are 'ropers and raiders'. Their ships are like huge floating castles, but are clumsy to steer. So the Spanish **galleons** will try to sail next to the enemy ships and tie themselves alongside with ropes and hooks. Then soldiers will jump onto the enemy ships and fight with swords, daggers and **muskets**. The heavy guns below decks will almost touch the other ships and will blow holes in their sides.

The ideal battle position for the Spanish – with the Spanish galleon (on the left) tied closely to the enemy ship.

Similarity and Difference

1. In your own words, describe how either an English or a Spanish ship's captain would try to defeat an enemy.

2. In your opinion, which fleet of ships, the English or the Spanish, stood the better chance of success? Explain your answer carefully.

3. Explain two ways in which Spain's fleet and England's fleet were different.

Over to You

1. Give one long-term cause and one short-term cause of Philip's planned attack on England.

2. What was his plan if his invasion was a success?

So what happened next?

King Philip's plan was for his fleet of 130 ships to sail up the English Channel to Calais and pick up Spanish soldiers waiting there. Then around 30,000 soldiers and sailors would cross the Channel, and capture London and Queen Elizabeth.

The Armada left Spain on 22 July 1588, but it was immediately spotted by a fast sailing boat heading for England. News that the Spanish were on their way reached England long before they arrived! Look at the cartoon and **Map B** to find out the rest of this amazing story.

1 130 Spanish ships set out, sailing close together in a **crescent** shape, which the English would find difficult to attack.

2 The Spanish are spotted off Cornwall on 29 July and **beacons** are lit on hilltops to warn people of a possible invasion. The English Navy chases the Spaniards for over a week but cannot sink a single Spanish ship.

3 The Spanish arrive in Calais, France, on 6 August. They wait for Spanish soldiers to join them but the soldiers are delayed.

4 Sir Francis Drake attacks the Spanish ships with the weapon they fear the most – fireships. Eight old ships are filled with straw, gunpowder, tar and barrels of pig fat and then set alight. They act like floating bombs and drift towards the Spanish, who panic when they see them.

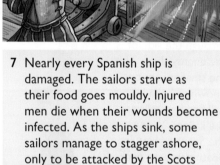

5 Frightened by the fireships, the Spanish ships scatter in ones and twos, over the North Sea. The fast English ships keep attacking.

6 The Spaniards flee north, towards Scotland. A sudden storm batters their ships as they struggle home around Scotland and Ireland.

7 Nearly every Spanish ship is damaged. The sailors starve as their food goes mouldy. Injured men die when their wounds become infected. As the ships sink, some sailors manage to stagger ashore, only to be attacked by the Scots and Irish.

▼ **MAP B** The route taken by the Spanish Armada in 1588. Only 67 ships made it back to Spain.

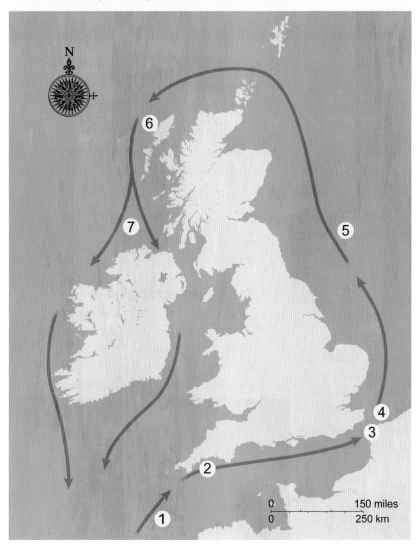

Key Words

beacon   colony
crescent   empire

▼ **INTERPRETATION C** From a book called *Elizabeth I and Tudor England* by Stephen White-Thomson (1984).

'The Spanish plan misfired for a number of reasons. The English were better sailors. Their ships were slightly smaller, could sail faster and had heavier firepower. The English also had better leaders. Lord Howard of Effingham and Sir Francis Drake were excellent commanders. The Spanish leader was the Duke of Medina Sidonia. He was seasick as soon as his flagship put out to sea. He was no match for his English rivals.'

Over to You

1 Sketch a map of the route taken by the Spanish Armada in 1588. Label your map with brief sentences, highlighting the most important events of the Armada's journey.

2 The following are all reasons why the Spanish Armada failed: bad weather; fireships; faster English ships; good English leadership; delay of Spanish soldiers at Calais.

   a Write down any other reasons you can think of.

   b Put all the reasons for the Spanish failure in order, starting with the most important.

   c Explain your choice of order.

3 Explain two consequences of the failed Spanish invasion of England in 1588.

Interpretation Analysis

1 Read **Interpretation C**. Summarise the reasons the author gives for the failure of the Spanish Armada.

2 How far do you agree with **Interpretation C** about the failure of the Spanish Armada?

Consequences of the failure of the Spanish Armada

- It showed that Queen Elizabeth could govern England in times of war, as well as peace.

- Elizabeth believed her island was safe from attack – but should always have a strong navy to protect it. She began to build up the navy and soon it would begin to venture out in search of valuable new land all over the world. In time, England would create **colonies** and trading companies that marked the start of the British **Empire**.

- For many Protestants in England (and in other places around the world) it made them believe that God was on their side. Catholicism became increasingly unpopular and was viewed as anti-English.

- Spain's failure proved that Spain was beatable. Spanish kings could no longer do as they wished.

1.6 Britain begins to build an empire

A period of great exploration and discovery began during Queen Elizabeth's reign. To begin, Elizabeth encouraged sailors to launch attacks on Spanish and Portuguese ships to steal gold, silver, jewels and silk. Later, in the 1570s and 1580s, she asked them to go out and claim new lands for England and make valuable trading contacts in these lands. Soon English people began to settle and live in these places. This was the beginning of what became known as the British Empire. An empire is a collection of communities, regions or countries controlled by one leading or 'mother country'.

Objectives

- Discover how and why the British Empire began.
- Examine the significance of key individuals in the growth of the British Empire.

Go, Gilbert, go!

In 1578, Elizabeth gave permission to an explorer called Humphrey Gilbert to travel to North America and build a settlement. The settlers hoped to farm, fish and perhaps find gold. However, Gilbert's ships were scattered by storms in the Atlantic Ocean and never reached North America. In 1583, Gilbert tried again. After landing in North America, he claimed hundreds of miles of land for the queen. But Gilbert made no attempt to form a colony because he lacked food and supplies, so he set off back to Britain – although his ship sank and he drowned. Today, however, the area around where Gilbert landed is regarded as the first part of the British Empire (see **A**).

New World settlers

In 1584, Queen Elizabeth sent another explorer, Walter Raleigh, to North America to set up a settlement. He founded the colony of Roanoke in 1587, but the settlers struggled. He sailed back to England for supplies but on his return found Roanoke mysteriously abandoned. However, in 1607, when King James I was on the throne, a group of settlers did manage to start new lives out in the 'New World'. They built homes and grew new crops like tobacco, sugar and cotton, which they sold to Britain, making lots of money. Before long, there were hundreds of British people living in North America, trying to make money and start a new life.

Money, money, money

Soon, British traders realised that if they bought popular (and cheap) items abroad and brought them back to Britain to sell at high prices, they could make huge profits. They travelled all over the world to bring exotic spices, luxury cloth, sugar, tea, coffee and fur back to Britain. Some even captured or bought human beings to sell as slaves. Sometimes traders built large trading stations in the foreign lands to keep themselves safe from local people. They often took lots of land around these stations, too.

▼ **INTERPRETATION A**
Sir Humphrey Gilbert cuts soil in 'Newfoundland' (as it was called) in 1583. The ceremony symbolised that the land was now English. The local people had no choice in the matter.

Fight, fight, fight!

Occasionally, the British would fight with a foreign power, like Spain or the Netherlands, and take some of their overseas land. In 1664, for example, the British seized a town called New Amsterdam from the Dutch. They renamed it New York after King Charles II's brother, the Duke of York. So, as a result of gaining land by either winning it or taking it, Britain managed to get control of several different areas in various parts of the world (see **B**).

▼ **MAP B** The early years of the British Empire, from the 1600s to the early 1700s.

1607: first successful British colony is started in North America

1713: Hudson Bay, a large area of Canada, becomes a British possession

1704: the British capture Gibraltar from the Spanish

1655: the British defeat the Spanish and take Jamaica

1642: sugar is first grown in the British colony of Barbados

1640s: the British set up trading stations in Africa to trade in **enslaved** people

1600: British first start trading in India

Meanwhile...
1573

British monarchs allowed sailors to rob foreign ships of goods and treasures, as long as they shared the wealth! Those who had permission were known as **privateers**. For example, Sir Francis Drake once returned to England with around 20 tons of gold and silver (worth over £5 million today). He gave most of this to Queen Elizabeth and kept a small percentage for himself. Those who kept the treasure to themselves were known as **pirates**. The most famous English pirate at the time was nicknamed 'Blackbeard' (his real name was Edward Teach).

Later on...

c.1800s

Over the next 200 years, the British Empire grew to become the largest empire the world had ever known. It was even bigger than the Roman Empire. At one point, Britain ruled over 450 million people living in over 50 areas (or colonies) including Australia, New Zealand, India and Kenya.

Over to You

1 Each of these dates is important in the early years of Britain's empire:

1607; 1587; 1664; 1642; 1713; 1600; 1655; 1583

Write the dates in order. Beside each date, write what happened in that year.

2 Look at **Interpretation A**.

a Describe what is happening in the image.

b What role did this person play in the early years of the British Empire?

Cause and Consequence

The growth of Britain's empire had several causes. Historians know that most events have a number of causes, and that these causes can sometimes be linked.

1 Explain how the following factors (reasons) helped the British Empire to grow:

   trade   wars   new crops

2 Explain connections between two of the following that are to do with the growth of the British Empire.

   trade   wars   new crops

1.7 What did Queen Elizabeth look like?

Our current monarch is known to millions of people all over the world – through appearances on television, in newspapers, and even on the money we use in the UK. But did ordinary people in Elizabeth I's reign know what their monarch actually looked like? How was Elizabeth I shown in paintings and described in writing?

Objectives

- Identify why it is so hard to know what Queen Elizabeth really looked like.
- Examine why Elizabeth controlled her royal portraits so carefully.

The power of portraits

In the sixteenth century, there was no television, Internet or daily newspapers to show ordinary people what Elizabeth I looked like. You might have been lucky enough to glimpse her as she toured around the country, but it was highly unlikely that an ordinary person would actually see her in person.

In order for ordinary people to know what she looked like, Elizabeth used portraits. However, she was a wise queen and she cleverly controlled the paintings the public saw. She did this to create an image of herself that would impress everyone.

The queen would have official portraits sent to artists to be copied. No other portraits were allowed. For years, the artist would copy these portraits every time an admirer wanted a portrait of the queen.

Look at the five portraits here (**B** to **F**) and see if you can match them to the descriptions (1–5).

▼ **SOURCE A** Written in the sixteenth century by Robert Cecil, one of Elizabeth's ministers, who describes how her portraits were controlled.

'Many painters have done portraits of the queen but none has shown her looks and charms. Therefore, she has asked people to stop doing portraits of her until a clever painter has finished one which all other painters can copy. Her Majesty, in the meantime, forbids the showing of any portraits which are ugly, until they are improved.'

Important visitors to England who met Elizabeth probably saw a very different person to the woman we see in the paintings. Some comments, written when the queen was over 60, are even quite insulting (see **G** to **I**).

Fact ✓

Elizabeth sat down to be painted only eight times – but over 200 paintings of her exist today. This shows just how many times artists were instructed to copy other paintings.

▼ **SOURCE B**

▼ **SOURCE C**

▼ **SOURCE D**

Painting descriptions

1 Painted in 1588, just after the Spanish had tried, and failed, to invade England. In the background are wrecked Spanish ships. Elizabeth's hand is on a globe to show she is one of the most powerful people in the world.

2 Painted soon after she was crowned. Elizabeth was about 25 years old. Note the crown, the orb (ball) and the sceptre (long stick), which are symbols of power and authority. Also look at all the jewels and gold-coloured cloth used to show how wealthy she is.

3 An engraving of Elizabeth, created when she was in her fifties. Notice how tired she looks.

4 Painted when she was in her sixties. Look carefully at her dress; it is covered in eyes and ears. What do you think the message is here?

5 Painted when Elizabeth was in her sixties. She is wearing a wig here.

▼ **SOURCE G** A French visitor, writing in 1597.

'On her head she wears a great red wig... Her face appears to be very aged. It is long and thin. Her teeth are yellow and unequal and there are less on the left than on the right. Many of them are missing and one cannot understand her easily when she speaks quickly. She is tall and graceful.'

▼ **SOURCE H** A German visitor, writing in 1598.

'Her face is oblong, fair but wrinkled; her eyes small, yet black and pleasant; her nose is a little hooked; her lips narrow; and her teeth black... She wears false hair and that red... her hands are small, her fingers long and her height neither tall nor short.'

▼ **INTERPRETATION I** Adapted from Susan Doran's book, *Elizabeth I and Her Circle*, published in 2015.

'Away from court, Elizabeth sent Edward a portrait of herself on 15 May 1549 in the hope that her likeness would remind him of her, and their old friendship. In the accompanying letter, her first to him written in English, she expressed her affection for her brother and hinted that she would like to be welcomed again at his court. The painting has not survived, but it probably showed her as deeply religious and studious.'

▼ **SOURCE E**

▼ **SOURCE F**

Over to You

1 Why were portraits of the queen so important for Elizabeth and her subjects?

   a Select one of the portraits (**Sources B** to **F**) on these pages. In your own words, write a detailed description of Elizabeth based on the picture.

   b If Elizabeth were to read your description, would she be pleased with what you have written? Explain your answer.

2 Explain why Elizabeth didn't allow 'the showing of any portraits which are ugly'.

3 Read **Sources G** and **H**.

   a Write down the details that both writers agree on.

   b Is there anything they disagree on?

   c Write a list of reasons why the writers might disagree.

4 Read **Interpretation I**. At the time the historian is writing about, Elizabeth had fallen out with her brother Edward, a deeply religious Protestant. How does she use a portrait to try to improve her relationship with her brother?

◐ Quick Knowledge Quiz

Choose the correct answer from the three options:

1 Who was Queen Elizabeth's mother?
   a Anne Boleyn
   b Catherine of Aragon
   c Jane Seymour

2 Elizabeth's half-brother and half-sister both became monarchs. What were their names?
   a Edward and Catherine
   b Mary and Edward
   c Henry and Mary

3 In what year did Elizabeth become Queen of England?
   a 1533
   b 1558
   c 1603

4 Queen Elizabeth's attempts to unite the country after the changes in religion under Henry VIII, Edward VI and Mary I are known by what name?
   a The Catholic Purge
   b The Queen's Quest
   c Religious Settlement

5 Which of the following relatives of Queen Elizabeth was kept in prison by her for nearly 20 years?
   a Mary, Queen of Scots
   b Mary Tudor
   c Lady Jane Grey

6 In 1586, what was the name of the man who plotted to kill Elizabeth?
   a Lord Darnley
   b Anthony Babington
   c Sir Francis Walsingham

7 In which year did the famous Spanish Armada sail towards England as part of Spain's plan to take over the country?
   a 1586
   b 1588
   c 1598

8 Who was the king of Spain during the Spanish Armada's attack on England?
   a Francis III
   b Philip II
   c Edward VI

9 In which year did Queen Elizabeth give permission for an explorer called Humphrey Gilbert to travel to North America and build a settlement?
   a 1578
   b 1584
   c 1598

10 What is the correct name for a collection of regions or countries controlled by one leading or 'mother country'?
   a colony
   b community
   c empire

 **Literacy Focus**

Writing in detail

1 Look at the paragraph below. It is a very basic answer to the question:

'Why did the Spanish attempt to invade England in 1588?'

The answer does not contain many specific, factual details. Rewrite the paragraph to include more detail – adding names, dates, examples and facts where possible. It might be a good idea to re-read pages 16–19 before you start this task.

> Two reasons are covered here. But what about other reasons? Why not mention the recent execution of Mary, Queen of Scots, or England's support for Protestant rebels in the Spanish Netherlands?

> Who was the Spanish king who ordered the attack?

> There were several reasons why the Spanish wanted to attack England in 1588. One reason was because the English had been attacking Spanish ships. Another reason was because the English had just sailed to Spain and attacked Spain's royal warships.

> Could you add some detail here? Why were the English so keen to attack the Spanish ships? (Clue: a rich prize…)

> Can you add more detail about the attack? Who led the attack? Where did the attack take place? How many Spanish warships were destroyed… and how?

Chronology

The ability to put events in the correct chronological order is vital in history. As you know, history is full of amazing stories – and to understand a story you must know the order in which things happened.

2 Put the following events in the correct chronological order so you can understand the 'big picture' of the Tudor monarchs:

- Nine-year-old Edward VI becomes king. He is a strict Protestant
- Henry Tudor becomes the first Tudor monarch, Henry VII
- Mary Tudor, Henry VII's eldest daughter, becomes queen – she is a strict Catholic
- Henry VII's son, Arthur, dies, leaving his younger son (also called Henry) as heir to the throne
- Elizabeth I becomes queen. She tries to find a 'middle way' in religion
- Henry VIII becomes king

History skill: Making inferences (source analysis)

Historians use sources to help them piece together the past and make sense of it. An important way that historians use sources is through **inference**: historians 'read between the lines' to work out what sources might be suggesting, rather than what is actually written or shown.

Imagine you have been asked an inference question:

> Give two things you can infer from **Source A** about Princess Elizabeth.

Look at **Source A**. On the left-hand side are examples of comprehension that *do not* answer the question. On the right-hand side are examples of inferences that *do* correctly address the question.

▼ **SOURCE A** This portrait of Princess Elizabeth was painted by the official royal painter in 1546, when Elizabeth was 13.

Comprehension: There is a book in the background.

Comprehension: She is wearing a lot of jewellery.

Inference: **I can infer** that Princess Elizabeth is trying to show that she is very rich. **Details in the source that tell me this** include the jewellery, which is full of precious stones. Only the very rich could afford such luxuries.

Inference: **I can infer** that Princess Elizabeth is showing that she is well educated. **Details in the source that tell me this** are the books in her hands and behind her. Only well-educated people would be able to read at this time.

The same methods can be used with written sources. Imagine you have been asked this inference question:

Give two things you can infer from **Source B** about Queen Elizabeth I.

▼ **SOURCE B** Comments by Queen Elizabeth in 1561 to Lord Maitland, a member of the Scottish Parliament.

'As long as I live, I shall be Queen of England. When I am dead they shall succeed me who have the most right... I know the English people, how they always dislike the present government and have their eyes fixed upon that person who is next to succeed.'

> **TIP:** Remember, Elizabeth had only been on the throne since 1558, so this was at the very start of her reign.

Comprehension: Elizabeth is the Queen of England. She says she knows the English people and that they always dislike the current government or rulers, and are looking forward to the next ruler.

> **TIP:** Comprehension is about understanding what information the source actually contains.

Inference: I can infer that Elizabeth is a determined woman. Her comment that she will be queen 'as long as I live' makes me think that she would die as queen rather than be forced to give up her crown.

> **TIP:** Inference is a valuable skill for historians – sources don't always tell us everything, so it is up to the skilled historian to 'read between the lines'.

Inference: I can infer that Elizabeth is a confident, intelligent woman. She says that she knows people are concerned about who will rule next, so she is determined to be a good leader and also find a successor who deserves the role she has.

Your challenge is to answer this source inference question:

> 1 Give two things you can infer from **Source C** about how Queen Elizabeth wanted to be portrayed. (10)
>
> 2 Give two things you can infer from **Source D** about Queen Elizabeth and her views of her reign as queen. (10)

▼ **SOURCE C** A portrait of Elizabeth I, painted around 1600. Many people think it was painted by Isaac Oliver, a well-known painter. It is known as the 'Rainbow Portrait' because of the rainbow Elizabeth holds in her right hand. She was around 60 years old when this was painted, but looks much younger.

This Latin translates as 'No rainbow without the Sun'.

She is wearing a crown.

A snake was a symbol of wisdom.

Rainbows are usually seen after stormy weather.

Eyes and ears pattern.

▼ **SOURCE D** Adapted from Queen Elizabeth's last speech to Parliament on 30 November 1601. It is known as the 'Golden Speech'. At this time, she had been queen for 43 years. When Elizabeth talks about her 'subjects', she is referring to the people she rules over.

'I do assure you there is no prince that loves his subjects better, or whose love can beat our love. And, though God has raised me high, this is what I think is the glory of my crown, that I have reigned with your love. Of myself I must say this: I never was any greedy, selfish or wasteful queen. My heart was never set on any worldly goods, but only for my subjects' good. There will never be a Queen who sits in my seat with more love for my country, care for my subjects, and that will sooner dedicate her life for your good and safety, than myself.'

> **TIP:** What does this source make you think about the queen and her reign? Read between the lines – what does it suggest about her?

For both questions, complete the tables below. Each question is worth 10 marks.

What I can infer from Source C (2)
Details in the source that tell me this (3)
What I can infer from Source C (2)
Details in the source that tell me this (3)

What I can infer from Source D (2)
Details in the source that tell me this (3)
What I can infer from Source D (2)
Details in the source that tell me this (3)

> **TIP:** Write down the reasons for your inferences. For example, if you think Elizabeth is trying to show that she is wise and that she sees everything, write down the details of the source that make you think this.

We are all different. We all look, dress and behave differently. We don't all have the same amount of money either: some people live in luxurious homes and follow the latest fashions, while at the other extreme some people are very poor. It was just the same in Tudor times. You could place people into groups, sometimes called **classes**. In 1587, an English priest called William Harrison published a book called *Description of England*. He wrote, 'we divide our people into four groups: **gentlemen**, **citizens**, **yeomen** and **labourers**.' But what did he mean?

Objectives

- Define the main groups that made up Tudor society.
- Examine how the poor were treated in Tudor society.

Read about the four groups mentioned in Harrison's book. Later on you will be asked to match each group to a house, a description of their life and a picture.

Who were the gentlemen?

Most of these people were very, very rich. They lived in huge country houses with lots of rooms in which to hold dinner parties, dances and music concerts. They owned lots of land and people paid them rent to farm it. Some gentlemen helped the king or queen to run the country. Even those who were not quite so rich still lived in large houses with plenty of land. This group made up about 5 per cent of the population. Although 'gentlemen' was the term used by William Harrison in his description, there were some women who had the same social status as gentlemen. They were known as 'ladies'.

Who were the citizens?

These people lived in towns and were still rich. Some made money from buying and selling goods, such as wool, jewellery, food, wine or cloth. These citizens were sometimes called **merchants**. They lived in fine town houses and had servants. They made up about 5 per cent of the population.

Who were the yeomen?

They were farmers. They either owned their land or rented land from a gentleman, or in some cases from a lady. They often lived in a medium-sized farmhouse and made quite a good living from farming crops (wheat or barley, for example) or cattle, pigs or sheep. They employed people to work on their farms and some even had servants. This group made up about 30 per cent of the population.

Who were the labourers?

These people were similar in status to the peasants of the Middle Ages. If they lived in the country – and most did – they would work on a farm. Some had their own small piece of land to grow their own vegetables and keep a few chickens. Some labourers lived in towns and might have worked as carpenters, tailors, shoemakers or bricklayers. Labourers made up about 60 per cent of the population.

Now study the following four photographs. Try to identify a home each for a gentleman (or richer lady), a citizen, a yeoman and a labourer.

HOME A

HOME B

HOME C

HOME D

citizen   class   gentleman
labourer   merchant   yeoman

Descriptions of Tudor homes

1   A timber-framed house, sometimes called a 'hall house' because of the large, open hall area inside. They were common in many parts of England, Wales, Ireland and Scotland, as well as in northern Europe. This one is in Bignor, Sussex.

2   These types of house were built with the materials that could be found nearby. This cottage, in Yorkshire, is built from stone and has a straw roof, but many were built with a timber frame with walls made from wattle (woven sticks) and daub (mud).

3   A large house in the centre of town. The person who lived here would be quite wealthy and could afford some luxuries, such as expensive clothes and fine wines. This town house is in Southampton.

4   This is Hardwick Hall, Derbyshire, the home of Elizabeth 'Bess' Hardwick. She married four times and rose to the highest levels of Tudor society. She was a friend of Queen Elizabeth I and one of the richest women of her time. She was a brilliant businesswoman who owned mines and a glass-making business. She became famous for her building projects, and her homes reflected her wealth and power. Built at a time when glass was a luxury, many people said Hardwick Hall was 'more glass than wall'.

Later on...

2018

In her book, *Black Tudors* (2018), historian Miranda Kaufmann describes how some black people worked for Tudor monarchs in important roles. John Blanke, for example, was a musician for both Henry VII and Henry VIII.

Over to You

1   a   Which group in Tudor society included tailors and bricklayers?

    b   Which group made up 30 per cent of the Tudor population?

2   Give one reason why the wealthiest people had such large homes.

3   Match images A–D with descriptions 1–4.

What about the poorest of the poor?

Even lower than the poorest labourers were the **paupers** – people who had no jobs and relied on charity. Some paupers were given permission to beg and wore special badges to show this. Others went to their local church to collect 'relief' – a few pennies to buy clothes or bread. Local people were taxed to pay for this. During Elizabeth's reign the population of England grew from 2.8 to 4 million. In the late 1500s, there were also bad harvests, food shortages and not a lot of jobs were available. All of this led to an increasing number of very poor people.

In 1601, Queen Elizabeth and her government introduced the first ever **Poor Law**. The new law divided the paupers into four categories. Each group was treated differently:

1 pauper children – given work and taught a trade
2 sick paupers – looked after in special homes
3 fit paupers – given work (they received food and drink as payment)
4 lazy, idle paupers – whipped, then sent to a **House of Correction** (a place where they were forced to work).

The Poor Law of 1601 said that poor people had to stay in their own town or village and not wander about. Each town or village had to appoint people to be 'Overseers of the Poor'. Their job was to collect money from people (a local tax, known as the 'poor rate') and make sure it was given to those in need. The aim of the Poor Law was to help those who were genuinely poor, but it still threatened punishment for those who were considered lazy and idle. This system of helping the poor remained largely unchanged for around 200 years.

Descriptions and pictures of Tudor classes

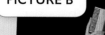
PICTURE A

PICTURE B

PICTURE C

PICTURE D

1 'Wine was brought back, and olive oil, currants, silk, clothes and dates. They were sold to a woman who then sold them in London.'

2 'The house has walls of earth, a low thatched roof, few rooms… a hole in the wall to let out smoke… they are very poor and have to labour hard for their living.'

3 'Every day she wears silks, velvets, satins and such like. She once gave away a pair of perfumed gloves with 24 small gold buttons, in each button a small diamond.'

4 'He eats well: bread, beer and beef, good food… full bellyfuls. He works hard: making hay, shearing corn, his workers are happy to farm for him.'

SOURCE A This illustration, from John Day's *A Christall Glass of Christian Reformation* (1569), shows a gentleman giving money to a beggar.

Key Words

House of Correction
pauper   Poor Law

Fact ✓

Richer people are often called the 'upper classes' while the poorer sections of society are sometimes referred to as 'lower classes'.

Significance

1 What was a pauper?
2 How were the poor looked after in Tudor times?
3 Significance can have a big impact on people at the time and can continue long afterwards. Based on what you have read on this page, how significant do you think the 1601 Poor Law was?

Over to You

1 In your own words, explain the meaning of the following:

   a gentleman   b citizen   c yeoman   d labourer.

2 Copy the chart below carefully.

   a Complete the chart by looking closely at the information on pages 30–33. Match the descriptions and pictures on these pages to the correct group or 'class' of people.

Class	Which home do you think they lived in? (Choose from Homes A–D)	Which description matches them? (Choose from Descriptions 1–4)	What do they look like? (Choose from Pictures A–D)
Lady			
Citizen			
Yeoman			
Labourer			

   b Now select one class and explain how you chose the descriptions and pictures for that class. For example, if you select a lady you might construct your sentences like this:
   - I think Picture _____ shows a lady because…
   - I think Home _____ would belong to a lady or gentleman because…
   - I think Description _____ is that of a lady because…

Not every child attended school in Tudor times. A Tudor child's education mainly depended on how wealthy their family was, as it wasn't free to attend school. Poor families couldn't afford school fees, and as a result, poor children would probably start work when they were five or six years old. But what were they missing out on? Was Tudor school life tough or a piece of cake?

Objectives

- Recall a typical day in a Tudor school.
- Compare today's schools with those in Tudor times.

Wealthy children often went to **grammar schools**, so called because they taught mainly Latin and Greek grammar. Latin was the language used by businessmen and merchants throughout Europe. So ambitious parents would make sure their child was taught at one of Britain's best grammar schools. Some free places were allocated to boys who were poor but clever.

The picture below is based on a classroom at a school near Chester called Bunbury Grammar School, which opened in 1594. Nearly every large town had a grammar school in Queen Elizabeth's reign. The key on page 35 will explain what's going on.

▼ **A** A typical school timetable. Lessons must have been dull – no computers, televisions, Internet or interactive whiteboards. Many lessons had to be learned off by heart.

6:00am – Day starts – Registration
6:15am – Prayers
7:00am – Latin grammar
9:00am – Maths
11:00am – Lunch (bread, beef, dried fruit, beer)
12:00pm – Greek grammar
2:00pm – Essays
3:00pm – Divinity (Religious Studies)
4:00pm – Homework given out
4:45pm – Prayers/Bible reading
5:00pm – Home time

Fact ✓

Most schools closed for two weeks at Christmas and two weeks at Easter. A school week was often Monday to Saturday – and there were no summer holidays.

Meanwhile...

In the countryside (where most people lived), most poor children worked on the farms. They did not go to school. If they lived in towns, children might be lucky enough to become an **apprentice** with a local tradesman, such as a blacksmith or shoe-maker.

Key

1 **School rules:** Tudor schools were very strict. Look at the list of school rules in **B** and compare some of your school rules to these.

2 **The birch:** A bundle of birch twigs or even a whip was used to hit children. A punishment session would be held once a week! Some school badges actually showed children being hit with a cane.

3 **A portrait:** A painting of the king, queen or the person who **founded** the school would often be displayed in the classroom. Does your school display any portraits or photographs of important people? Bunbury School was founded by Thomas Aldersey (1521–1598), a wealthy cloth merchant.

4 **Printed books:** Each student was expected to bring their own Bible to Bunbury Grammar School. Why do you think that many of the other books were kept behind the teacher?

5 **Girls in school:** Girls were allowed to study at Bunbury until they were nine, or they had learned to read English. It wasn't common to see girls in a classroom and many were educated at home.

6 **Children studying:** What lesson do you think is taking place here? Children wrote with a **quill pen**, made from a feather, and often read out loud from a **hornbook** (which looked like a wooden bat). One side would have the alphabet and the Lord's Prayer on it. The other side was left blank for practising writing or maths.

7 **Teacher:** Sometimes called a schoolmaster. Teachers were always men and could be very strict. In one school, a particularly strict teacher used to whip students every morning in winter, just to warm himself up!

8 **Toys:** Balls, spinning tops and hoops were used at break times.

9 **Costs:** Parents had to buy candles in the winter so their children could read – and they had to buy any additional books they might need too. Books for one year in school might cost over £10, which was about as much as a teacher earned each year!

Key Words

apprentice   birch   found
grammar school   hornbook   quill pen

▼ **B** Actual school rules from England – Manchester Grammar School and Oundle School had rules like these.

School rules

You will be beaten for:

- arriving late
- not learning a passage from the Bible off by heart
- forgetting your books
- hitting another pupil
- playing with dice or cards
- going to an alehouse at lunchtime
- losing your school cap
- making fun of another pupil
- stealing, swearing or lying
- wearing a dagger or bringing a stick or a bat to school – only meat knives allowed.

Over to You

1 Describe each of the following:
 a birch   b quill pen
 c hornbook   d grammar school.

2 Why did so few poor children go to school in Tudor times?

3 Imagine you are a student at a Tudor version of your school. Using the information provided on these pages, write a paragraph describing your typical school day. The title should be, 'A day in the life of (insert name) at (insert name) Grammar School.'

4 Look at **B**, the list of school rules.
 a Which of the 'offences' on the list would you not be punished for in your school now?
 b Explain why you wouldn't be punished.

Change and Continuity

1 Make a list of five similarities and five differences between your school and a school in Tudor times.

2 In what ways have schools changed since Tudor times?

How did people have fun in Tudor times?

There was no television or radio in Tudor times. People couldn't go to the cinema, play computer games, go on their mobile phones, or stream music online. Instead, they had to make their own entertainment. Some Tudor games and sports will be familiar to you, but not others! So how did the Tudors have fun?

Objectives

- Recall different types of Tudor entertainment.
- Examine how and why Tudor entertainment differed from the types of entertainment we enjoy today.

Go to public executions:
Many Tudor people loved to see criminals being killed: they enjoyed watching the expressions on each criminal's face, and complained if the executioner worked too quickly! Poorer criminals were usually hanged; richer ones were beheaded with a sword.

Play shin-hacking:
Two people would stand opposite each other in their biggest, heaviest boots. They took it in turns to kick each other as hard as they could. The person left standing won.

Bet on blood sports:
A bear or a bull would be tied to a post and attacked by a pack of dogs. Sometimes two cockerels would be forced to attack each other after having their beaks sharpened and their legs fitted with metal blades. People would bet on the results. Some successful bears, such as Harry Hunks, Tom of Lincoln and Blind Robin, became as famous as some footballers and pop stars are today.

Watch the strolling players:
Groups of actors ('strolling players') travelled from village to village and acted out well-known stories or plays. They also brought news and gossip. Often, they were joined by acrobats, jugglers, musicians and puppeteers. Plays soon became so popular that special theatres were built.

Join in a football match:
One village or town would take on another. The ball (a pig's bladder full of sawdust and peas) would be carried, kicked and thrown across the land between the two villages. The winning 'team' was the one that got the ball into the centre of the other village.

Play cudgels:
Two people would stand opposite each other, each holding a heavy stick. They took it in turns to hit each other. The person left standing won.

Go to the fair:
There were no roller-coaster rides or arcade games. Instead, a fair was a large noisy market full of goods to buy, food to eat and entertainment to watch (or join in with). Fire-eaters, tightrope walkers, sword-fighting and dog racing were all popular, as were most of the other sports and entertainments on these pages.

Fun-loving nation

Ordinary Tudors had tough lives and worked long hours. So, when they had any spare time, most wanted some serious fun! Drinking, singing, playing games and dancing were as popular then as they are now. And it wasn't just ordinary people – kings, queens and nobles enjoyed sport and entertainment of all types too. **Source B** describes the many entertainments enjoyed by rich and poor.

Key Words blood sports   cudgels   shin-hacking   strolling players   Whitsun

▼ **SOURCE A** The 'Cotswold Olimpick Games' started in 1612 and were held every year during **Whitsun**. In this drawing people can be seen sword-fighting, playing shin-hacking and throwing javelins.

▼ **SOURCE B** Adapted from a book, written in the 1600s by Edward Chamberlayne, called *The Present State of England*, in which the author explains how wealthy and ordinary citizens have different hobbies.

'The rich gentlemen also have their parks, horse-races, hunting, fishing, hawking, duck-hunting, cock-fighting, tennis, bowling, billiards, chess, draughts, cards, dice, quizzes, stage plays, dancing, singing and all sorts of musical instruments. The citizens and peasants have handball, football, skittles, golf, cudgels, bear-baiting, bull-baiting, bow and arrow, throwing, bowling, leaping, wrestling and ringing of bells. Among these, cock-fighting seems to all foreigners too childish and unsuitable for the gentry, and for the common people bull-baiting and bear-baiting seem too cruel, and for the citizens football very uncivil, rude, and barbarous within the city.'

▼ **INTERPRETATION C** A modern historian writes about the Tudor people's love of such 'sports' as bear-baiting and cockfighting.

'It does seem strange that the Tudor people who so much admired beauty in music, poetry, drama and architecture should have taken such delight in cruel, blood-thirsty "sports" which involved the torture of animals.'

Over to You

1 a Which forms of Tudor entertainment seem unpleasant or cruel to us today, or have been made illegal?

   b Why do you think some of these sports and entertainments have been banned?

2 Why would a group of strolling players coming to town be such an exciting event in Tudor times?

Knowledge and Understanding

1 Look at **Sources A** and **B**. Make a list of all the sports and entertainments in these sources.

2 Sort them into two lists:
   a Cruel and dangerous
   b Not cruel or dangerous.

3 'All types of entertainment in Tudor times were cruel and dangerous.' How far do you agree with this statement? Hint: Find examples that support the statement – and examples that oppose (don't support) it.

And now for your Shakespeare lesson...

We've all heard of William Shakespeare, and most people can name a few of his plays. Many are still performed around the world today, and some of them have been made into films. But what made this man so famous? And why do we still study his work at school?

A trip to the theatre

One of the most popular types of Tudor entertainment was watching actors perform a play. Queen Elizabeth would often get a group of actors to visit one of her palaces to act for her. In 1576, an actor named James Burbage saw a chance to make some money and built the first successful permanent theatre, in Shoreditch, just north-east of London. Burbage made a fortune and soon other theatres were built nearby, such as the Globe and the Swan (see **A**). By 1600, watching a play was popular among both rich *and* poor.

Superstar playwrights

The popularity of the theatre led to people earning a living by writing new plays. Many of these **playwrights** are still well known today, such as Christopher Marlowe and Ben Jonson. But by far the most famous is William Shakespeare.

Shakespeare is thought to have started writing plays in 1588. He wrote at least 37 and even acted in some of them. His plays are famous all over the world. They are important because they not only show us how people lived and thought in Tudor times, but also because Shakespeare wrote about everyday human emotions, such as love, hate and jealousy. Ben Jonson wrote that '[Shakespeare] was not of our age, but for all time'. We all experience the feelings Shakespeare wrote about and people can relate to them whatever century his plays are set in.

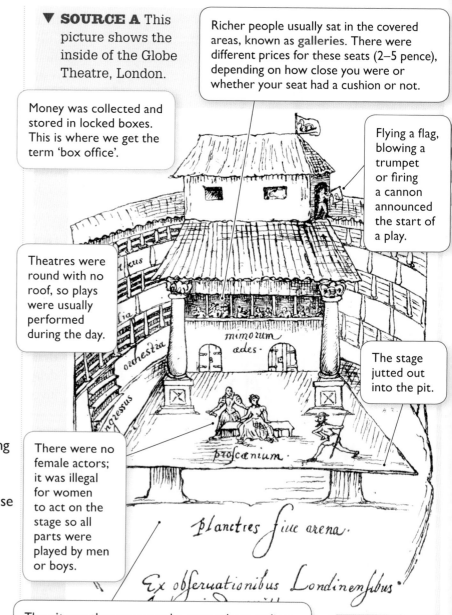

▼ **SOURCE A** This picture shows the inside of the Globe Theatre, London.

Richer people usually sat in the covered areas, known as **galleries**. There were different prices for these seats (2–5 pence), depending on how close you were or whether your seat had a cushion or not.

Money was collected and stored in locked boxes. This is where we get the term 'box office'.

Flying a flag, blowing a trumpet or firing a cannon announced the start of a play.

Theatres were round with no roof, so plays were usually performed during the day.

The stage jutted out into the pit.

There were no female actors; it was illegal for women to act on the stage so all parts were played by men or boys.

The **pit** was the area near the stage where ordinary people could stand and watch for only a small price – one penny. This was around the same price as a loaf of bread, and the low cost was one of the reasons why the theatre was so popular.

Pies, beer, fruit and soup could be bought during the performance.

In 1989, archaeologists found the remains of the Rose Theatre in London. They discovered that the floor area was littered with fruit seeds and hazelnut shells. Some historians think that this shows what people ate at the theatre – in the same way that people today sometimes eat popcorn at the cinema.

▼ **INTERPRETATION B** Fiona Shaw, an actor and television presenter on BBC'S *Greatest Britons* series, 2002.

'Engineering gets us from A to B; science helps us to understand what's around us; but Shakespeare does what no one else has done. He makes us understand our thoughts and feelings and what could be more useful in our lives than that?'

▼ **INTERPRETATION C** Adapted from a 2009 online article in the *Guardian* newspaper by journalist Peter Beech, who has a degree in Shakespearean Studies from King's College London.

'I've got a confession to make which some of you may find upsetting: I'm just not that into him. In my experience, reading or watching Shakespeare is, by turns, baffling, tiring and frustrating. It does not offer unparalleled insight into universal human truths. Don't get me wrong, Shakespeare's writing isn't exactly torture - but it is out of touch, and we read him, I'm convinced, out of habit.'

Over to You

1 a In what way was James Burbage an important figure in theatre history?

   b Why do you think theatre is less popular today than it was in Tudor times?

2 Describe the sights, sounds and smells that a visitor to a theatre would have experienced in Shakespeare's time.

Key Words   gallery   pit   playwright

Macbeth examines ambition and guilt.

King Henry V looks at courage, heroism and togetherness.

Key themes in Shakespeare's plays

Julius Caesar deals with power and betrayal.

Romeo and Juliet is about falling in love – which has never gone out of fashion!

▼ **SOURCE D** This portrait is said to be of William Shakespeare (1564–1616), painted by the English artist John Taylor around 1610.

Interpretation Analysis

1 Look at **Interpretations B** and **C**. Sum up what each interpretation says about Shakespeare.

2 Study **Interpretations B** and **C**. They give different views about Shakespeare's plays. What is the main difference between the views?

The modern cosmetics industry is big business. There are thousands of products available to change the appearance (and smell) of our bodies. Skin care, hair care, deodorants, makeup and fragrances are just some of the things that are sold in shops and online. This vast range of products was not available in Tudor times – but rich women in particular still wanted to look a certain way. Many women made their own cosmetics, often with disastrous effects.

Objectives

- Describe what some rich Tudor women did to their skin to create the 'perfect face' and why.

To be considered beautiful and wealthy, a Tudor woman needed pure white skin, ruby red lips, rosy cheeks, bright eyes and fair hair. A rich woman wanted white skin because she didn't want anyone to think that she needed to spend time outside working and getting a tanned face. And as you will find out, rich Tudor women did many things to gain the 'perfect face'. Ordinary Tudor women, working out in the fields on farms, did not go through the same beauty regime.

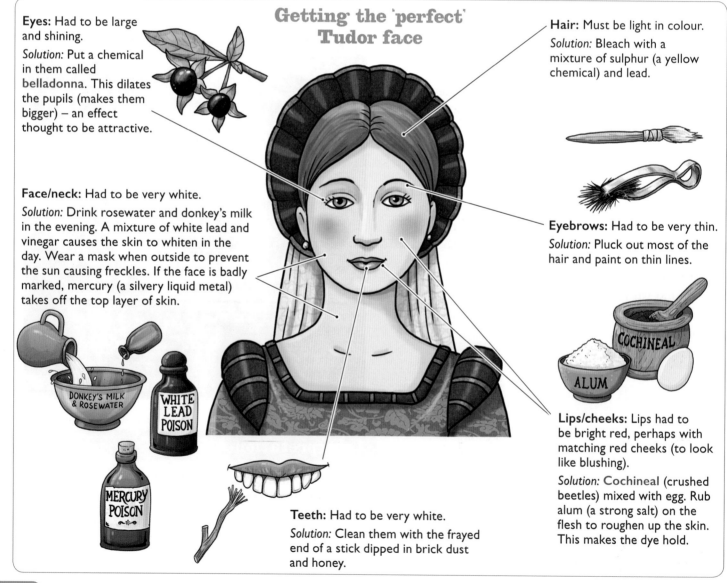

Getting the 'perfect' Tudor face

Eyes: Had to be large and shining.
Solution: Put a chemical in them called **belladonna**. This dilates the pupils (makes them bigger) – an effect thought to be attractive.

Face/neck: Had to be very white.
Solution: Drink rosewater and donkey's milk in the evening. A mixture of white lead and vinegar causes the skin to whiten in the day. Wear a mask when outside to prevent the sun causing freckles. If the face is badly marked, mercury (a silvery liquid metal) takes off the top layer of skin.

DONKEY'S MILK & ROSEWATER

WHITE LEAD POISON

MERCURY POISON

Hair: Must be light in colour.
Solution: Bleach with a mixture of sulphur (a yellow chemical) and lead.

Eyebrows: Had to be very thin.
Solution: Pluck out most of the hair and paint on thin lines.

COCHINEAL

ALUM

Lips/cheeks: Lips had to be bright red, perhaps with matching red cheeks (to look like blushing).
Solution: **Cochineal** (crushed beetles) mixed with egg. Rub alum (a strong salt) on the flesh to roughen up the skin. This makes the dye hold.

Teeth: Had to be very white.
Solution: Clean them with the frayed end of a stick dipped in brick dust and honey.

Having a bath

The Tudors didn't bathe often. Bathing was a rather complicated process. Unlike today, where we can jump in the shower or run a quick bath, most Tudors would have to fill a large wooden tub with several buckets of water which had been warmed up by the fireplace. Queen Elizabeth, for example, who was regarded as being extremely clean, bathed around four times a year. To cover up their smells, many Tudors carried scented items around with them and wore lots of expensive perfume imported from the East.

Fact ✓

At the age of 29, Queen Elizabeth became ill with smallpox, which left scars on her face. She began to apply thicker white makeup to cover up the scars – and because she was so influential, women began to copy her.

When the makeup is removed

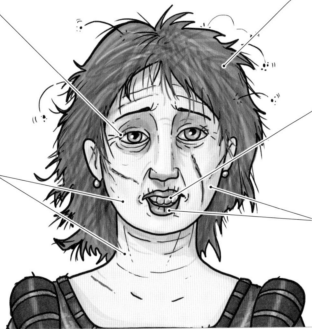

Eyes: Belladonna was made from Deadly Nightshade (a plant), which is extremely poisonous and damaged the eyes of the user. It fogged their vision so they couldn't see properly.

Face/neck: White lead was extremely poisonous. It caused people to have wrinkles and, even worse, open sores that didn't heal. A lotion made from mercury – a very harmful chemical – caused the skin to peel like flaking paint. People using it hoped that the new layer of skin underneath, which would have been very painful to touch, would be whiter than the last.

Hair: Bleaching with sulphur and lead would cause the hair to fall out. Until that happened, a woman would pile her hair on top of her head. It would have been full of lice and other vermin because she rarely washed it.

Teeth: Many people over the age of 20 had smelly mouths, full of black teeth. As well as removing stains, the brick dust removed the enamel on the teeth, leaving them exposed to decay.

Lips/cheeks: Cochineal was one of the safest substances used (we still use it today in red cake icing – enjoy!). Alum, however, made the skin very rough and scarred.

Over to You

1 Why did rich Tudor women want very white skin?

2 a Using a full page in your book, draw the outline of a woman's face. Around the face, make a brief note of your five favourite/most interesting Tudor beauty tips. Add the title 'My Top 5 Tudor beauty tips'.

  b Using another full page, draw the outline of the face of a modern girl or boy. Around the face, make a brief note of your five favourite/most interesting modern beauty tips (don't be shy, we all try to look after our hair, teeth and faces). Add the title 'My own Top 5 beauty tips'.

Change and Continuity

1 a Listed below are some chemicals and substances that Tudor women used. Write them out in your book. Next to each one, write down what each was used for. For example: Belladonna – a chemical made from Deadly Nightshade, used to make Tudor women's eyes shine.
  - belladonna
  - cochineal
  - white lead
  - brick dust
  - sulphur
  - mercury

  b Now write down the effects each had on a Tudor woman's face.

2 Explain one way in which a Tudor beauty regime was different from a modern one.

Tudor Masterchef

Most of us get up, eat our meals, and go to bed at similar times each day. We call this our routine – a well-established pattern of behaviour we follow almost all the time. Our routine includes the usual types of food and drink we have throughout the day. But what routines did people follow in Tudor times? Did daily life differ between rich and poor?

Objectives

- Examine Tudor daily routines and meals.
- Compare these routines with modern daily routines.

Simple meals for country workers

In Tudor times, the average country worker got up just before sunrise and worked until around 4pm. At busy times of the year, such as harvest, work would go on later, with men, women and children working in the fields until it was too dark to see. Workers would stop a couple of times each day for a break, eating a breakfast of bread and beer (known as ale) at 7am and a lunch of bread, cheese and ale around 11am.

The main meal of the day was around 6pm. People usually ate bread (again) with a kind of stew (called pottage), which was mostly made up of vegetables such as turnips, cabbages, parsnips, onions, carrots and peas. The poor ate very little meat, but sometimes they caught rabbits or fish, or had chicken or bacon. It was only the rich who could afford to buy (or hunt for) meat. This routine had not changed much for many hundreds of years.

Fine dining for the rich

The rich got up early too, around 5am, and ate breakfast around 7am. Like ordinary country workers, breakfast would consist of bread and ale, but a rich family's breakfast table might include meat or fish too.

Dinner time was around 12 noon and consisted of lots of courses, served one after the other. Beef, pork, mutton (sheep meat) and fish would be offered, but more unusual foods such as roasted pigeon, seagulls, lobster and peacock might appear as well. Salads and fruit pies were common, all washed down with ale, wine, sack (a very strong wine) and cider. Food was eaten with a spoon and a sharp pointed knife. Supper, consisting of the same sorts of food and drink as dinner, might also be eaten in the late afternoon or early evening.

▼ **SOURCE A** A dinner menu for a well-off family from a 1575 book called *A Proper New Book of Cookery*. Note that there were very few vegetables in their daily diet.

'The first course: pottage or stewed broth, boiled meat or stewed meat, chicken and bacon, powdered [finely chopped salted] beef, pies, goose, pig, roasted beef, roasted veal, custard. The second course: roasted lamb, roasted capons [chickens], roasted conies [rabbits], chickens, peahens, baked venison, tart.'

▼ **SOURCE B** These top tips for Tudor table behaviour have been adapted from a 1534 handbook of manners for children called *De Civitate*.

- Do not sit down until you have washed.
- Undo your belt a little if it will make you more comfortable; because doing this during the meal is bad manners.
- Once you sit, place your hands neatly on the table; not on your plate and not around your belly.
- Don't shift your buttocks left and right as if to let off some blast. Sit neatly and still.
- Children are sometimes allowed to stand to take their food.
- Children should not stay for the whole meal, but once they have eaten enough, pick up their plate, salute, and leave.
- Don't wipe your fingers on your clothes; use the napkin.
- If someone is ill mannered by ignorance, let it pass, rather than point it out.

In the mid-1600s, the three most common hot drinks – tea, coffee and cocoa – were introduced. Cocoa came from Mexico, coffee from Arabia and tea from China. Also, at this time, some people had started to use forks – some with eight prongs!

▼ **C** A wealthy Tudor family enjoy their dinner.

Key

1 Walls were plastered; painted cloths or tapestries often hung on them

2 Rushlight, made from rushes soaked in grease; it burned very slowly

3 Some plates made from thick pottery or pewter (made from tin and lead); in richer families plates might be made from silver

4 Oak chest, sometimes contained valuable family items like silver candlesticks or gold plates

5 Spoons and knives were used, but diners still ate much of their food with their fingers; forks were rarely used until the mid-1600s

6 Two carved chairs for parents, sometimes cushions added for comfort

7 Stools or benches for children, but they were allowed to stand up to eat

8 Stone paving slabs covered in mats made of rushes to make it more comfortable

9 Trestle table, covered by a tablecloth

10 Apple pie

11 Leg of mutton

12 Roast pigeon

13 Roast beef

14 Ale was the main drink

15 Bread

16 Hot meat pies

17 Cheese

18 Pickled herrings

19 Fish plate containing pike, eels, salmon and carp

Over to You

1 a What is meant by the term 'daily routine'?

   b How is your daily routine different from, or similar to, that of people in Tudor times?

2 Imagine you've been invited to go for a meal at the home shown in the drawing. Describe what it's like and what you ate. Take time to describe the room as well as the meal. Use **Sources A** and **B** to help you, too.

Similarity and Difference

1 Explain two ways in which the daily routines and diets of country workers and the rich were different.

Tudor crime and punishment

During the Tudor period the number of poor and unemployed people increased. Many had to wander the streets looking for food and shelter. While most wanted to find work and provide for themselves, a small number found that they could use tricks to get people to give them money. Who were these beggars, and what did they do to get money? How did the people in power deal with them and other criminals? And how were criminals punished?

Objectives

- Discover how some of the poorer people in Tudor times tried to make money.
- Examine how Tudor society dealt with sturdy beggars.
- Analyse why and how torture was used during the Tudor period.

Poverty in Tudor times

The first Tudor king, Henry VII, banned his rich barons from keeping private armies, so lots of men lost their jobs as soldiers. Also, many large landowners started to keep sheep on their land rather than allow farmers to rent it and grow crops. This meant fewer jobs, so farmers and their families had to fend for themselves. Later, when Henry VIII closed all the monasteries, the increasing number of poor people couldn't even go to the local monks for help. Also, during Queen Elizabeth's reign there were bad harvests, so fewer jobs were available working in the fields.

All this led to an increase in the number of beggars, or **vagabonds**. They were a mixture of unemployed soldiers and farmers, women and children, and the old and sick. A small number of these vagabonds who were fit enough to work used tricks to con people into giving them money. They were tough and devious, and became known as '**sturdy beggars**' – and they were seen as a major social problem in Tudor times.

Different types of sturdy beggar

In about 1567, a man named Thomas Harman wrote a best-selling book warning against the dangers of sturdy beggars. He described 23 different types, some of which are detailed here.

Counterfeit Crank

A Counterfeit Crank would trick people into believing they were unwell with a condition known at the time as the 'falling sickness'. They would mimic the symptoms by biting on soap so that it looked like they were frothing at the mouth, and then they would pretend to have a seizure. There was no known cure at the time so many people had sympathy for those with this condition, and would offer Counterfeit Cranks money.

Clapper Dudgeon

Clapper Dudgeons would cut their skin to make it bleed and tie dirty rags over the wounds to make them look even worse. They hoped people would feel sorry for them and give them money for 'medical attention'.

Gangs of thieves and their tricks

A woman, known as a 'Baretop Trickster' would take off some of her clothes to trick a man into going into a house with her. Once inside, there would be a gang of thieves waiting to rob him.

Tom O'Bedlam

'Tom O'Bedlam' described someone who would behave in an unusual way and follow people around. They might carry a stick with a piece of meat attached to the end or spend hours barking like a dog. Why do you think people gave them money?

▼ **SOURCE A** This picture of baretop tricksters appeared in a warning leaflet in the 1500s.

▼ **SOURCE C** An illustration from a book by Thomas Harman, written in 1567, which warned people about thieves and tricksters. The two men pictured are the same person. On the left, Harman shows the man in his ordinary clothes – but on the right, he pictures him in the clothes he wears when he dresses as a trickster known as a 'Counterfeit Crank'.

▼ **SOURCE B** These other sturdy beggars were featured in Harman's book about them, which was written in about 1567.

- Bristler – would use specially weighted dice ('bristles'), which would land on whichever number the bristler chose, in order to cheat at gambling.
- Cutpurse – a pickpocket who would creep up behind you, cut a hole in your pocket or bag and steal the contents.
- Angler – fixed a hook to a long stick and stole clothes from washing lines.
- Dummerer – pretended to be deaf and dumb, hoping people would feel sorry for him or her.
- Priggers or prancers – horse thieves.
- Rufflers – ex-soldiers who beat people up to get their purses.

Fact ✓

Sturdy beggars developed their own language, a kind of slang known as **canting**. They used it to speak secretly on busy streets. Amazingly, some 'canting' words managed to work their way into everyday use. For example, booze (meaning 'alcohol'), peck (meaning 'food' – ever said you were 'peckish'?), duds (meaning 'clothes') and lift (meaning 'steal') will still be recognisable to some of you today.

Over to You

1 Why did the number of poor people increase in Tudor times?

2 It is 1575 and you work as a printer in a large town. The mayor has asked you to design a leaflet warning visitors about the dangers of sturdy beggars. Your leaflet should include details about some (or all) of the sturdy beggars mentioned on these pages and about how they might try to trick someone.

How were sturdy beggars and vagabonds dealt with?

Dealing with sturdy beggars became one of the country's major issues. They were thought to be behind all sorts of crime and, in 1531, the government took action.

Some old and sick people were given a special licence to beg. Those who weren't would be whipped if they were caught begging. If they were caught a second time, they had a 2.5cm hole bored through their ear. The third time meant death by hanging.

Gradually, it became clear that most vagabonds were just genuinely poor and unemployed people who were looking for work. In the late 1500s, various laws were passed that ordered each district or parish to provide money for the poor. Queen Elizabeth supported the first official Poor Law in 1601.

Keeping law and order

Remember, not all crime was committed by sturdy beggars – crimes were committed by all sorts of people for all sorts of reasons. There was no police force, but some towns had groups of men known as **watchmen** (often controlled by a **constable**) who looked out for criminals. **Justices of the Peace** tried to investigate crimes, gather information and hold trials.

Most guilty people were either fined or faced some sort of public humiliation, such as the stocks or being whipped. People accused of more serious crimes were tried in large towns. They had to defend themselves in front of a judge and jury. Like in medieval times, punishments could be very harsh and public executions (usually hanging) were common. In 1532, for example, a cook was boiled to death in a cauldron for trying to poison the Bishop of Rochester.

▼ **C** How Tudor beggars were treated

Date of law	King or queen	Action
1495	Henry VII	Beggars went in stocks for three days, then sent back to their birth place or previous residence.
1531	Henry VIII	Some 'worthy' poor, old and sick given a licence to beg. Others whipped and sent back to where they came from. Harsher punishments for repeat offenders.
1547	Edward VI	Beggars whipped and branded with a V (for vagabond) on forehead. Also enslaved (made a slave) for two years. If they offended again or tried to escape, they were executed (this law remained in force for three years before it was changed back to the 1531 law because it was viewed as too severe).
1601	Elizabeth I	Local taxes used to help the poor. Poor people who refused to work imprisoned in a House of Correction. Beggars whipped until they bled, and sent back to where they came from.

Tudor torture

Justices of the Peace did not just deal with crime. These government-appointed men were also busy with other duties, such as looking after roads and bridges, checking alehouses and reporting people who continually failed to attend church. As a result, the government sometimes used other ways of getting information, catching criminals and foiling plots. One way was to employ spies, but this was time-consuming and costly. A much more brutal solution was to use torture. So what were some of the more barbaric torture techniques?

Fact ✓

There were prisons, but they tended to be places where people were held before their trial or while awaiting punishment. Unlike today, they were very rarely used as a punishment in their own right.

The rack: A prisoner was stretched for hours on end. Often, their tendons and ligaments would tear and their shoulders would become dislocated.

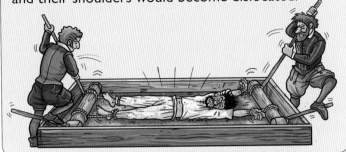

The Spanish donkey: Weights were attached to a prisoner's legs while they sat astride the wooden 'donkey'. More weights were applied until the prisoner confessed.

The press: A prisoner would lie under wooden or metal boards while heavy stones were placed upon them. If a prisoner failed to own up to their crimes, another heavy rock would be placed on them.

The Scottish boot: A prisoner's foot was placed in a heavy metal boot and wooden wedges were hammered down the sides. Gradually, the leg and anklebones would be crushed and splintered into pieces.

Skeffington's irons: These were specially designed to keep the prisoner in a very uncomfortable position. Either they owned up to the crime... or their back was broken.

The Judas cradle: A prisoner was hung above a cone pyramid and then lowered onto it. The sharp tip of the cone was forced up between the prisoner's legs.

Over to You

1 Explain the difference between a watchman and a Justice of the Peace.

2 a Here are five ways that sturdy beggars were punished: whipped; branded; hanged; put in a House of Correction; made into a slave; helped. Write down the one you think was the most suitable punishment and explain your choice.

  b Why do you think we do not punish poor people and beggars today?

3 a Why did the Tudors favour torture over the use of spies?

  b Do you think that torture was a good way to find out whether or not a person was guilty? Why or why not?

Knowledge and Understanding

1 Why do you think Tudor kings and queens treated sturdy beggars so brutally?

2 Describe two measures taken by Tudor monarchs to deal with sturdy beggars.

⟳ Quick Knowledge Quiz

Choose the correct answer from the three options:

1 In 1587, William Harrison published a book in which he divided the people of England into four groups: gentlemen, citizens, yeomen and... ?

   a   celebrities
   b   royalty
   c   labourers

2 In Tudor times, people who had no jobs and relied on charity were called... ?

   a   paupers
   b   pensioners
   c   parishioners

3 In Tudor schools, children sometimes wrote with a pen made from a feather. What was this called?

   a   a hornbook
   b   a quill pen
   c   a fountain pen

4 A popular game at this time involved two people standing opposite each other, each holding a heavy stick. They took it in turns to hit each other. What was this game called?

   a   shin-hacking
   b   bog-snorkelling
   c   cudgels

5 Groups of actors who travelled from village to village and acted out well-known stories or plays were known by what name?

   a   strolling players
   b   influencers
   c   walking wanderers

6 Who built the first successful permanent theatre in Shoreditch, London in 1576?

   a   Ben Jonson
   b   William Shakespeare
   c   James Burbage

7 In a Tudor theatre, the covered areas usually occupied by richer people were known by what name?

   a   galleries
   b   pits
   c   alleyways

8 What substance, made from crushed beetles, was rubbed on the cheeks and lips of some richer Tudor women?

   a   cochineal
   b   belladonna
   c   Deadly Nightshade

9 What was the name of the stew commonly eaten by poorer people in Tudor times?

   a   porridge
   b   pottage
   c   pigeon

10 What was a 'sturdy beggar'?

   a   a Tudor con-artist or trickster
   b   a poor farmer
   c   a famous Shakespeare character

Literacy Focus

Spelling, punctuation and grammar

1   The sentences below don't make much sense. Some words are misspelled, and some sentences need capital letters, full stops and apostrophes.

   a   Copy out each sentence, correcting the spelling and adding punctuation as you write.

   • in tudor sociaty the poor people were known as paupers
   • paupers were the most feared group in tudor times
   • in 1601 a poor law was introduced that treid to help them
   • the law sed that poor people hat to stay in their own town or villige and not wander from one plaice to another
   • each town or village had to apoint people to be responsable for the poor
   • their job was to collect money from poeple a local tax known as the 'poor rate' and make sore it was given to those in need
   • this job was the best job in tudor society
   • this sistem of helping the poor remianed largely unchanged for around 200 yeers

   b   Underline the factual sentences in blue and the sentences that contain opinion in red.

> **TIP:** Remember, a fact is definitely true and can be backed up with evidence. For example, 'Elizabeth became queen in 1558'. An opinion is how someone feels – it is their belief about something. For example, 'Elizabeth was the best queen ever'.

Vocabulary check

2   In each group of historical words, phrases or names below, there is an odd-one-out. When you think you have identified it, write a sentence or two to explain why you think it doesn't fit in with the other words in its group. The first one has been done for you – but remember, there may be several different correct answers. The skill here is to be able to justify why you have made your choice.

   a   Henry VIII   Edward VI   Mary I   Elizabeth I

   Henry VIII is the odd one out because he is the father, while the others are his children.

   b   gentlemen   citizens   labourers   engineers
   c   Divinity   Greek grammar   Business Studies   Latin grammar
   d   Blood Sports   Harry Hunks   Tom of Lincoln   Blind Robin
   e   Fortune   Rose   Globe   London
   f   Macbeth   Shakespeare   Romeo and Juliet   Julius Caesar
   g   lipstick   rosewater   donkey's milk   mercury
   h   cocoa   coffee   tea   ale
   i   vagabond   bristler   ruffler   counterfeit crank

2 History skill: Similarity and difference

Even though there could be similarities in people's lives in the past, there were probably differences too, even if they lived in the same period of history. Historians often call this diversity.

TIP: For example, a farm worker and a town merchant had to follow the same laws and might get the same illnesses, but they would live in very different houses and eat different foods.

Comparing similarities and differences

Here is one way to answer a question on similarity and difference. Imagine you have been asked:

> Explain two ways in which the diet of rich people and poorer people in Tudor times were similar. Explain two ways in which they were different.

1 **Recap:** Make some notes on the different types of food and drink eaten by both groups in Tudor times. You might want to turn to pages 42–43 for help. Don't just think about the differences, think about the similarities too.

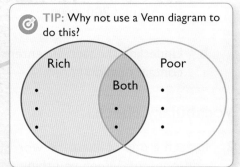

TIP: Why not use a Venn diagram to do this?

Rich   Both   Poor

2 **Think deeper**: In your recap, you probably spotted the following:

- People had different experiences. For example, rich people tended to eat more meat than poorer people. Can you think of reasons why?

- Sometimes it is possible to find both similarities and differences in the same example. Both rich and poorer people got up at roughly the same time and enjoyed the same types of food (bread and ale), but a rich family's breakfast table might include meat or fish too!

- Mealtimes show the subtle differences that took place. Both rich and poorer people had three meals per day – but the main meal of the rich was around lunchtime, while the main meal of poorer people was at the end of the day, when they had finished working in the fields.

3 **Write:** After identifying these similarities and differences, start writing your answer. Here is one way to structure an answer, using some sentence starters:

> There were several similarities in the diets of rich people and poorer people in Tudor times. One of the main similarities is related to the types of food they ate.
>
> At breakfast time, for example, both rich and poorer people would have the same basic type of food and drink — bread and ale.
>
> Mealtimes were an example of both similarity and difference. For example...
>
> The diet of a poorer person would mainly consist of...
>
> However, a richer person's diet was different. For example...
>
> The reasons why they had different diets were...

Assessment: Similarity and difference

Your challenge it to answer this question about similarity and difference.

1 Explain two ways in which the lives of the upper and lower classes in Tudor times were similar. Explain two ways in which they were different. (20)

🎯 **TIP:** Richer people are often called the 'upper classes', while the poorer sections of society are sometimes referred to as 'lower classes'.

You could use the steps below to help you structure your answer.

1 **Recap:** What have you learned about the upper and lower classes in Tudor society? Look at pages 30–43 for help. Remember to consider not just the clothes they wore or the homes they lived in – you could look at other aspects of their lives too, such as the following:

- **Tudor society:** What different groups made up Tudor society? How did the upper classes lead their lives? What about the lower classes?

- **Schools:** Did both classes have the same access to education?

- **Sport and entertainment:** How did the different classes enjoy themselves? What were the similarities and differences?

- **Diets and daily routine:** Were they the same for both classes?

🎯 **TIP:** Why didn't many poorer people in Tudor society go to schools like the one on pages 34–35?

🎯 **TIP:** Theatre is a good example of both similarity and difference in the same topic. Both upper and lower classes went to the theatre – but had slightly different experiences of it!

2 **Think deeper:** In step 1 you made notes on the *diversity* of life in Tudor times. Now start organising these notes into an answer. You could:

- Write about different *types of people*. You could start with the upper class and write about their lives. Then you might look at other classes of people.

- Or, look at different *areas of life*. So you might start with the diversity of homes, and then move on to jobs, for example, and describe how jobs and job opportunities were different.

Whichever way you choose, you need to have a structure to your answer.

🎯 **TIP:** In History we make generalisations. In other words, we sometimes talk about the 'upper class' as one general group. A good historian will know that within the upper class, some will be richer than others and experiences will be different (that's diversity, after all), but generalisations are useful to us because they help us reach conclusions. However, it's always important that we back up these conclusions with evidence from what we have learned.

3 **Write:** You may use the sentence starters below to help you get started.

There were many differences in class and the way people lived in Tudor times. One of the main differences is related to the type of home people lived in. For example, people in the lower classes, such as ordinary labourers...

However, people in the upper classes lived in different types of home. For example... (5)

Another difference was the types of job that people did. For example, many people in the lower classes... (5)

There were other differences in the way people lived their lives too. For example... (5)

There were also some similarities in the way different classes lived. For example... (5)

King James I: the scruffy Stuart!

In early 1603, Queen Elizabeth became seriously ill with a lung disease. She had never married or had any children, and her advisers were worried about who would rule after her. In the final days of her 44-year reign, Elizabeth's advisers suggested her third cousin, James VI of Scotland, as her successor. Elizabeth nodded and raised her hand in agreement.

Objectives

- Explain why the throne of England passed to the Scottish royal family.
- Identify what England's new Scottish king believed about his 'Divine Right'.

Exit the Tudors, enter the Stuarts

In the early hours of 24 March 1603, Elizabeth died. A messenger called Robert Carey jumped on a horse and galloped up to Scotland to tell James. So James VI, King of Scotland, also became James I of England – one man with two countries to rule. Several weeks later, dirty, tired and injured after a fall on the way, the 36-year-old king arrived in London. The crowds that cheered him were witnessing one of the most famous changes of royal family in English history. The Tudor period had ended and now a new Scottish family, the Stuarts, had arrived to rule England.

James I: 'the scruffy Stuart'

Name: James Stuart	**Age:** 36
Job title: King James I of England and King James VI of Scotland	

Early career: He was a successful king of Scotland. He managed to control powerful lords and highland chiefs whenever they showed any sign of rebellion. He appointed royal judges to hold regular criminal trials. He invited weavers from abroad to teach Scottish clothmakers how to make better cloth that could be sold abroad, and encouraged gold, silver and coal mining. He also managed to keep control of the Scottish (Protestant) Church.

Intelligence: James was a clever man who wrote several books. His favourite subject was witchcraft. He also wrote about the dangers of smoking tobacco, which was a new fashion at the time.

Beliefs about being king: He believed that God had chosen him to be king, and that he was answerable to no one except God – an idea called the **divine right of kings**. As a result, he thought he could do no wrong.

Hygiene and manners: James never washed and he swore all the time. People also said that he picked his nose a lot.

▼ **INTERPRETATION A** A description of James I (VI) written in 1650 by Sir Anthony Weldon in his book *The Court and Character of James I*. Sir Anthony had worked for James but was sacked by him in 1617. He wrote this when the Stuart family no longer ruled the country.

'He was fat. His eyes were large, ever rolling after any stranger that came into his presence. His tongue was too large for his mouth. His drink came out of each side of his mouth and dribbled back into his cup. He never washed his hands. He was crafty and cunning in small things but a fool in important matters.'

James and religion

When James arrived in England in 1603, he knew that one of his most important problems would be religion – it had troubled England's kings and queens for years, and people still quarrelled about it. Queen Elizabeth had worked hard to stop arguments between Catholics and Protestants.

However, when James met up with Church leaders in 1604, he failed to impress them. Some strict Protestants were so unhappy with the meeting that they left England forever. James also angered the Catholics when he ordered all their 'troublesome' priests to leave England. One small group of Catholics was so angry that they decided to launch one of the most famous murder plans in history – the Gunpowder Plot (see pages 56–59).

James and Parliament

The new king also managed to fall out with Parliament. James needed Parliament to help him rule – but didn't want them to argue with him about anything. When Parliament refused to collect money for the king, James sent all the politicians home… for ten years!

He then asked his friends for help running the country – and found other ways to get money, such as through selling land and titles. However, although he managed to find ways to get lots of cash, James was very quick to spend it – and by the time of his death in 1625, the king was nearly **bankrupt**.

Key Words   bankrupt   Divine Right of Kings

▼ **B** James quickly labelled himself King of Great Britain, although England and Scotland still ran their own affairs. In 1606, a competition was held to find a new flag that united both countries – the Union Flag.

These designs were rejected.   The first Union Flag – 1606.

Fact ✓

When James met with Church leaders at Hampton Court Palace in 1604, it was agreed that a new English translation of the Bible was needed. The *King James Bible*, as it became known, remained unchanged for 300 years and is the most printed book in history.

Over to You .ııl

1 On Queen Elizabeth's death, why was the King of Scotland asked to become King of England?

2 a In your own words, explain what is meant by the 'Divine Right of Kings'.

  b Why do you think James was so keen on the Divine Right of Kings?

  c Can you think of ideas why Parliament might not agree with this idea?

3 a Look at the fact file on James I, paying particular attention to the portrait. Write a description of James I's appearance, based on what you see.

  b Give a reason why this painting might not show the truth about James.

Interpretation Analysis

1 Read **Interpretation A** and summarise the writer's view of King James.

2 Explain why the writer might think this way.

Remember, remember the fifth of November!

Remember, remember the fifth of November
Gunpowder, treason and plot.
I see no reason why gunpowder, treason,
Should ever be forgot...

Some of you may have heard this poem. It concerns an event so famous that millions of people still remember it – over 400 years after it happened. That legendary event is the Gunpowder Plot of 1605.

Objectives

- Recall at least five accepted facts about the Gunpowder Plot.
- Identify the role of key individuals in the story of the Gunpowder Plot.

The plot has all the ingredients of a brilliant crime story – a plan to kill a king, gunpowder, betrayal, prison, torture, gun battles, hangings and fireworks! Some of you will know the story already. But do you know the full story? What led to the plot? Was it successful? What happened to the plotters?

How did King James I treat Catholics?

In 1605, there were laws passed against people who were Catholic. King James had even ordered Catholic priests to leave England or face execution. A small group of Catholics decided that they wanted James dead. They hoped a new king or queen would treat them better.

The plot

Every year, the king or queen officially opened Parliament and most of the powerful people in the country would go to watch. This ceremony still takes place today. In 1605, Parliament was due to be opened on 5 November. The plot was to blow up the king during this ceremony, seize his young daughter, Elizabeth, and place her on the throne instead of James. The plotters would make sure that she was helped by Catholic advisers.

The plotters

The leader was Robert Catesby, a strict Catholic who had gambled away much of his family's wealth. He was joined by Thomas and Robert Winter, Christopher and John Wright, Thomas Percy, and of course Guy – or

Guido – Fawkes. Guy was an experienced soldier who was used to handling explosives. He would be responsible for lighting the gunpowder to be placed under Parliament. There were many others who knew of the plan too.

▶ **SOURCE A** An image by a Dutch artist that appeared in leaflets soon after the plot was discovered, in late 1605. It is unlikely that the artist ever saw the plotters.

What went wrong?

On 26 October 1605, a mysterious letter arrived at the house of a man called Lord Monteagle. Monteagle was due to attend the opening of Parliament on 5 November. The note contained a warning and Monteagle immediately took the note to Robert Cecil, who was the king's chief adviser. Cecil took the letter to the king (see **B**).

▶ **SOURCE B** The mysterious letter sent to Monteagle on 26 October 1605 contained this warning.

'I would advise you... to devise some excuse to shift your attendance at the Parliament... they shall receive a terrible blow this Parliament and yet they shall not see who hurts them'

In the early hours of 5 November, the cellars below Parliament were searched. A tall, brown-haired man was found hanging around. He was holding a lantern and had a watch and matches. He said his name was John Johnson and that he worked for Thomas Percy. He was brought before King James but refused to answer any of his questions. The king then ordered that he be taken to the Tower of London and questioned. After two days of torture he gave his real name as Guido Fawkes. After another two days he told his torturers that he was there to blow up Parliament. After another six days, he named the other plotters.

What about the others?

When the other plotters realised the plan hadn't worked, they barricaded themselves into Holbeche House, near Dudley, in the Midlands. They tried to dry out some of their wet gunpowder near a fire and, not surprisingly, it blew up. The noise from the explosion alerted the king's troops, who were searching nearby. After a shoot-out in which both Catesby and Percy were killed by the same bullet, the surviving plotters were arrested and taken to London. However, some would say Catesby and Percy were the lucky ones…

The punishment

After a quick trial, the survivors, including Guy Fawkes, were sentenced to death. They were dragged through the streets of London, hanged until they were nearly dead, cut down, cut open, and their insides were pulled out and burned on a fire in front of them. Then their corpses were cut into pieces and put on display around the country.

Fact ✓

Guy Fawkes was probably dead before his punishment ended. As he climbed up the scaffold steps with the hangman's noose around his neck, he jumped off head first and broke his neck. The execution carried on regardless.

Source Analysis ★

1 Look at **Sources A** and **C**. Describe the images. Use no more than 15 words for each image.

2 How useful are **Sources A** and **C** for an enquiry into the Gunpowder Plot?

▼ **SOURCE C** From a leaflet published in 1605 in the Netherlands, by Dutch artist Cornelis Visscher; it shows the terrible punishments for the plotters.

Over to You ▂▃▅

1 Explain what the plotters hoped to achieve by blowing up King James.

2 Write down the names of all the people connected to the story of the Gunpowder Plot – and the role each played. For example, Lord Monteagle was sent the letter warning him of the plot to blow up Parliament.

3 Read **Source B**. In your own words, explain the meaning of the letter.

4 a Why do you think King James ordered such a nasty execution for the plotters?

   b 🖊 Imagine you were in London to witness the execution of Guy Fawkes and the remaining plotters. Write a letter to a friend describing the events. Use **Source C** to help you. Remember, at the time most people were pleased that the plot had failed.

5 How do many people remember the Gunpowder Plot today?

3.3 Were the Gunpowder Plotters framed?

For hundreds of years, people believed the official government story of the Gunpowder Plot. This is the story that you read on pages 56–57. However, in recent years, some historians have found it difficult to accept this story. It has been argued that Robert Cecil, the king's minister and adviser, found out about the plot and even encouraged it. Cecil was a Protestant who wanted to make Catholics as unpopular as possible. What better way to do this than uncover a Catholic plot to kill the king?

Objectives

- Assess evidence related to the Gunpowder Plot.
- Justify whether you think Robert Cecil knew about the plot all along.

Look carefully through the following **evidence**. Your task as a history detective is to hunt for clues, piece them together, and try to establish a clear picture of the plot to kill King James.

Evidence A

The 36 barrels of gunpowder were kept in a cellar next to Parliament. The cellar was rented to Thomas Percy by John Whynniard, a friend of Robert Cecil. Whynniard died suddenly and unexpectedly on the morning of 5 November.

Evidence B

All supplies of gunpowder were kept under guard in the Tower of London. The records for 1604 are missing.

Evidence C

Lord Monteagle took the mysterious warning letter to Robert Cecil on 26 October. The cellars below Parliament weren't searched until at least a week later.

Evidence D

One of the plotters, Francis Tresham, was Monteagle's brother-in-law. He was not caught straight away but was captured on 12 November. He died of a mysterious illness on 22 December, locked away in the Tower of London. Some said he'd been poisoned.

▼ **INTERPRETATION A** From *Look and Learn*, a 1960s children's magazine. The magazine was designed to appeal to 9- to 14-year-olds and was packed with facts and colour stories that covered all sorts of topics, including history. This image was painted by Ron Embleton, one of the magazine's best-known artists. The title of the image is 'The truth about the Gunpowder Plot'.

Evidence E

The source below is based on the views of a Catholic visitor to London in 1604, According to him, Robert Cecil said:

'The king is too kind to Catholics. This gives great offence to others. We cannot hope for good government while we have a large number of people who obey foreign rulers as Catholics do. The Catholic priests preach that Catholics must even kill the king to help their religion.'

Evidence F

The sources below show two examples of Guy Fawkes' signature while he was in the Tower of London. This one was written just after his arrest:

This one was scribbled a few days later.

Why do you think the signatures are so different?

Key Words evidence

Fact ✓

Historians can never really be sure about certain events. The Gunpowder Plot is a good example of this. Some historians will say that the evidence proves that Robert Cecil knew about the plot all along. Others will say it proves we can't be sure. These disagreements are one of the things that make studying history so fascinating.

Evidence G

The source below is part of Thomas Winter's confession, read out at the trial. He was one of the main plotters. The original confession has never been seen. A copy was written out by Robert Cecil for the trial.

'We were working under a little entry to the Parliament house. We under-propped it with wood. We bought the gunpowder and hid it in Mr Percy's house. We worked another two weeks against the stone wall, which was very hard to get through. At that time we called in Christopher Wright. About Easter we rented the cellar. After this Mr Fawkes laid into the cellar 1000 sticks and 500 bundles of firewood.'

Evidence H

Holbeche House was surrounded on 7 November, only two days after Fawkes was captured. According to the government report, it took two days of torture to get Fawkes to reveal his real name, let alone his part in the plot (another two days) and the names of the plotters (a further six days).

Over to You

Now you have read all the evidence, it is time to put together your theory about the Gunpowder Plot.

Step 1 Find evidence that the plotters were framed:
Can you find any evidence of a connection between the plot and Robert Cecil? Did Cecil try to hide anything? Perhaps he even tried to stop people from talking? Do you think he knew details of the plot before it happened? Make notes on what you have discovered.

Step 2 Find a motive:
The king was not very popular at the time. Can you find any evidence to suggest why Cecil would 'set up' Catholic plotters and only catch them at the last minute? Write down your findings.

Step 3 Think!
Can we trust the evidence? Is there any reason not to trust the confessions of the plotters who were caught? Are they reliable? If not, why not? Write down the ideas that you have.

Step 4 Time to wake up your mind, history detective! Were the plotters framed?
Write a short paragraph outlining your theory. Was Cecil involved in setting up the plotters? Be sure to back up your ideas with some of the evidence.

People in Tudor and Stuart England were very superstitious. The day Queen Elizabeth was crowned, for example, was specially selected only after the stars had been studied for several weeks. Despite the fact that scientists were uncovering more and more about the world, people still didn't understand how animals could suddenly drop down dead or why a field of crops might fail. On many occasions, when bad things happened in a town or village, it was concluded that a witch might be at work. Witches, people thought, were the Devil's helpers, always doing evil things and helping sinners find their way to hell.

Objectives

- Outline why witchcraft was so widely believed in.
- Identify how people were accused of witchcraft.

The king's favourite subject

King James I was very interested in witchcraft and wrote a book suggesting different ways to catch witches. He wrote that all witches had strange marks on their bodies where they fed their 'familiars'. A familiar was a small creature – a toad or a cat, for example – that sucked on the witch's blood every night. The familiar, James wrote, was really the Devil in disguise. In fact, all sorts of 'witch-spotting' tips were published – they had no shadow, they talked to themselves, their hair couldn't be cut, they couldn't say the Lord's Prayer without making a mistake, and many more.

James told Parliament to pass strict laws against anybody who was thought to be a witch and, in 1604, witchcraft became a crime punishable by hanging. Over the next 100 years, thousands of people were accused of witchcraft. The majority were poor, elderly women – after all, they were the most likely to live alone with a pet and have marks on their body from a lifetime of hard work!

A witch trail

In James I's book, he claimed that one of the best ways to identify a witch was to 'swim' them. This was a kind of trial. The accused would have their arms tied in front of them and a rope wrapped around their waist. They would then be thrown into a pond that would have been 'blessed' by a priest. It was thought that if the accused floated, they must be a witch because the 'pure' water didn't want them. They would be hanged. If they sank, the 'pure' water wanted them so they must be pure themselves and couldn't possibly be a witch – they were declared innocent (but drowned in the process).

▼ **SOURCE A** This woodcut by an unknown artist from around 1600 shows accusers 'swimming' a suspected witch.

Witch-hunting

Witch-hunting was at its height in East Anglia between 1645 and 1646. An unsuccessful lawyer named Matthew Hopkins set up his own witch hunt, claiming that he had the Devil's list of witches. Hundreds of people were rounded up as a result of his enquiries – most were women over the age of 50. He had 68 people put to death in Bury St Edmunds in Suffolk, and 19 hanged in Chelmsford, Essex, in a single day. In fact, during this time, there were more cases of witchcraft in Essex courts than of any other crime, apart from theft.

During the seventeenth century, about 2000 people were hanged as witches in England, Wales and Scotland before the 'witch craze' finally began to die down. Witchcraft ceased to be a crime in 1736. Britain's last victim, Janet Horne, was executed for witchcraft in 1727. She had been accused of turning her missing daughter into a flying horse.

Key Words   familiar

Earlier on... 1486

One book on witches, known as *The Hammer of Witches*, was a guide on how to identify, hunt and interrogate witches. For over 100 years, except for the Bible, the book sold more copies than any other book in Europe after its publication in 1486.

▶ **SOURCE B** A coloured version of a page from a book published in England in 1647. It shows Matthew Hopkins (known as the 'Witch Finder General') surrounded by 'familiars'.

▼ **SOURCE C** This German illustration, dated 1555, shows witches burning on a bonfire. Around 200,000 people were tortured, burned or hanged for witchcraft in Europe between 1500 and 1750.

Over to You

1 Write down five facts about the Witch Finder General.

2 Imagine the Witch Finder General himself is coming to your town and you want to impress him. Design a booklet that gives details about your town's efforts to catch witches. Include:
   - information about spotting a witch
   - successful convictions
   - drawings to show your witch trials.

3 Why do you think people in Tudor and Stuart times were so ready to believe in witchcraft and witches?

Source Analysis

1 Look at **Source A**. In your own words, explain how the 'swimming test' was meant to identify a witch.

2 Do you think this was a fair test? Write down the reasons for your answer.

3 Look at **Source B**. Why has the artist drawn so many animals?

4 How useful are **Sources A** and **B** to a historian studying the belief in witchcraft in Tudor and Stuart times?

For thousands of years, North and South America (and the people who lived there) were unknown to Europeans. But by the fifteenth century, Europeans from a variety of countries began to sail to and later settle in the 'Americas'. During Tudor and Stuart times, several groups from England did this too. So who were they? Why did English become the most common language used in North America? And why are so many place names in North America so familiar?

Objectives

- Describe the early days of European settlement in America.
- Explain why the English settled in North America during the Stuart period.

Read the following cartoon strip carefully to find out about the early years of European settlement in America and how the English began to dominate in North America.

1 **Indigenous peoples** had lived in North America for thousands of years.

Great civilisations like the Maya, Aztecs and Incas could be found in Central and South America too.

2 In 1492, Christopher Columbus became the first recorded European to reach the Americas. He was an Italian who was sponsored by Spain.

Other famous sailors followed Columbus but it was Spain and Portugal that began to dominate European exploration.

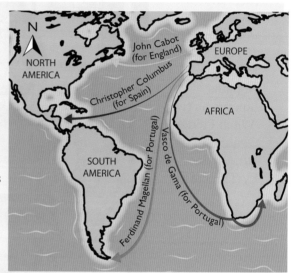

3 By the mid-1500s, Spain controlled most of the trading routes to Central and South America. It also controlled lots of land, including areas now called Cuba, Panama, Jamaica, Chile, Ecuador, Peru and north-west Argentina.

Spain became even richer because it found gold in its new colonies and traded in tobacco, potatoes, tomatoes, cotton, sugar and rum from its colonies.

4 English explorers concentrated on the northern parts of the world. They didn't find gold in North America, but found plenty of cod in the seas there.

In 1553–54, explorer Sir Hugh Willoughby tried to get around Russia to India for access to the rich trade in spices, tea and gemstones. Willoughby's attempt failed, but later Richard Chancellor (in 1554) managed to get to Moscow and set up trade links. Martin Frobisher (in 1576–78) and John Davis (in 1585–87) tried to find a route (known as the 'Northwest Passage') to the east by sailing around the top of Canada.

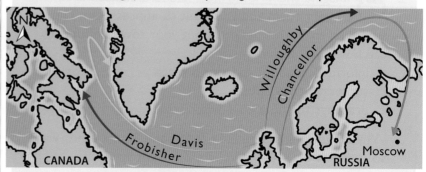

5 The quest to find trade routes and set up trade links and colonies continued. In 1584, Queen Elizabeth had given permission to one of her favourite explorers, Walter Raleigh, to start a settlement – or colony – in North America.

The new settlement was called Virginia after a name Elizabeth was known by – the Virgin Queen.

7 In April 1607, a group of British settlers tried again to settle in America by moving to Virginia on the East Coast.

They named their new settlement 'Jamestown' in honour of Stuart King James I – but they initially struggled to survive.

By September 1607, half of the 104 colonists had died from disease and there was ongoing conflict with the local indigenous people whose land had been invaded. However, after many years of struggle Jamestown began to grow and is recognised as North America's first permanent English

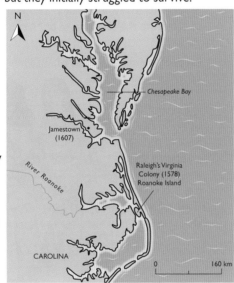

Later on...

Many Americans today are very proud of the settlers of 1620 who are known in American history books as the 'Pilgrim Fathers' or 'Founding Fathers'.

Over to You

1 Explain how each of the following dates is important in the story of European settlement in the Americas:
   - 1492
   - 1584
   - 1585
   - 1587
   - 1590
   - 1607
   - 1620.

2 a Who were the 'Pilgrim Fathers'?
   b Suggest a reason why they were called 'Pilgrim Fathers'.

---

6 In 1585, over 100 male settlers (or colonists) from England tried to start new lives in this new English colony but there was no good harbour, no easy way to grow food, and the local **American Indians** often fought against them. The settlers soon returned to England.

In 1587, Raleigh tried to start a second colony in North America. This group included women and children. However, the supply ships that Raleigh sent to the colony failed to arrive. When help finally got there in 1590, all the settlers had mysteriously vanished.

8 In September 1620, another group of settlers (102 men, women and children) tried to start a new life in North America. Of the initial settlers in Stuart times, this group probably established the strongest early settlement.

Thirty-five of the travellers were Puritans, unhappy with King James I, who would not accept their ideas about religion. A person who undertakes a religious journey is known as a 'pilgrim' so the Puritans were sometimes called 'pilgrims'.

Fact ✓

Puritans were members of the Church of England (Protestants) but they believed that still more change in religion was needed. They felt that the Protestant Church allowed too much sin to take place, like playing football on a Sunday when people should be praying. Puritans tried to lead 'pure' lives.

9 Life in their new homes was hard for the British settlers of 1620. They struggled to grow food – crops of wheat and peas failed. During the first winter, 51 settlers died from diseases such as pneumonia.

But the settlers were determined to survive and in the spring of 1621 they received help from an unexpected source.

10 It is said that a local American Indian named Squanto, who had been acting as an interpreter between the settlers and local indigenous people, showed the settlers how to plant 20 acres of corn and six acres of barley successfully.

He advised them how to fertilise the soil – with dead fish! From then on the settlers knew how to farm successfully, and life started to improve.

11 In 1621, to celebrate their successful harvests – and to give thanks for their good fortune – the Plymouth settlers tucked into a feast of turkey and goose. Around 90 indigenous people joined them, bringing lots of food.

12 This celebration meal is still remembered in the United States of America today. In Canada, 'thanksgiving' is also celebrated – to celebrate the safe voyage of Martin Frobisher to Canada in 1576–78.

Every November, millions of American families have a day off work and school, and sit down to a meal of turkey, cranberry sauce and pumpkin pie. It is called 'Thanksgiving Day'.

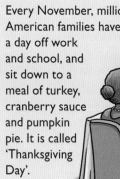

13 The success of the 1620 settlers encouraged others to leave Britain and move to what they regarded as the 'New World'. By 1624, over 120 people, including more settlers from Britain, were living in Plymouth, New England.

They were joined by settlers from other countries, including France and the Netherlands. In fact, Dutch settlers were responsible for building a town called New Amsterdam... later renamed New York.

14 Despite settlers from many other nations moving to this area of North America, it was the British who began to dominate the area and take over more and more land.

Soon, products grown there, such as tobacco, cotton and sugar, began to flood into Britain, making some people on both sides of the Atlantic Ocean very rich.

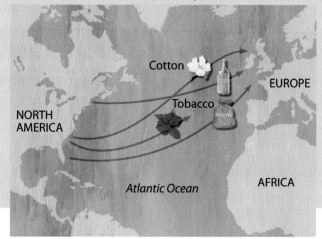

15 By the early 1700s, there were 13 British colonies along the East Coast of North America, remembered today by the 13 stripes on the American flag.

It was now clear that British men, women and children – and so the English language – were firmly rooted in North America.

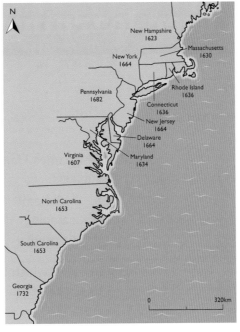

N

New Hampshire 1623
Massachusetts 1630
New York 1664
Rhode Island 1636
Pennsylvania 1682
Connecticut 1636
New Jersey 1664
Delaware 1664
Virginia 1607
Maryland 1634
North Carolina 1653
South Carolina 1653
Georgia 1732

0   320km

▼ **SOURCE A** A list of things that a settler family was advised to take to America, printed in 1630. 'Victual' is food and drink. 'Apparell' is clothing. * means you could miss it out if you couldn't afford it.

Victual.
Meal, one Hogshead.*
Beefe, one hundred waight.
Porke pickled, 100. Or Bacon 74. pound.
Butter, two dozen.
Cheese, halfe a hundred.
Salt to save Fish, halfe a hogshead.

Apparell.
Shooes, six payre.
Boots for men, one payre.
Leather to mend shooes, foure pound.
Irish Stockings, foure payre.
Shirts, six.
Handkerchiefes, twelve.*

Tooles which may also serve a family of foure or five persons.
One English spade.
One steele shovell.
Axes 3, one broad axe, and 2 felling axes.
One woodhooke.
One hammer.

For Building.
Lockes for Doores and Chests.
Hookes and twists for doors.

Over to You ◾◾◾

1 Complete the following sentences with accurate terms:
  a The settlers of 1620 struggled to begin with, but it is said they were helped by a local named _____ .
  b The North American celebration known as _____ is linked to early English settlers in North America.
  c By the early 1700s, there were _____ English colonies in North America.
  d Products grown in the colonies, such as _____ and _____ , were imported to Britain.

2 Look at **Source A**.
  a List five foods, five items of clothing and five tools that settlers had to take with them.
  b Why did some settlers not have to take as much as others?
  c Why do you think the settlers had to bring so much equipment and food?

3 Imagine you are a settler who has briefly returned to Britain. People are constantly asking you what it is like in the 'New World'. Prepare a speech to give to a group of people who are unsure whether to take the trip. Try to convince them that travelling with you on your return journey is a good idea.

Causation

1 Explain two causes of English settlement in North America.

Quick Knowledge Quiz

Choose the correct answer from the three options:

1 In what year did Queen Elizabeth die?

   a 1601

   b 1603

   c 1605

2 King James I of England was also King of Scotland. But what was his title in Scotland?

   a James IV

   b James V

   c James VI

3 King James I believed that God had chosen him as king and that he was answerable to no one except God. What was this belief called?

   a Godly Choice

   b Divine Right of Kings

   c God on Earth Theory

4 Who was the leader of the Gunpowder Plotters?

   a Robert Catesby

   b Thomas Winter

   c Guy Fawkes

5 Who received a mysterious note in October 1605 warning him not to attend the opening of Parliament?

   a Lord Thatcher

   b Thomas Percy

   c Lord Monteagle

6 What was the name of the house where some of the main plotters ran away to after Guy Fawkes was captured?

   a House of Commons

   b Holbeche House

   c Himley Hall

7 King James I famously wrote a book on which subject?

   a witchcraft

   b camping

   c painting

8 In 1584, which Englishman was given permission by Queen Elizabeth to start a colony in North America?

   a Robert Cecil

   b Walter Raleigh

   c David Pilgrim

9 What name are the people who went to start a new life in North America in 1620 famously known as?

   a Pilgrim Fathers

   b America's Angels

   c The First Pilgrims

10 By what name was New York originally known?

   a New England

   b New Amsterdam

   c New Brunswick

 **Literacy Focus**

Linking things together

When writing historical narratives, it's really important that the story *flows*. It's vital to get things in chronological order, but it's also useful to be able to use a variety of **connectives** to improve your work. Connectives are 'joining words' used to connect one part of text with another to form longer sentences and improve the flow of your writing.

> When King James became King of England, many Catholics were unhappy with the way they were being treated. James was a Protestant and many Catholics did not see him as the rightful king. In November 1605 a group of Catholic plotters planned to blow him up with gunpowder when he went to open Parliament. The plotters would then seize James's young daughter. Her name was Elizabeth. They would place her on the throne instead of James. The plotters would make sure that she was helped by Catholic advisers.

⏱ **TIP:** This paragraph is simply a collection of short, sharp sentences. Look at the paragraph below to show how connectives have improved it.

Look at the improved paragraph below:

> When King James became King of England, many Catholics were unhappy with the way they were being treated. **Also**, James was a Protestant and many Catholics did not see him as the rightful king. **As a result of this**, in November 1605 a group of Catholic plotters planned to blow him up with gunpowder when he went to open Parliament. **In addition**, the plotters would then seize James's young daughter, Elizabeth, **and then** place her on the throne instead of James. **Furthermore**, she would be helped by Catholic advisers.

1 Now it's your turn. Add connectives to improve the paragraphs.

> In October 1605, a man called Lord Monteagle received a note warning him not to attend Parliament. Monteagle took the note to Robert Cecil, the king's chief advisor. Cecil took the letter to the king.
>
> In the early hours of 5 November, the cellars below Parliament were searched. Guy Fawkes was found there next to the gunpowder. He was brought before King James. He refused to answer any questions. The king ordered Fawkes to be taken to the Tower of London and tortured.

Word bank: connectives

If you want to emphasise something:
- Most of all
- Above all
- Especially
- Notably
- In particular

If you want to add something:
- And
- In addition
- Furthermore
- Also
- As well as

If you want to give an example or illustrate a point:
- For instance
- For example
- These include
- Such as
- As revealed by

If you want to show cause or effect:
- As a result
- Because
- Therefore
- This led to
- Consequently

If you want to compare:
- Equally
- Similarly
- Likewise
- In the same way
- Compared to

If you want to contrast:
- In contrast
- On the other hand
- However
- Alternatively
- Whereas

If you want to put a sequence together:
- Firstly
- Secondly
- Finally
- Then
- Subsequently

3 History skill: Source analysis

A **source** is a piece of evidence from the period of time you are studying. Sources are incredibly useful to historians for finding out about a past event, person, or development.

What can sources tell you?
When trying to understand what a source can tell you, it's important to think about the following:

1 **Content:** What is actually written or pictured in the source? What does it tell us about the event or the person? What does it *not* tell you?

TIP: If you are thinking about what the source is not telling you (in other words, the 'limitations' of the source), make sure you clearly say how this could limit your understanding of the topic.

2 **Caption:** If there is a caption or label with the source, it will tell you about where the source comes from, or where it originates from (also known as the 'provenance'). The caption will help you to place the source within the events you are studying.

3 **Context:** This is where you think back to what you already know about the topic. Is the source accurate? Does it match with what you have learned about the person or event it describes?

4 **Conclude:** Now use your answers from steps 1–3 to answer the question and summarise what the source tells you.

Now spend some time looking through the following two sources. Imagine you have been asked:

1   What can **Source A** tell us about the punishments of the Gunpowder Plotters?

2   What can **Source B** tell us about the punishments of the Gunpowder Plotters?

Use the two sources and your own knowledge to support your answer.   (20)

▼ **SOURCE A** Adapted from an eyewitness account, reported on 31 January 1606 in *The Weekly News*, an early type of newspaper.

Caption: The person saw the event happening.

Context: I know that Johnson gave a fake name when he was first discovered in the cellars underneath Parliament.

'Last of all came the great devil of all, Guy Fawkes, who also called himself Johnson, who should have lit the gunpowder. His body was weak with torture and sickness, and he only just got up the ladder, yet with much effort, by the help of the hangman, went high enough to break his neck by the fall. He made no speech, but crossed himself and prayed, and then met his end upon the gallows and the block, to the great joy of all the spectators that the land was ended of so wicked a villain.'

Context: I know Fawkes was tortured before confessing to his role in the plot.

Content: I learn about the process of execution.

Content: There was a crowd watching, who cheered.

▼ **SOURCE B:** From a leaflet published in the Netherlands in 1605, created by a Dutch artist, Cornelis Visscher, which shows the terrible punishments for the plotters.

Caption: One limitation is that we have no evidence that Vissher was there, so might have to be careful with what he has drawn.

Caption: It was done soon after the events, but created in the Netherlands.

Content: A large crowd gathered to watch.

Content: This shows us details of the execution – it took place on a scaffold.

Context: I know that the plotters were hung, drawn and quartered – this is the 'drawn' process.

After you have gone through this process with the sources, summarise what they can tell you about the topic. Now turn to the next page to have a go at answering this type of question.

Your challenge is to answer these source analysis questions:

> 1   What can **Source A** tell us about the views of James VI of Scotland/James I of England?
>
> 2   What can **Source B** tell us about the views of James VI of Scotland/James I of England?
>
> Use the two sources and your own knowledge to support your answer.   (20)

▼ **SOURCE A** Adapted from a speech by King James VI of Scotland (also King James I of England), at Whitehall Palace, London in March 1609.

'Monarchy is the greatest thing upon earth. Kings are rightly called gods since, just like God, they have power of life and death over all their people in all things. They are accountable to God only... so it is a crime for anyone to argue about what a king can do.'

▼ **SOURCE B**: An image from a book written in 1597 by King James VI of Scotland/James I of England called *Daemonologie*. The book covers James' ideas on magic, sorcery and witchcraft. The image shows four suspected witches kneeling in front of the king at a witch trial in Scotland in 1590.

You can use the example sentence starters to help you answer the question for each source. Complete all the steps for Source A before moving on to Source B. Each source is worth 10 marks.

1 Content: What does the content of each source tell you about the views of King James?

One thing I learned from the content of Source A is... Another thing I learned is... **(3)**	One thing I learned from the content of Source B is... Another thing I learned is... **(3)**

2 Caption: What do the captions tell you? Who made the sources? Why do you think they made them?

One thing the Source A caption tells me is... Another thing is... **(3)**	One thing Source B caption tells me is... Another thing is... **(3)**

3 Context: Does the information in the sources match with what you already know about the views of King James?

One thing I already know about the views of King James is... This (matches/doesn't match) with what Source A says about... **(3)**	Another thing I already know about the views of King James is... This (matches/doesn't match) with what Source B says about... **(3)**

4 Conclude: Now summarise what the sources tell you.

Source A tells us... I know this because... **(1)**	Source B tells us... I know this because... **(1)**

Why did the English start fighting each other?

In 1642, thousands of Englishmen went to war. But they weren't about to fight the French, the Spanish or any other foreign army. They went to fight other English people. England was at war with itself. We call this a **civil war**. So what made the English turn against each other? What were the short- and long-term causes of the conflict? And what were the two sides called?

Objectives

- Define the term 'civil war'.
- Examine the causes of the English Civil War.

In most wars, there are two sides facing each other. The English Civil War was no different. On one side were the Stuart King Charles I and his followers, known as the **Royalists**. On the other side were the men of Parliament and their followers, known as the **Parliamentarians**. For many years, Parliament had worked with the monarch, but now they were at war against the king. Parliament was meant to help make laws, discuss wars and raise taxes. However, James I, and then his son Charles I, began to argue regularly with Parliament. They thought that Parliament was there to serve them… but Parliament thought differently. It thought that the monarch was there to serve his or her country. The argument ended in war. Look carefully at some of the key issues that caused it.

I became the king when my father James I died in 1625. As the king, I can do as I like. and expect total obedience from the people I rule. This is because the 'divine right of kings' means God appointed me, and no one can oppose me. Parliament thinks it can control its king by keeping me short of money. Parliament must be stopped… even if it means war.

King Charles I

If Charles needs money, Parliament must get it for him. He is their king and God has put him on the throne. Parliament must allow a king to act like a king. But Parliament doesn't give Charles enough money and even ordered the execution of two of his personal advisers. Parliament must be stopped… even if it means war.

William Cavendish, a rich lord

John Hampden, a Member of Parliament

Running the country is a difficult job and Parliament has been helping kings and queens for years. We like helping to make decisions, but Charles only uses us to collect taxes for him. When we last refused to get him any more money, he sent us all home for 11 years between 1629 and 1640 and ruled without us. He only asked us back because a Scottish army invaded and he needed money to raise an army. The reason they invaded was Charles's fault too, because he'd told the Scots to use a new prayer book they didn't like. Charles must change his ways… even if it means war.

The two sides prepare for war

The final straw came in December 1641 when Parliament sent Charles a long list of complaints about him and his way of running the country. He was furious. In January 1642, he took 300 soldiers to London to arrest the five most troublesome Members of Parliament. However, when he got there, they had all escaped. Charles then left London and headed north to collect his army together. His wife, Henrietta Maria of France, went to the Netherlands to sell the crown jewels to pay for the war. Parliament started to bring its own army together. The English Civil War was about to begin.

There are more of us Puritans than ever before. We are strict Christians and our 'pure' way of worship is becoming popular. Many Puritans are Members of Parliament now. Charles has married a young Catholic princess. Is he trying to make the country more Catholic? We must stop him... even if it means war.

Harriet Vane, a Puritan

Emma Short, a farm worker

I work very hard to make a good living. But Charles takes taxes from us without even asking Parliament for permission or agreement. His most recent idea was to reintroduce an old tax known as the ship tax. This tax had been collected in the past to raise money for warships — but it was only collected from people living near the sea. Now Charles is making everyone pay it, even if they don't live by the sea! And we're not even at war, so the risk of invasion is low. Charles must be stopped... even if it means war.

I will have to fight for Charles because my landlord told me to. He told me that Charles was appointed by God and I don't want to go against God's wishes. If Parliament is against Charles, they must be against God. They must be stopped... even if it means war.

Nicholas Farrall, a merchant

Over to You

1 Define the following terms:
   a Royalist
   b Parliamentarian
   c divine right.

2 What is the main difference between an ordinary war and a civil war?

3 Copy the following statements into your book. Beside each, write either the word 'Royalist' (if it would be the view of a supporter of the king) or 'Parliamentarian' (if this view would be held by a supporter of Parliament). Are any statements appropriate for both sides?
   a The king is chosen by God – he has a divine right to rule.
   b Parliament's job is to follow the king's commands.
   c No king of England should marry a foreign Catholic.
   d The king is there to serve his country – not the other way around!
   e One man cannot govern an entire nation.
   f This ship tax is unfair and illegal.

Causation

1 Look at each of the cartoons on these pages. In no more than 20 words, summarise the thoughts of each one.

2 For each one, say whether you think they are a Royalist or a Parliamentarian.

3 Explain why the English Civil War broke out in 1642. You may use the following in your answer:
   • the Ship Tax
   • the actions of Parliament.
   You must also use information of your own.

On 22 August 1642, King Charles gathered his army together and stuck his Royal Standard (a big flag) into a field near Nottingham. It was the signal that the English Civil War had started. So what kind of people made up Charles's army? And who dared to fight against their king? How did the two armies fight and work out who was on each side?

Objectives

- Examine which sections of society supported each side in the Civil War.
- Describe the different types of soldiers and summarise how they fought.

Who was on each side?

Ordinary people rarely chose which side they were going to be on. They supported the side that got to their town or village first, or the side their local landowner supported. Friends would sometimes end up fighting friends, families might fight against their own relatives, and so on. Ordinary people were also forced to provide food and give shelter to any soldiers that arrived in their town or village. Many people suffered as their homes, possessions and land were destroyed by the visiting soldiers. Some people starved because the soldiers took their food.

While some people were forced to fight for one side or another, others knew exactly who they would fight for. The rich lords and country gentlemen usually fought for the king. Catholics also tended to support the king (and his Catholic wife). His support was strongest in the north of England, Wales, Devon, Cornwall and Somerset. Parliament was most popular in the south, especially in London and other large towns and ports. Most merchants, businessmen and Puritans also fought for Parliament.

The Royalists were known as **Cavaliers**. 'Cavalier' comes from the Italian word *cavaliere*, which means soldier on horseback. The Cavaliers were known for their long hair and stylish clothes.

The Parliamentarians were nicknamed **Roundheads** because of their simple, short 'bowl-cut' hairstyles.

The armies

The richer gentlemen on each side went into battle on horseback. The **cavalry**, as soldiers on horseback are known, wore steel breastplates over their leather coats. They tried to break through the enemy lines by firing their **pistols** and cutting men down with their swords.

Ordinary people on each side joined either the **pikemen** or the **musketeers** (see page opposite). Soldiers without horses were known as **infantry** or foot soldiers. As you couldn't easily tell who your enemy was by their appearance or language, both sides wore brightly coloured strips of cloth. The Royalists wore red **sashes** and the Parliamentarians wore yellow ones. That way, you could clearly see who was on each side.

The musketeers

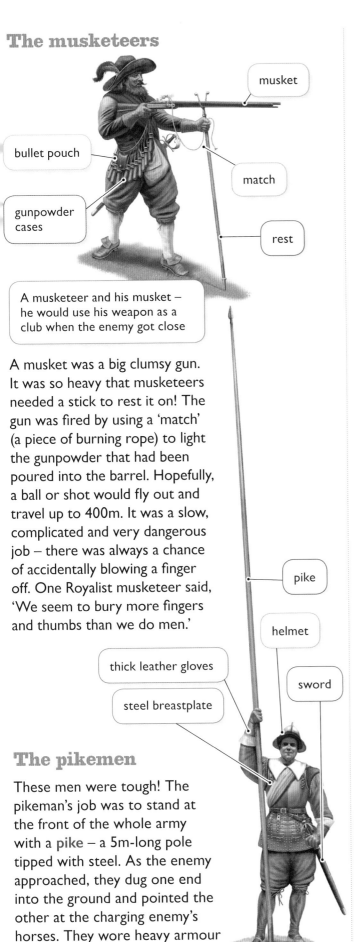

musket

bullet pouch

match

gunpowder cases

rest

A musketeer and his musket – he would use his weapon as a club when the enemy got close

A musket was a big clumsy gun. It was so heavy that musketeers needed a stick to rest it on! The gun was fired by using a 'match' (a piece of burning rope) to light the gunpowder that had been poured into the barrel. Hopefully, a ball or shot would fly out and travel up to 400m. It was a slow, complicated and very dangerous job – there was always a chance of accidentally blowing a finger off. One Royalist musketeer said, 'We seem to bury more fingers and thumbs than we do men.'

pike

helmet

thick leather gloves

sword

steel breastplate

The pikemen

These men were tough! The pikeman's job was to stand at the front of the whole army with a **pike** – a 5m-long pole tipped with steel. As the enemy approached, they dug one end into the ground and pointed the other at the charging enemy's horses. They wore heavy armour and also carried a sword.

A pikeman and his pike

Revolution, Industry and Empire: Britain 1558–1901

Key Words

ally   Cavalier   cavalry   infantry   musketeer
pike   pikeman   pistol   Roundhead   sash

Lots of fighting

There were over 600 different clashes between Cavaliers and Roundheads during the English Civil War. Sometimes the Cavaliers won, sometimes there was no clear winner and, on other occasions, the Roundheads claimed victory. One Royalist general and his troops even changed sides – but forgot to change their old red sashes to the new Roundhead yellow ones. They were all shot by their new **allies**.

Over to You

1 Complete the sentences below with an accurate term.
   a The English Civil War began in August _____ .
   b The rich lords and country gentlemen usually fought for the _____ .
   c London and many other large towns and ports usually supported _____ .
   d The Royalists were known as Cavaliers and Parliamentarians were nicknamed _____ .

2 a Look at the pictures of the pikeman and the musketeer. On which side did each fight? Explain how you made your choice.
   b Choose either a pikeman or a musketeer and explain how this soldier would fight.

3 Write a job description for either a musketeer or a pikeman, in order to try to recruit more men for your army. Try to include the following:
   • details of the job and responsibilities
   • equipment supplied
   • hazards of the job
   • benefits of the job.

Knowledge and Understanding

1 Define the following:
   a cavalry b infantry c musketeer d pikeman
2 Describe two features of the armies that fought in the English Civil War.

What was new about the New Model Army?

The first great battle of the Civil War – Edgehill, 1642 – ended in a draw... just! The commanders of Parliament's armies were shocked by their troops' lack of discipline and skill. This was the first fighting that many of the soldiers had seen, and they had been given very little training. In the chaos of battle, orders were ignored and soldiers fled in panic. The king's cavalry were experienced and well trained, and very nearly wiped out Parliament's forces. So what changes did the Roundhead commanders make to their forces? And what was it like to live and fight in the **New Model Army**?

Objectives

- Summarise why Parliament needed to improve its army.
- Examine the impact of Parliament's new fighting force.

In order to upgrade its army, Parliament decided to create a new fighting force – England's first truly professional army, which was known as the New Model Army. Oliver Cromwell (a Member of Parliament from Cambridgeshire) had argued in Parliament the army should be improved – and a Yorkshire politician named Thomas Fairfax was given the job of reorganising and training the soldiers.

The secret of success

While Cromwell was not in overall command of the New Model Army (Fairfax was), he was in charge of the cavalry, a vital component of an army at this time. All the training and discipline paid off at the Battles of Marston Moor (1644) and Naseby (1645). Both were major victories for Parliament and, at Naseby, the king's army was all but destroyed by a series of complicated moves and brave attacks by Cromwell's men. On 5 May 1646, Charles realised he had no defence against Parliament's troops. He went to Scotland and surrendered, hoping he would be safe there. But the Scots sold him to Parliament for a massive £400,000!

Charles was brought to London for peace talks but soon escaped and managed to persuade the Scots to support him. Soon, more fighting broke out (this is sometimes called the 'Second Civil War'), but it didn't last long. The king's troops (who had been joined by Scottish soldiers) were beaten in August 1648 and the king was recaptured and brought to London (again). So what was Parliament going to do with him this time?

New Model Army Soldier

metal 'pot helmet'

leather coat

metal breastplate

sword

leather boots known as 'bucket tops'

leather gloves

▼ **SOURCE A** Adapted from a letter written by Cromwell after the Battle of Edgehill in 1642 to his cousin (and fellow Roundhead) John Hampden, about Hampden's soldiers.

'Most of your soldiers are old decayed men... the Royalist soldiers are gentlemen's sons, younger sons, persons of quality. Do you think that such low-level and mean fellows will ever be able to beat gentlemen that have honour, courage and determination? You must get men of a spirit... that is likely to go on as far as a gentleman will go, or else I am sure you will be beaten still.'

▼ **INTERPRETATION B** This view of the New Model Army is taken from a History textbook, *History Alive Book 1*, by Peter Moss (1980). It mentions Prince Rupert, the nephew of Charles I. He was put in charge of the Royalist cavalry and, apart from Charles himself, was the most famous Cavalier of the whole war.

Key Words

New Model Army

'These men were strictly trained and strictly disciplined. But above all, they fought for God. Singing hymns, they charged into battle and their discipline proved too much for Rupert's cavalry, for although the cavaliers were good horsemen, they were not always good soldiers.'

▼ **SOURCE C** There was a tough code of discipline in the New Model Army. These are some examples of their rules from a 1642 document called 'Laws and Ordinances of War established for the better conduct of the Army'.

Laws of the Army

Duties to God
- Let no man blaspheme [speak disrespectfully about Christianity] upon pain to have his tongue bored with a red-hot iron.
- Cursing – Nasty language shall be punished with loss of pay.
- Neglecting worship – All those who often and wilfully absent themselves from church services and public prayer will be punished.

Duties towards Superiors and Commanders
- Resisting against correction – No man shall resist, draw, lift or offer to draw, or lift his weapon against any officer.
- Seditious [criticising Parliament] words – None shall utter any words of sedition and uproar, or mutiny, upon pain of death.

Moral duties
- Unnatural abuses – Any abusive or extremely violent behaviour shall be punished with death.
- Theft – Theft and robbery, exceeding the value of 12 pence, shall be punished with death.

Duties towards civilians [ordinary people not involved in the fighting]
- Waste and extortion [using force to take something] – No soldiers who march through the country shall waste, spoil or extort [take by force] any victuals [food/drink] or money, from any person, upon pain of death.

- Taking of horses – No soldier shall take a horse or wrong the farmers or cattle or goods, upon pain of death.

Duties in camp and garrison
- Swerving from the camp – No man shall depart a mile out of the army camp without licence [permission], upon pain of death.
- Offering violence to Victuallers [people who sell food and drink] – No man shall do violence to any that brings victuals to the camp, upon pain of death.
- Whosoever shall in his quarter [the place where the soldiers lived], abuse, beat, frighten his landlord, or any person else in the family, shall be punished.

Duties in action
- Flying – No man shall abandon his fellow soldiers, fly away in battle, upon pain of death.
- Flinging away arms – If a pikeman throws away his pike, or a musketeer his musket, he or they shall be punished with death.

Over to You

1 Why did Parliament need a New Model Army? Try to use **Source A** to help you in your answer.

2 Who was given the job of training the new army?

3 According to the sources and interpretation, what sort of men did Parliament want fighting for them?

4 Was the New Model Army a success? Explain your answer.

Source Analysis

1 Look at **Source C**. This list was made public and pinned up around England. Why do you think Parliament did this?

2 How useful are **Sources A** and **C** to a historian studying the success of the New Model Army?

Why was King Charles I sentenced to death?

King Charles I and his Royalists lost the Civil War. England faced an uncertain future but nobody expected what happened next. At 2pm on 30 January 1649, Charles had his head chopped off! But how did this happen? And who sentenced him to death?

Objectives

- Discover how and why King Charles I was put on trial.
- Analyse the key events of the trial.

By 1647, Charles's troops had been beaten and he was being kept prisoner by Parliament. But he managed to escape, get another army together, and persuade the Scots to fight on his side. However, in August 1648, Cromwell's army defeated the king's forces at Preston, and Charles was once again taken prisoner.

Many Members of Parliament (MPs) felt they couldn't trust the king any more and met to discuss what to do with him. Out of the 286 MPs, 240 thought Charles should be given another chance. However, when they next met for discussion, those same 240 MPs were stopped from entering Parliament by Cromwell's troops. This left 46 MPs to vote about what to do with the king. By 26 votes to 20, it was decided that Charles should be put on trial for treason. A jury of 135 top lawyers and judges were chosen to try him.

Firstly, the list of charges was read. It said that Charles was a **traitor**, a murderer and an enemy of England.

▼ **SOURCE A** The crimes that Charles was charged with.

'Charles Stuart, King of England... traitorously waged a war against Parliament and the people. He renewed the war against Parliament in 1648. He is responsible for all the treasons, murders, burnings and damage caused during these wars.'

The main judge leading the trial, John Bradshaw, asked Charles to say whether he pleaded 'guilty' or 'not guilty' to the charges.

Charles laughed at Bradshaw. He refused to accept that the court had any legal right to put him on trial at all.

▼ **SOURCE B** The king's response to the charges.

'I want to know by what power I am called here. I want to know by what authority, I mean lawful. There are many unlawful authorities in the world, thieves and robbers on the highway... Remember, I am your king, your lawful king... I have a trust committed to me by God.'

Day 1

The trial in Westminster Hall, London, began on Saturday 20 January 1649

Charles was brought to court by armed soldiers. There were meant to be 135 judges but only 67 turned up.

He refused to remove his hat, but nobody forced him to.

Day 2

Monday 22 January 1649

On the second day, 70 judges turned up. The king again refused to plead 'guilty' or 'not guilty'.

This is not a proper court of law. The courts of England are my courts and under my control. How can the king be put on trial in his own court?

Tuesday 23 January 1649

On the third day, 71 judges turned up. Once again, Charles refused to plead and was taken away after just a few minutes in court.

> I do not know why I am here. There is no law to make your king your prisoner.

24–26 January 1649: The judges met without Charles for the next few days. They decided to write down a plea of 'guilty' even though Charles had chosen not to answer any of their questions properly.

There were many angry people who came to watch. Some thought that the court had no right to put the king on trial.

> No one should be tried in this court!

> The king cannot be tried by any court!

Witnesses were called to give evidence.

▼ **SOURCE C** A witness at the trial.

'King Charles once saw some of Parliament's troops being badly treated by Royalists. He said, "I do not care if they cut them three times more, for they are my enemies."'

▼ **SOURCE D** Another witness at the trial.

'Here is a letter from King Charles to his son. He is asking his son to get a foreign army together to invade England. Charles wants foreigners to kill Englishmen. He can't be trusted... he's a traitor.'

traitor

The verdict and sentence

On the final day, 68 judges turned up. Charles tried to make a statement but wasn't allowed to. Bradshaw pronounced the king 'guilty' and read out the sentence.

> It is the duty of any king to talk with Parliament frequently. You did not do this. You failed in your duties as king. This started the war.

The punishment

> Bradshaw wore a metal-lined hat during the trial. Why do you think he did this?

> This court does judge that Charles Stuart, as a traitor, murderer and a public enemy, shall be put to death by the severing of his head from his body.

The execution date was set for Tuesday 30 January 1649. The death warrant (a signed piece of paper that confirms that a person will be executed) was signed by 59 judges.

Over to You

1 Throughout the trial, Charles refused to take his hat off, interrupted and even laughed at what was being said. Why do you think he behaved like this?

2 It is 1649 and you have got a seat in court to watch the trial of Charles I. Write a letter to a friend about the events of days 1 and 2. Remember to follow the conventions of a letter, including your school's address and the date. Hint: Choose whether you are a supporter of Charles *or* a supporter of Parliament. Your letter should reflect your feelings. For example, a supporter of Charles might think his refusal to take his hat off was brave. Someone against him might think this was disrespectful.

3 Write another letter to your friend about the events of days 3–7, including your opinion of the verdict.

Around 2pm on Tuesday 30 January 1649, King Charles I was executed. His head was cut off with an axe outside Whitehall Banqueting House in London, in front of a large crowd. This event shocked many people and changed how the country was run. How did the execution happen, and what do we know about it?

Objectives

- Examine the details of Charles I's execution.
- Evaluate sources relating to the execution.

Before the execution

Charles had spent the few days since his trial at one of his royal palaces in London. His execution was planned for around 12 noon, so early in the morning he went for a walk through St James's Park with his pet spaniel. He ate some bread, drank some red wine and dressed in his finest clothes (all black). He also wore a blue sash – a sign of royalty – and then walked the short distance to the Whitehall Banqueting House.

Fact ✔

It was a cold January day and Charles wore two shirts because he didn't want to start shivering from the cold. He didn't want the public to think that he was trembling with fear.

Problems with the executioner

The execution was delayed because the usual executioner refused to do it. Then 38 other men were each offered £100 to do it. One by one they refused. Eventually, two men agreed to do it in disguise. They wore masks, wigs and false beards, and to this day their identity is a mystery.

The time arrives

Eventually, shortly before 2pm, the king stepped onto the black cloth-covered scaffold, took off his jewels and his cloak, and then tucked his hair into a cap. He spoke calmly to those men near to him, kneeled down to pray and then put his head on the block.

After one clean chop, one of the axemen held up Charles's head for all to see. An eyewitness said, 'There was such a groan by the thousands then present, as I never heard before and desire I may never hear again.'

After the king's body had been taken away in a wooden coffin, some people paid to dip their handkerchiefs in the blood left on the ground. Others tried to break off pieces of the scaffold covered in his blood. Some of the soldiers guarding the scaffold made a fortune that day! After the execution, big questions loomed over the nation: what would happen to the country now? With no king, what would Parliament do?

Why did many people support the execution?

People were motivated to support the execution by many factors. Some were very unhappy with the way Charles had been running the country. As far as many were concerned, Charles's defeat in battle was a sign that God was against him. Others simply wanted an end to the taxes they had endured under his reign. For many, though, the major factor in support of his execution was the fact that Charles had made a deal with Scottish forces to invade England and start the war all over again (the Second Civil War). Oliver Cromwell, for example, who until this point was willing to make a deal with Charles, described this action as a 'prodigious [major or epic] treason'.

▼ **SOURCE A** Adapted from a short speech made by the king while he stood on the scaffold before his execution on 30 January 1649. Later, the speech was printed out and read by people all over England.

'I never did begin the war with Parliament... They began war upon me... if anybody will look at the dates of what happened... they will see clearly that they began these unhappy troubles, not I... therefore I tell you I am the martyr of the people.'

► **SOURCE B**
A lawyer called John Rushworth was in the crowd at Charles's execution in January 1649. He wrote an account of what happened (adapted).

'The scaffold was hung round in black... the axe and block were in the middle of the scaffold... "I shall be very little heard by anybody here," began the King, speaking from notes he had taken from his pocket... He protested his innocence of beginning the war... Then the King took off his cloak... laid his neck upon the block; and after a little pause, stretching forth his hands, the executioner at one blow cut his head from his body.'

Key Words

martyr

► **SOURCE C**
This painting of the execution was painted by an unknown Dutch artist soon after the event.

Over to You

1 a Why do you think so many people refused to execute Charles? Give as many reasons as you can.

  b Why did the executioners finally agree to do it?

2 Look at **Source A**.

  a Summarise what Charles is saying.

  b Did Charles think he was guilty or not? Write down the words and phrases that show he did or did not think he was guilty.

3 Look at **Source C**.

  a You will notice four smaller pictures surrounding the main one. Describe each of the smaller pictures.

  b Why do you think the woman in the main picture has fainted?

  c Suggest reasons why some people dipped their handkerchiefs in the king's blood.

Causation

1 Look at the following reasons why Charles was put on trial and executed. Rank the reasons in order – from most important reason why he was executed, to least. Explain your choice.

  a Charles married the Catholic Henrietta Maria. This offended many English Protestants.

  b He ruled without Parliament, which upset the MPs.

  c He would only reassemble Parliament when he wanted to raise funds because he ran out of money.

  d He joined forces with Scotland and invaded England in an attempt to win the war. Many thought this was treason.

  e Charles was disrespectful to Parliament and never seriously tried to make peace, which led many people to think him arrogant (and stupid).

2 'The main reason why Charles was sentenced to death was because he upset Parliament.' How far do you agree?

4.6 Cromwell: the man who banned Christmas

When King Charles I was executed in January 1649, the country became a **republic** – a country without a king or queen. Things would stay like this for the next 11 years. So what was life like in the republic? If there wasn't a king or queen, who made all the laws and decisions? And why did Cromwell disapprove of Christmas so much?

Objectives

- Define the words 'republic' and 'Interregnum'.
- Discover how the country changed under Cromwell.
- Explain why Christmas celebrations were banned.

Who rules?

Without a king or queen, people looked towards the most powerful man in the country to guide them. That person was Oliver Cromwell, the leader of the army that had beaten King Charles's men (see **A**).

Who was Oliver Cromwell?

Cromwell was a Member of Parliament and a brilliant army leader. He was also a Puritan. Puritans were strict Christians who read the Bible closely, as they believed it taught them how to live their lives. They tried to lead simple lives, wear plain clothes and eat ordinary food. They didn't like sports and entertainment because they thought these distracted people from worshipping God. By the 1650s, there were lots of Puritans in the country, including Oliver Cromwell.

Parliament rules... or does it?

To start with, Parliament ruled the country – but soon the politicians began to argue among themselves. So Cromwell, who was greatly respected by many, closed Parliament and decided to run the country himself. From 1653 he was called **Lord Protector** and was paid a huge salary of £100,000 a year (over £10 million in today's money). Cromwell divided the country into 11 districts and appointed a **Major-General** to run each one. These men were strict Puritans and introduced many new laws that aimed to 'improve' people's behaviour. **B** shows some of the things that were banned.

Fact ✓

A proposed law in 1650 tried to stop women wearing make-up, and swearing was outlawed.

▼ **INTERPRETATION A** In this painting, Oliver Cromwell is looking at the body of King Charles I. The French artist Paul Delaroche is well known for painting famous historical events that he did not witness and may have been only legends... so this scene may not have actually happened. It was painted in 1849.

▼ **B** Puritan rule was very strict and laws like the ones below made the Puritan rulers increasingly unpopular.

BANNED!

By order of the Major-General

- Football banned
- Inns shut
- Bear-baiting stopped
- Theatres closed
- Maypole dancing stopped
- Gambling banned

What about Christmas?

The Puritans banned several traditional feast days, such as May Day. They also believed that Christmas celebrations were sinful, and that there was no mention in the Bible of God calling on people to celebrate in such a way! Strict laws banned anyone from holding or attending a Christmas church service. From 1656, shops and markets were told to stay open on 25 December – and soldiers were ordered to patrol the streets, confiscating any food they discovered being prepared for a Christmas celebration. Interestingly, Cromwell himself wasn't a particularly strict Puritan. He drank alcohol, played bowls and liked music and hunting!

Fed up!

By 1658, Cromwell and the Major-Generals were becoming very unpopular. Many ordinary people didn't want to live by these strict laws any more.

In September that year, Oliver Cromwell died. So what would happen to the country next?

Key Words

Interregnum   Lord Protector   Major-General   republic

Fact ✓

The time when England was a republic is known as the **Interregnum**. It comes from the Latin words *inter*, meaning 'between', and *regis* or 'king', so it means the period *between kings*.

▼ **SOURCE C** Lucy Hutchinson was an English poet and author, and a strong Puritan. She was once one of Cromwell's strongest supporters, but wrote this in around 1670.

'Cromwell exercised such power that the whole land grew weary of him, while he set up a company of silly, mean fellows, called Major-Generals. These ruled according to their wills by no law but what seemed good in their own eyes, imprisoning people, punishing some that were innocent.'

▼ **SOURCE D** A Dutch painting from the 1600s. Puritans led simple lives, wearing plain clothes (usually black and white) rather than bright, fashionable ones. They wanted simple churches too – plain glass replaced stained glass, church bells were removed, candlesticks were melted down and organs smashed up.

Over to You

1 Write a sentence to explain the following words:
   a republic
   b Interregnum.

2 a What was the difference between the Lord Protector and a Major-General?
   b Why do you think Cromwell gave himself the title of 'Lord Protector'?
   c Why do you think the Major-Generals were so unpopular with some people?

3 a Who are the two men featured in **Interpretation A?**
   b Many historians don't think this scene actually happened. So why do you think the artist painted it?

Change

1 Write a paragraph explaining how the following changed during the Interregnum:
   a churches
   b entertainment.

2 In what ways did the lives of people in England change during the Interregnum?

4.7 Why does Cromwell divide opinion?

Oliver Cromwell is one of the most famous people in British history. Apart from Queen Victoria, more streets in Britain are named after him than anyone else. Yet one of the reasons why Cromwell is so well-known is because he divides opinion. To some he was a great man who, as Lord Protector, changed the way Britain was run and made it a safer and fairer place to live. But to others he was a power-hungry monster who made Britain a worse place to live. So what do you think?

Objectives

- Examine a variety of opinions about Oliver Cromwell.
- Justify the sort of reputation you think Cromwell deserves.

▶ **SOURCE A**
This statue of Cromwell stands outside the House of Commons in Westminster, London. In a 2002 BBC survey of the British public, Cromwell was voted one of the Top 10 'Greatest Britons' of all time.

Look through the following pieces of information, opinions and interpretation about Oliver Cromwell's time as leader of the country. Think about whether they support the view that Cromwell was a great man or not. Do some opinions contain both positive *and* negative views? Or neither?

A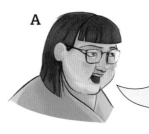

> Cromwell rose to become a brilliant soldier and a respected politician. And he promoted people based on their abilities, not on who their parents were or how much money they had.

B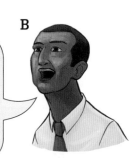

> Cromwell was one of the politicians that supported putting King Charles on trial in 1649. He said it was better for the country that Charles was executed because he couldn't be trusted and wasn't prepared to work with Parliament.

C

> Cromwell helped improve the army. The army was both feared and respected by France and Spain, which made the country safer and stronger.

D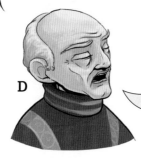

> During Cromwell's reign, sports and entertainment that ordinary people thoroughly enjoyed were stopped — theatres were closed and music, gambling and dancing were banned. Boys caught playing football on a Sunday were whipped!

E

> Cromwell himself enjoyed music, hunting and playing some sports. At his daughter's wedding, there was dancing and violins were played.

F Cromwell ended a war with the Netherlands and sorted out issues with Portugal. He made a deal with France against Spain, which led to him capturing Jamaica in the Caribbean and Dunkirk in France, which the Spanish were using as a naval base.

G Cromwell sometimes put his personal enemies in prison and acted without Parliament's agreement. He was against the idea of allowing all ordinary people to vote.

H In Ireland in 1649, Cromwell and his large army slaughtered at least 5000 people who refused to support him. This included men, women and children. Thousands of Irish children were enslaved and sent to the Caribbean. Even today, Cromwell is known to many as the 'curse of Ireland'.

I In 1290, all Jews were expelled from the country during the reign of King Edward I. During the Interregnum, Cromwell allowed Jews to come back and worship how they wanted to.

J Cromwell wanted Parliament to rule the country. But in 1653, when the politicians tried to restrict people's freedom to worship how they wished, Cromwell said that was wrong and dismissed Parliament.

K Without Parliament, Cromwell ruled on his own (from 1653 to 1658) — a bit like a king! The country was divided into 11 areas, each with its own Major-General, who set taxes and made laws. They were very unpopular.

Over to You

1 a Make a list of opinions that show Cromwell in a positive way.

   b Make another list of opinions that show him in a negative way.

   c Have you struggled to place some in either category? If so, which ones? Explain why.

2 What is your opinion of Oliver Cromwell? Do you support the view that he was 'great' or do you have a more negative opinion of him? Explain your view.

3 In museums, exhibits often have short explanations about what they show, called 'captions'. Imagine you've been asked to write a museum caption on Cromwell for a newly discovered portrait of him. Try to sum up what sort of person Cromwell was in no more than 100 words.

▼ **INTERPRETATION B** Adapted from historian Dr David Smith from the University of Cambridge.

'Oliver Cromwell is a unique figure in British history. He is the only example in British history of a republican head of state. He divided opinion at the time, and has continued to do so ever since. For some, he is a hero: a champion of freedom who stood up against the complete authority of Charles I. For others (especially in Ireland), he is a villain: a religious fanatic who was brutal to anyone who opposed him. Some see him as someone with strong beliefs and principles; others as a hypocrite and power-seeker. One thing is clear: regardless of whether you love him or loathe him, it is impossible to ignore Oliver Cromwell.'

Interpretation Analysis

Read **Interpretation B**.

1 Summarise the historian's views on Cromwell.

2 How far do you agree with this interpretation of Oliver Cromwell?

The monarchy returns – but what happened to Cromwell's head?

Oliver Cromwell died of **malaria** in September 1658. His funeral was the biggest ever seen. Around 30,000 soldiers escorted his coffin to Westminster Abbey, London, where it was buried. But Cromwell's body didn't stay there long! A few years later Cromwell's body was dug up… and his head was cut off. Why did this happen – and what happened to his head over the next 300 years?

Objectives

- Explain how England became a monarchy once more.
- Discover how and why King Charles II sought revenge after 1660.

Cromwell Junior

After Oliver Cromwell's death, his son Richard was made Lord Protector. But he didn't really want the job and would rather have been left alone to work on his farm. Unable to stop the arguing between Parliament and the army, Richard resigned after only a few months, in May 1659.

A new Charles returns

After a few more months of confusion, Parliament asked Charles I's son (also called Charles) to return from abroad to become king. So in 1660, the nation had a monarchy again. And one of King Charles II's first actions was a brutal one. He decided to kill the men who had killed his father.

Hunting the 'king killers'

In 1649, 59 people had signed the death warrant for King Charles I. By 1660, 21 of them were already dead, including Oliver Cromwell and the main judge, John Bradshaw. The new king ordered that the bodies of the leaders should be taken out of their coffins and publicly hanged at Tyburn (near Marble Arch in London today). Afterwards, their heads were cut off and stuck on spikes outside the building where Charles I's trial had taken place. Their bodies were thrown into a pit.

But Charles II didn't stop there. While some of the men who had signed his father's death warrant had escaped abroad, many others were still in Britain and were arrested. Several died in prison, but 9 of the **regicides** (a person who kills a monarch) were executed.

So what about Cromwell's head?

The story of Oliver Cromwell's head, which was stuck on a spike outside Westminster Hall in London, is fascinating – and disgusting.

1658: Cromwell dies.

c.1685: Cromwell's head stays on the pole for over 20 years but is eventually blown off in a storm. A soldier named Barnes finds it, takes it home, and hides it in a chimney.

1660: King Charles II becomes king and wants to punish Cromwell, who is already dead! Cromwell's body is removed from Westminster Abbey and hanged at Tyburn. His head is then stuck on a 6m pole nearby.

1702: As Barnes lies dying, he tells his family where he hid the famous missing head. It is sold and eventually ends up in a museum in London.

1738: The museum owner dies and the head comes into the possession of Samuel Russell, an actor. He pays his rent by charging people to see it.

Key Words

malaria   regicide

Over to You

1 Why do you think Charles II wanted to punish all the men involved in his father's death, including the ones already dead?

2 Read the story of Cromwell's head once more.
   a Why do you think soldier Barnes hid the head?
   b Why do you think Josiah Wilkinson was so convinced he had bought Cromwell's head?
   c What evidence did the doctors have in 1934 that the head was Cromwell's?
   d Why do you think the head was finally buried in secret?

3 Explain why England became a monarchy again in 1660.

Later on...

1980s

Historians are confident that they know the story of Cromwell's head, but mystery still surrounds what happened to the rest of his body! Experts think that it was probably thrown in an unmarked grave near Tyburn. In the 1980s, builders found several skeletons without skulls buried near where Cromwell's body was supposedly buried... but no one could be sure if one of them belonged to him!

Significance

1 How significant was the Interregnum? Hint: If something is significant in history, it means it was important at the time, it affected a lot of people because important changes took place, and it is still important today.

Fact ✓

There were a number of conditions placed on Charles's return – he had to agree not to take revenge on Parliament's army and to continue with Cromwell's policy of religious tolerance. He also had to promise to share power with Parliament.

1787: When Russell gets into debt, he is forced to sell the head. Twelve years later, a group of businessmen buy it for £230 (over £7000 in today's money). It goes on display in Bond Street, London.

OLIVER CROMWELL'S HEAD

1934: A descendant of Wilkinson allows the head to be examined by experts. A 109-page report is written, stating that the head had definitely been chopped off and that the pimples and warts match portraits of Cromwell. It is concluded that the head is indeed Oliver Cromwell's.

1960: Wilkinson's descendant decides the head should be buried properly. It is given to Cromwell's old college in Cambridge where it was buried secretly. It is still there today.

c.1814: The head is sold to a man named Josiah Wilkinson. He keeps it in a box, wrapped in silk. Wilkinson writes that there is an ear missing, a hole in the top of the head where a spike has been, and axe marks on the neck.

Quick Knowledge Quiz

Choose the correct answer from the three options:

1   A supporter of King Charles I during the English Civil War was known as what?

   a   a Royalist
   b   a Roundhead
   c   a Parliamentarian

2   The English Civil War began in which year?

   a   1638
   b   1642
   c   1646

3   A section of an army with soldiers who fight on horseback are known as what?

   a   infantry
   b   cavalry
   c   musketeers

4   During the English Civil War, supporters of Parliament often wore which colour sashes?

   a   red
   b   blue
   c   yellow

5   Which of the following is *not* a well-known battle of the English Civil War?

   a   Dunkirk
   b   Naseby
   c   Edgehill

6   What was name of the professional army created by Oliver Cromwell to take on the king's men?

   a   Old Contemptibles
   b   Cromwell's Cavaliers
   c   New Model Army

7   Who was the main judge at the trial of King Charles I?

   a   Matthew Wilson
   b   Charles Stuart
   c   John Bradshaw

8   On which date was King Charles I executed?

   a   14 October 1666
   b   30 January 1649
   c   6 June 1642

9   What was the title of the head of state in England between 1653 and 1659, a position first held by Oliver Cromwell?

   a   Lord Protector
   b   Home Secretary
   c   Lord Chancellor

10 The period in history when England was a republic is also known as what?

   a   the Renaissance
   b   the Interregnum
   c   the Reformation

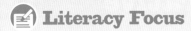 **Literacy Focus**

Note-taking

Note-taking is a vital skill. To do it successfully, you must pick out all the important (key) words in a sentence. The important words are the words that are vital to the meaning (and your understanding) of the sentence. For example, in the sentence:

> *A civil war is a war between two groups of people in the same country. The English Civil War, which began in 1642, was a conflict between a group known as the Royalists, led by King Charles I, and the men of Parliament and their followers. This group was known as the Parliamentarians.*

… the important words are: civil war; conflict between groups in same country; English CW; began 1642; between Royalists; leader King Charles I; vs Parliament; AKA Parliamentarians.

The original paragraph was over 50 words long – but the shortened version is fewer than 25 words long and contains abbreviations. Note-taking like this will help your understanding of events – and provides you with a great revision exercise.

1   Write down the important words in the following paragraphs. These important words are your notes.

- Ordinary people rarely chose which side they were going to be on. They supported the side that got to their town or village first, or the side their local landowner supported. Friends would sometimes end up fighting friends, families might fight against their own relatives, and so on.

- Ordinary people were also forced to provide food and give shelter to any soldiers that arrived in their town or village. Many people suffered as their homes, possessions and land were destroyed by the visiting soldiers. Some people starved because the soldiers took their food.

- The rich lords and country gentlemen usually fought for the king. Catholics also tended to support the king (and his Catholic wife). His support was strongest in the north of England, Wales, Devon, Cornwall and Somerset.

- Parliament was most popular in the south, especially in London and other large towns and ports. Most merchants, businessmen and Puritans also fought for Parliament.

- The richer gentlemen on each side went into battle on horseback. The cavalry, as soldiers on horseback are known, wore steel breastplates over their leather coats. They tried to break through the enemy lines by firing their pistols and cutting men down with their swords. Ordinary people on each side joined either the pikemen or the musketeers.

4 History skill: Write a narrative account (causation)

Historians use the term 'causes' to describe the things that made events happen. Most events have a number of causes. Also, events have **consequences** – the results or effects of something. Like causes, there can often be several consequences.

Writing about the causes and the consequences of an event can help historians create a well-explained story. A good story, or a narrative account, should:

* show off your knowledge of a period in history

* show that you can get a story in the right chronological order (so it makes sense)

* explain why things happened (cause) and what they led to (consequence).

How to write a narrative account

Here is one way to write a narrative account:

1 **Plan:** Firstly, it is important to make sure you know the key events. What should you include? What should you leave out? Make a plan of the main events.

2 **Check order and add detail:** To tell the story in a logical way, organise the key events in your plan in the right order. Don't forget to add some dates to the events.

3 **Write your story:** When you are sure of the order of events, it's time to start writing the story down. Don't forget to add details to the events.

4 **Make links:** To improve your narrative, you need to make sure that your story is not just a detailed description. Try to link events together, to show the causes and consequences of why and how things happened. This helps you to show that you know how the different parts of the story are connected and moves you beyond a collection of detailed facts. These 'linking' words and phrases are called 'connectives'.

TIP: For example, you may have studied the Spanish Armada of 1588. There were a number of causes of Spain's attack on England, including the news that Mary, Queen of Scots (a Catholic, like Spain's King Philip II) had been executed by England's Queen Elizabeth.

TIP: Using the Spanish Armada example again, a consequence of the Spanish defeat might be that it showed that Queen Elizabeth could govern England in times of war, as well as peace.

TIP: You can use words and phrases like:

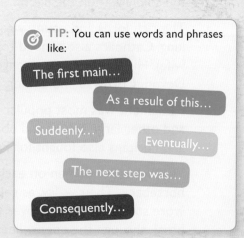

The first main...

As a result of this...

Suddenly...

Eventually...

The next step was...

Consequently...

Your challenge is to answer this narrative account question:

> Write a narrative account of the events during the reign of Charles I (between 1625 and 1642) that led to the start of the English Civil War.
>
> You may use the following in your answer:
>
> • the Divine Right of Kings
>
> • the introduction of the Ship Tax.
>
> You must also use information of your own.　　　　(20)

The steps below will help you structure your answer. Use the sentence starters to help you get started.

1   **Plan:** Make a list of the main events and causes in the build-up to the outbreak of the Civil War. You have been told about two causes (the Divine Right of Kings and the introduction of the Ship Tax), but there are others.

> **TIP:** You might want to re-read pages 72–73.

> **TIP:** An important aspect of writing a good narrative account is to demonstrate your own knowledge.

2   **Check order and add detail:** Organise the events you listed in chronological order. Can you add any dates to the events?

3   **Write your story:** Write about the events in the right order by using your answers in step 2.　　　　(15)

4   **Make links:** Try to connect the events together. It's important that your account *flows*.　　　　(5)

> **TIP:** For example, when describing the difficult relationship between Parliament and Charles that led to the outbreak of the Civil War, you might write:
>
> Parliament felt that Charles only used them to collect taxes for him. Eventually, Parliament refused to collect taxes for him. As a result, he stopped Parliament between 1629 and 1640 and ruled without it. However, he was forced to ask it to meet again because a Scottish army invaded and he needed money to raise an army...

5.1 Who was the Merry Monarch?

29 May 1660 was a special day for King Charles II, the son of Charles I. Firstly, it was his thirtieth birthday. Secondly, it was the day he returned to London after living abroad for almost ten years. Thousands lined the streets of London, Europe's largest city. The country had a king once more. How did life change under Charles II?

Objectives

- Explain how, when and why Charles II became king.
- Compare Cromwell's nation with the 'Merry Monarch's'.

The return of the king

England had been without a king since 30 January 1649, the day Charles I was executed. After this, the country was ruled by Parliament for a time and then by Oliver Cromwell, a politician and leader of the army. But Cromwell's strict religious views didn't make him popular. He closed down pubs and theatres, and banned most sports. He even banned Christmas and Easter celebrations and replaced them with days of fasting! Before he died in 1658, he picked his son Richard to carry on running the country. But Richard couldn't control the army or Parliament, and didn't really want the job. So, in 1660, Parliament asked Charles I's son to become king – and Britain became a monarchy again.

The Merry Monarch

Charles II couldn't have been more different from Cromwell. He brought back all the sports and entertainments that had been banned and soon earned the nickname of the 'Merry Monarch'. Charles himself could often be seen racing down the Thames in a yacht, gambling on horses at Newmarket, visiting the theatre, or playing 'pell mell' (a game combining hockey, golf and croquet) in the streets. Once again, Christmas, May Day and harvest time were celebrated. Most people were very happy with these changes.

Earlier on...

While the rest of Britain did not have a king from January 1649, Scotland had, in fact, already claimed Charles II as their king as soon as Charles I was executed. Charles II was the grandson of James VI of Scotland, who had become James I of England after Elizabeth I died.

▼ **SOURCE A** A painting of the magnificent procession through London to celebrate Charles II's coronation.

▼ **INTERPRETATION B** From a review of historian Malcolm Gaskill's book about Charles II (2009).

'Charles liked riding and tennis, and loved jokes and gossip. But his passion was women. His sleazy attitude, and the court's eye-popping behaviour, harmed the king's image.'

▼ **SOURCE C** During Stuart times, the River Thames often froze solid and 'Frost Fairs', like the one shown here in 1683, were held on it. Charles II would attend regularly.

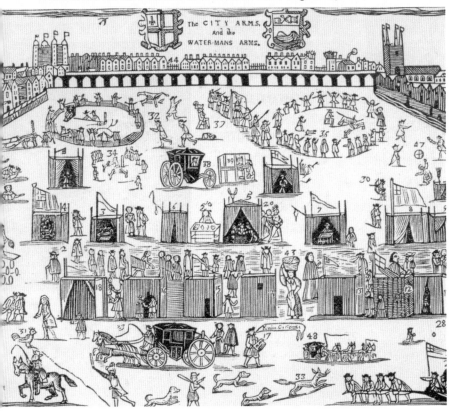

The serious side

Charles II had a serious side too. He encouraged scientific experiments and loved art, design, mathematics, drama and music. He was also careful to build a good relationship with Parliament because he didn't want there to be another civil war.

Religious freedom?

One of the most positive things about life under Cromwell was that he allowed people to worship in almost any way they wished. Charles II hoped that there would be some religious freedom too, but Parliament was not so keen. In 1664, it banned all religious services except those of the Church of England, which was now England's official religion.

Key Words   Restoration

Carefree... but heir-free

Charles II was married to a Portuguese princess named Catherine, but had lots of affairs with other women. His mistresses produced at least 14 (yes, 14!) children between them, but none could be king or queen after Charles's death. This is because, by law, the heir must be a child born from the king and his wife. Charles's wife, Queen Catherine, had no children, so when Charles died, he would be replaced as king by his younger brother, James.

Over to You

1 Why do you think Charles II was nicknamed the 'Merry Monarch'?

2 Charles II's return as king in 1660 is known as the **Restoration**. Why do you think it was called this?

3 Explain why Charles's brother was to become king after Charles's death and not one of Charles's children.

4 Look at **Source C**.
   a Make a list of all the different activities you can see. Here are three to start you off:
   • dogs hunting a fox
   • archery
   • a man selling knives and combs.

Change and Continuity

1 When Charles II became king in 1660, there were huge parties that went on for many days. List as many reasons as you can why people might have been so happy.

2 Explain two ways in which Cromwell's nation and the Merry Monarch's nation were different. You might want to look at pages 82–85 to remind yourself of life in Cromwell's England.

5.2A How deadly was the Great Plague?

A **plague** is a fast-spreading killer disease. In Tudor and Stuart times, plague struck many times. In 1536, a plague killed 18,000 people in Britain. In 1603, 40,000 people died and a further 35,000 died in 1625. But one of the worst outbreaks happened in 1665. This plague killed up to 100,000 people in London alone and thousands more around the country. It became known as the 'Great Plague'. What caused it? How did people try to control it? And what was its impact?

Objectives

- Discover what people knew about the spread of plague and disease in seventeenth-century Britain.
- Recall the symptoms of the Great Plague.
- Examine the impact of the plague.

The diary of Samuel Pepys

Much of what we know about the impact of the Great Plague on London comes from the diary of a man called Samuel Pepys (pronounced 'peeps'). He was a London MP who wrote in his diary almost every day from 1660 to 1669. His diary (which still survives) tracks the spread of the plague and gives a very personal account of the tragedy. Read some extracts from the diary below.

▶ **SOURCE A**
A portrait of Samuel Pepys, painted by John Hayls in 1666 shortly after the Great Plague hit London.

▼ **SOURCE B** Adapted versions of Pepys's diary entries for the summer of 1665.

7 June
'The hottest day that I have ever felt in my life. In Drury Lane I saw two or three houses marked with a red cross and the words "Lord have mercy upon us" written on the door. This worried me so much that I bought a roll of tobacco to smell and chew.'

17 June
'I was riding in a coach through the street when my driver drove slower and slower before stopping. He told me that he felt sick and could hardly see where he was going. I felt very sorry for him – did he have the plague?'

29 June
'I travelled on the river today and saw wagons full of people trying to leave the city. I might move my wife up to Woolwich where there is no plague – but I will remain working in my office. I hear the church bells ring five or six times a day for a funeral.'

20 July
'Walked home past Redriffe, where the sickness is; indeed, it is scattered almost everywhere. 1089 people died of plague this week.'

8 August
'Poor Will, the man who used to sell us ale, his wife and three children died, all of them on the same day. 4000 people died in London this week, 3000 of the plague.'

12 August
'The king and queen are to leave London and go to Salisbury. God preserve us!'

31 August
'The mayor said that all fit people should be indoors by 9pm, so the sick can exercise and have some fresh air at night.'

3 September
'I bought a new wig but I have been afraid to wear it until now. It might have been made from the hair of a dead plague victim!'

20 September
'What a sad time it is to see no boats on the river; and grass grows all over the roads, and nobody but poor wretches in the streets!'

What were the symptoms?

There are different kinds of plague, each with a different cause. Historians cannot quite agree on the type of plague that hit London in 1665 but most think it was the **bubonic plague**. It gets its name from the 'buboes', or huge round boils, which appeared in a victim's armpit or on their groin. There were lots of other nasty symptoms too (see the cartoon).

▼ **C** Some people had all these symptoms and still survived – but most people suffered a painful death within a week.

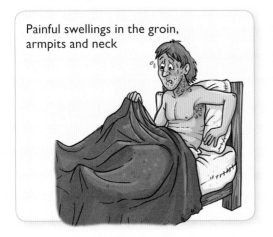

Painful swellings in the groin, armpits and neck

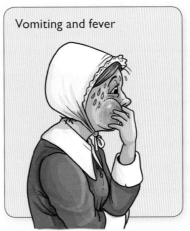

Vomiting and fever

Dizziness and hallucinations (seeing things that aren't really there)

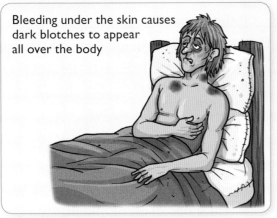

Bleeding under the skin causes dark blotches to appear all over the body

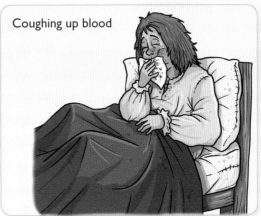

Coughing up blood

What did people at the time think caused the Great Plague?

People came up with all sorts of suggestions for what caused the plague. Some thought it was caused by the positions of the planets, or sent as a punishment from God. Others said it was spread by touching a cat or a dog. The most common explanation, though, was that it was caused by poisonous air (**miasma**). As a result, it was common for people to smoke a lot, chew tobacco, or carry around bunches of flowers to get rid of the 'bad air'!

Later on...
1951

In 1951, the stories from the diary were made into a musical called *And So To Bed* – the title came from the way Pepys ended his diary each day.

Over to You

1 Describe the symptoms of the plague.

2 Re-read Samuel Pepys's diary entries carefully and answer the following questions.

   a What do you think the red crosses and the writing on people's doors meant?

   b Why do you think Pepys bought a roll of tobacco to smell and chew?

   c How might the plague spread around the country?

3 Why are diaries like the one kept by Pepys useful to historians?

The real cause of the Great Plague

In 1665, people didn't understand what caused the plague or how to treat it properly. Today, one of the most common theories about the plague was that it was caused by germs that lived in the blood of black rats and in the fleas on their bodies. The fleas would hop onto humans, bite them, and pass on the disease.

Historians think that plague-infected rats and fleas brought the disease to England aboard boats bringing goods from the Netherlands. The plague germs, the fleas which carried them, and the black rats which carried the fleas, flourished in the filthy, overcrowded streets of London and several other towns.

How did people try to deal with the plague?

There were many theories about the cause of the plague – and just as many strange suggestions for how to 'cure' it and to prevent it from spreading.

Earlier on... 1348

Many of the beliefs about the causes of the 1665 Great Plague (and the unusual suggestions to prevent and cure it) are very similar to what you might have studied on the Black Death of 1348. This shows that people's understanding of disease had not developed much between the fourteenth and seventeenth centuries.

Attempts to control the plague

Although it wasn't known how and why the disease spread, many people at the time began to notice two things. Firstly, there were more plague victims in the dirtiest, filthiest areas of London. And secondly, a person was more likely to get the plague if they had been in contact with a person who was already infected. As a result, the Mayor of London and his council passed a series of rules and regulations to try to stop the spread of plague (see E).

▼ **SOURCE D** As soon as the plague appeared, so did con artists (known as **quacks**) selling fake potions and pills that they claimed could cure or prevent it. The advice here has been adapted from an information sheet published at the time.

Famous and effective MEDICINE to treat the PLAGUE

To avoid the plague:

Place a gold coin in vinegar for one day. Then put the coin in your mouth and keep it there.

Smoke tobacco to keep away the poisonous air that carries plague.

Wear a dead frog around your neck.

Carry a lucky rabbit's foot or another lucky charm.

If the plague is in your house:

Wrap the victim in woollen blankets, until they are very sweaty. Then cut a live pigeon in half and rub it on the boils. The boils should begin to shrink.

Place a live frog next to a boil. The frog will suck out the poison, swell up and explode.

Drink plague water – a special mixture of 22 herbs, mixed with white wine and brandy. You can buy this in shops all over London.

▼ **SOURCE E** Adapted from the rules and regulations issued by the Mayor of London in 1665

To prevent the spread of the plague:

- Houses containing any plague victims should be boarded up and marked with a large cross and the words 'Lord have mercy on us'. No one can leave or enter the house for a month after the last victim has died or recovered. The house will be guarded.
- The dead are only to be buried at night in special plague cemeteries.
- Victims' clothing should be burned.
- Pubs and theatres to be closed.
- Homeowners must sweep the streets outside their homes.
- Dogs and cats are to be killed and all animals are banned from the city.

SOURCE F Each week the number of dead and the cause of death were written on a **Bill of Mortality**. This one covers 12–19 September 1665.

The Diseases and Casualties this Week.

Abortive	4	Imposthume	8
Aged	45	Infants	22
Bleeding	1	Kingsevil	4
Broken legge	1	Lethargy	1
Broke her scull by a fall in the street at St. Mary Woolchurch	1	Livergrown	1
		Meagrome	1
		Palsie	1
Childbed	28	Plague	4237
Chrisomes	9	Purples	2
Consumption	126	Quinsie	5
Convulsion	89	Rickets	23
Cough	1	Rising of the Lights	18
Dropsie	53	Rupture	1
Feaver	348	Scurvy	3
Flox and Small-pox	11	Shingles	1
Flux	1	Spotted Feaver	166
Frighted	2	Stilborn	4
Gowt	1	Stone	2
Grief	3	Stopping of the stomach	17
Griping in the Guts	79	Strangury	3
Head-mould-shot	1	Suddenly	2
Jaundies	7	Surfeit	74
		Teeth	111
		Thrush	6
		Tissick	9
		Ulcer	1
		Vomiting	10
		Winde	4
		Wormes	20

Christned	Males — 90	Buried	Males — 2777	Plague — 4237
	Females — 81		Females — 2791	
	In all — 171		In all — 5568	

Increased in the Burials this Week ———— 249
Parishes clear of the Plague ——— 27   Parishes Infected ——— 103

The Assize of Bread set forth by Order of the Lord Major and Court of Aldermen,
A penny Wheaten Loaf to contain Nine Ounces and a half, and three
half-penny White Loaves the like weight.

SOURCE G A drawing of a plague doctor from the 1600s. When visiting victims, every part of the doctor's body would be covered and he would place perfume or spice inside his mask to avoid the bad air. The costume often worked because the thick leather protected them from fleas.

Mask with glass visor, beak stuffed with perfume or spices

Stick to keep people away

Leather gloves to avoid skin contact with the sick

Long leather coat

Key Words   Bill of Mortality   quack

The impact of plague

Most rich Londoners – lawyers and merchants, for example – moved away from London. King Charles II also left in July 1665. Parliament was postponed and court cases were moved to Oxford. By the end of that summer, it was mainly the poor who were left. The city changed from a busy, crowded centre of trade to a place where grass started growing in the streets. Some people were forced to beg for food because the plague had affected business so badly.

Despite the Mayor's attempts to limit the spread of the plague, up to 100,000 Londoners died. It has been estimated that over half a million people across the country were killed. By December 1665, the plague had started to die down, but another disaster was about to strike… the Great Fire of London!

Over to You

1 How do historians think the plague of 1665 might have got into Britain?

2 a List three measures that were taken to try to prevent the spread of the plague.

   b For each of the measures you have chosen, explain whether you think they would have been effective or not. Explain your answer.

3 Look at **Source G**. Write a sentence or two to explain why the plague doctor is dressed in this way.

4 Make a list of the ways that the Great Plague made an impact on London.

Source Analysis

1 Look at **Source F**. What was a 'Bill of Mortality'?

2 a How many people died of the plague?

   b How many people died and were buried 'in all' during this week?

   c Work out what percentage of people were killed by the plague during this week.

   d What do you think is meant by: 'aged', 'grief', 'suddenly' and 'teeth' as causes of death?

3 How useful is **Source F** to a historian studying the Great Plague?

Was the Great Fire of London an accident – or arson?

On Sunday 2 September 1666, a fire started in London, not far from London Bridge. Over the next three days it blazed out of control across the city, destroying more than 13,000 homes and 88 churches. What caused the fire to start? Was it an accident, or did someone start it deliberately (a criminal act known as arson)? And how did it manage to spread across so much of London?

Objectives

- Describe how the Great Fire devastated London.
- Explain why the fire spread so quickly.

Samuel Pepys, the famous diarist, lived a bit further away from London Bridge. When he first saw the flames, he wasn't too worried. However, it later became clear that this fire was serious (see **A**).

▼ **SOURCE A** From Samuel Pepys's diary, written in 1666.

2 September
'Walked to the Tower and got up on one of the high places… I did see the houses at the end of the street on fire… The lieutenant of the Tower tells me it began this morning in the king's baker's house in Pudding Lane… we saw the fire grow… in the most horrid, bloody flame, not like the fine flame of an ordinary fire. It made me weep to see it. The churches, houses and all on fire, and flaming at once, and a horrid noise the flames made, and the cracking of houses at their ruin. So home with a sad heart.'

Fact ✓

With the fire fast approaching, Samuel Pepys rushed to save some of his precious belongings by burying them in his garden – including a big piece of cheese.

The fire spreads

As the day went on, the fire got worse and worse. London's buildings were packed close together, so the fire spread quickly. In addition, most of the buildings were made of wood, which had dried out during the long, hot summer of 1666 and so they burned easily.

There was no fire brigade at that time, either. There were attempts to fight the fire by pouring on water, but this made little difference.

London's burning

By the evening of Sunday 2 September, Charles II was so concerned that he ordered houses in the path of the fire to be pulled down. The idea was to create 'fire breaks' to stop the fire spreading to more houses. But the man in charge of stopping the fire – the Mayor of London – was struggling with the king's orders. People didn't want to lose their homes so they only allowed their houses to be pulled down at the last moment. And by then it was too late – the piles of wood and plaster just caught fire too.

▼ **INTERPRETATION B** A painting of the Great Fire from the late 1670s. Note the people loading up carts and running from the flames.

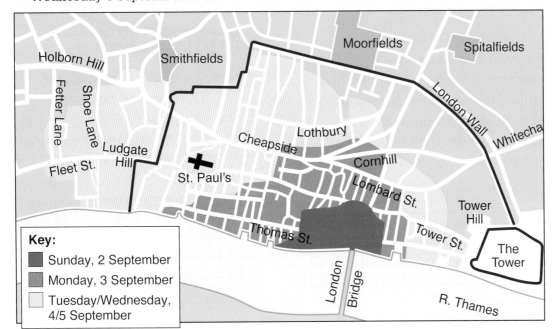

▼ **MAP C** A map showing the spread of the fire from Sunday 2 September to Wednesday 5 September 1666.

A city in fear

Strong winds fanned the fire for the next few days. Thousands of terrified Londoners loaded their possessions onto carts and fled the city. On Wednesday, the king ordered whole rows of houses to be blown up with gunpowder. The gaps created by the explosions stopped the fire spreading so quickly and by Thursday the fire was dying down. But the heart of Europe's largest city had been reduced to ashes. Amazingly, the number of officially recorded deaths as a result of the fire is low (six), but around 100,000 people were made homeless. John Evelyn, another well-known diarist, even wrote, 'London was, but is no more.'

So who started the Great Fire of London?

Today, historians are sure that the fire started in a small bakery, run by Thomas Farriner, near Pudding Lane, not far from London Bridge.

But many people at the time didn't believe it was an accident. They suspected a foreign plot, or a Catholic plot. Right after the fire had died down, rumours spread throughout the city and people were attacked at random. A Swedish man was nearly hanged by an angry crowd and a French visitor was beaten with an iron bar. Another Frenchman was nearly beaten to death by people who thought he was carrying fireballs (they were, in fact, tennis balls!). Then, a week after the end of the fire, a Frenchman named Robert Hubert was arrested on suspicion of starting the fire. He even confessed that he had thrown a fire bomb through Farriner's bakery window. He was found guilty and hanged in October 1666. However, Hubert could not have had anything to do with the fire – he wasn't actually in the country when the fire began. His confession was probably extracted after hours of torture. Hubert's conviction and execution shows how keen people were at the time to find someone to blame – and Hubert was a convenient **scapegoat**.

1 Suggest reasons why people were so ready to blame Robert Hubert for starting the fire.

2 Plan an exhibition for primary school children about the causes and impact of the Great Fire. You will need to include: what happened; what damage was done; how people tried to fight it; some different opinions about who was to blame; the reaction of the authorities. Think about the maps, exhibits and materials that you might use. You might want to work in a small group or with a partner for this.

Knowledge and Understanding ⭐

1 When and where did the Great Fire start?

2 Outline how the Great Fire of London started and spread across the city.

London: a city reborn

The Great Fire of 1666 had a great impact on the city of London – it destroyed around five-sixths of it, including many filthy, stinking streets and alleys full of dirt and disease. Planning for the rebuilding of the city began soon after the fire was finally out. Who was involved in these plans and how did they change London?

Objectives

- Recall the impact of the Great Fire of London.
- Examine how London was rebuilt after the Great Fire.

New plans

King Charles II asked for plans for a new city, and within weeks, several **architects** had written up their ideas. Most of the plans, including those by well-known scientists and thinkers such as Christopher Wren and Robert Hooke, wanted a city with broad, straight streets, wide-open spaces and magnificent new brick or stone churches and homes.

However, some of these big ideas were ignored. The people whose homes had been destroyed wanted them built quickly and in exactly the same places as their old ones. Few people wanted to – or could afford to – give up their land to make London a nicer place to live. However, the king did insist on some important changes, and a 'new' London emerged from the ruins.

New rules for a new London

- Building new homes out of wood is **banned**.
- All new houses should be built of **brick** or **stone**.
- All new streets must be **wide**.
- Houses over 9m wide are only allowed on main streets.
- 100 streets must be **widened**.
- The filthy Fleet River will be covered over and some new common **sewers** will be built.

A new London

By 1676, a new city was taking shape. London looked like it had been planned properly – with rows of houses all the same height and made from the same building materials. Cleaner streets meant fewer rats and fleas. Stone buildings meant less chance of fire. Never again was there a plague or fire on the same scale as those of 1665 and 1666.

One of Wren's most popular ideas was his plan for more than 50 new churches. The most famous, St Paul's Cathedral, took 35 years to build (see **A** and **B**). Wren's designs became sought after and by the time he died in 1723 he had been involved in many other magnificent buildings, including colleges and hospitals.

▼ **INTERPRETATION A** Adapted from a 2016 article, 'How the Great Fire shaped modern London', by architectural journalist Ike Ijeh for *Building* magazine.

'London is a city defined by a relentless cycle of destruction and redevelopment... and yet the Great Fire of London probably remains the greatest single driver of architectural change in the capital's history. With London essentially a blank canvas a new **baroque** style was applied to new churches, hospitals, monuments, houses and palaces and it is a style that we still associate with London today... Had it not been for the Great Fire of London, there's a chance we may never have had iconic buildings like the Old Bailey, Admiralty Arch, County Hall and of course St Paul's Cathedral.'

A new idea

Insurance companies started up as a result of the Great Fire. Before the fire, if your house burned down, you paid for it to be rebuilt. In 1680, the first insurance company (the 'Fire Office') was set up. A house owner could pay small sums of money to 'insure' their property. If a fire started, the employees of the insurance company would put out the fire using their own fire engine. Other insurance companies soon started and by 1690 one in ten houses in London was insured.

▼ **SOURCE B** A 1710 image of St. Paul's Cathedral. It was the tallest building in London from its construction until 1962. The dome is the second largest in the world and Wren used latest engineering techniques in its construction. When he died in 1723, Wren was the first person to be buried in St Paul's Cathedral.

1675

Meanwhile...

Other new buildings during the era of the Restoration illustrate an increased interest in science. Charles II was a great supporter of the latest scientific inventions and technology, and showed this when he ordered the building of the Royal Observatory at Greenwich, London. It was designed by Wren.

1723

Later on...

Wren is buried in St Paul's. On his grave are the words 'Si monumentum requiris, circumspire' – they mean, 'If you seek his monument, look around you.'

Key Words   architect   baroque   sewer

▼ **SOURCE C** St Paul's Cathedral today.

Over to You

1 a How much of London was destroyed by the Great Fire?
   b What sort of city did people such as Wren and Hooke plan?
   c Can you suggest reasons for these ideas?
   d Why were some of their plans not used?
   e Do you think the description on Wren's grave is an appropriate one?

2 Look at **Interpretation A**. What point does the writer make about the impact and influence of the Great Fire?

3 Summarise the style of house-building during the Restoration period.

Consequences

1 What is insurance – and how is it linked to the Great Fire?

2 Explain two consequences of the Great Fire.

⟳ Quick Knowledge Quiz

Choose the correct answer from the three options:

1 In which year did Charles II return to London to become monarch after ten years living abroad?

    a 1649

    b 1660

    c 1665

2 Which of the following was a popular nickname for Charles II?

    a the Cool King

    b Cheeky Charlie

    c the Merry Monarch

3 When did the Great Plague of London occur?

    a 1660

    b 1665

    c 1666

4 What was the name of the famous diarist who recorded events of both the Great Plague and the Great Fire?

    a Samuel Pepys

    b Adrian Mole

    c Christopher Wren

5 Each week the number of dead and the causes of death were written out and displayed around London. What were these lists called?

    a Death Warrants

    b Mortal Engines

    c Bills of Mortality

6 On which day did the Great Fire of London begin?

    a Sunday 2 September 1665

    b Sunday 2 September 1666

    c Wednesday 5 September 1666

7 The Great Fire started in the home and business of Thomas Farriner. But what was his job?

    a butcher

    b baker

    c candlestick-maker

8 Why did the king order houses in the path of the fire to be pulled down?

    a to force people to leave London

    b to create 'fire breaks' to stop the fire spreading to more houses

    c because he was unhappy with the design of some of London's houses

9 Approximately how many houses did the Great Fire destroy?

    a 3,000

    b 30,000

    c 13,000

10 What was the name of the architect who designed many of London's new churches, including St Paul's Cathedral?

    a Christopher Wren

    b Christopher Robin

    c Robert Hooke

Literacy Focus

Writing detailed answers

When writing answers, it is very important that you structure your paragraphs properly and support what you write with evidence. One way of doing this is to use the PEEL paragraph writing approach.

> Your point should include:
>
> **P**oint: Make your point.
>
> **E**vidence: Back your point up with supporting evidence and examples.
>
> **E**xplanation: Explain and elaborate how the evidence supports your point.
>
> **L**ink: Link it to the following point in the next paragraph or link it back to the question.

1   The paragraphs below show the beginning of an answer to the question:

Explain two consequences of the Great Fire of London.

The PEEL paragraph writing approach is used to explain one of the consequences – fear and suspicion. Use the approach to explain the other consequence – the destruction of the city and the new London that emerged afterwards.

Point: Here, the two consequences are *pointed* out in the first paragraph.

One consequence of the Great Fire of London was the fear and suspicion that swept through London. Another consequence was the destruction of the city and the building of a new one within a few years.

The fire spread rapidly because London's buildings were made of wood and the houses were packed close together. After the long, hot summer of 1666, the wood was very dry and it burned easily. Attempts to put out the fire failed and soon thousands of terrified Londoners loaded up their possessions onto carts and fled the city. As soon as the fire began to die down, many people couldn't believe it was an accident and suspected a foreign or Catholic plot. All over London, foreigners and Catholics were beaten by angry mobs, indicating just how worried Londoners were. A French Catholic named Robert Hubert was even hanged for starting the fire – and he wasn't even in the country when it began! His death, and the attacks on others, as well as the fact that many people simply ran away from London, show that one of the major consequences of the Great Fire was fear and suspicion.

Another consequence of the Great Fire was the destruction of the city and the new London that emerged afterwards...

Evidence: Fear and suspicion has been identified as one of the consequences – now the answer is going into more detail.

Explanation: Detail is added here, which supports the point that one of the consequences was suspicion of who started the fire.

Link: This sentence links back to the question.

Now it's time for you to complete the answer. Complete a detailed answer on the second consequence. Use pages 98–101 to help you. You might like to think about short-term and long-term consequences here too. The destruction of London was the short-term consequence – but the new London that was rebuilt was a long-term consequence.

History skill: Source analysis (historic environment)

Historians need to be able to think deeply about a particular place at a particular time in history. This is sometimes known as a study of the 'historic environment'. For example, historians might examine the relationship between a place, and the historical events and developments that happened there.

Responding to questions about sources and the historic environment

Here is one way to answer questions about sources and the historic environment. Imagine you have been asked:

> 1 Describe two features of the Great Plague.
>
> 2 How useful are **Sources A** and **B** for an **enquiry** into the impact of the Great Plague on London in 1665? Explain your answer, using both sources and your knowledge of the historical context.
>
> 3 How could you find out more about the impact of the Great Plague? Name two sources (other than **Sources A** and **B**) you could use, and explain your reasons. (20)

> ⊙ **TIP:** To describe a feature of the Great Plague, you might write:
> - The plague was a fast-spreading killer disease. In 1665, it killed up to 100,000 people in London alone.

1 **Describe features:** When asked to describe 'features', you are simply asked to name an important characteristic or part of a place or an event, and include supporting information for each as well.

2 **The usefulness of sources:** A source might be useful because it reveals something new, explains why events turned out the way they did, or reveals why people acted or thought in a particular way at the time.

You can use the following steps to help you judge how useful a source can be:
- **Content:** What does the source say – or show? What does it tell you? What does it *not* tell you?
- **Caption:** A caption can tell you about where the source comes from, or where it originates from (also known as the 'provenance'). Was the person there at the time? What are their views or background? Use the provenance to get you thinking about the reasons why the source was created.
- **Context:** Think back to what you already know about the topic. Does it match with what you have learned?
- **Conclude:** Now use your answers from the previous steps and judge: How useful are the sources for an enquiry into the topic? You can conclude by saying:
  The source is... for an enquiry into... because...

> ⊙ **TIP:** You can pick one of the phrases below that you think fits best in the sentence:
>
>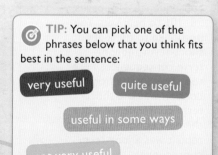
>
> very useful   quite useful   useful in some ways   not very useful

Key Words   enquiry

3 **Find out more:** The final question asks how you might investigate a topic in greater detail. Imagine this is **Source A**:

▼ **SOURCE A** Adapted from the diary of Samuel Pepys, a Londoner who wrote a diary almost every day from 1660 to 1669. His diary (which still survives) tracks the spread of the plague and gives a very personal account of the tragedy.

31 August 1665

Up, and set to putting several things in order before I move to Woolwich [outside London], the plague deaths having a great increase this week beyond all expectation, of almost 2000... Thus this month ends, with great sadness upon the public through the greatness of the plague, everywhere through the Kingdom almost. Every day, sadder and sadder news of its increase... As to myself, I am very well; only, in fear of the plague...

For a historian, **Source A** provides very useful detail about the impact of the plague, from someone who was there at the time and witnessed what happened.

- But what other sources (as well as this one) might you use to find out more about the impact of the plague?
- You would also need to explain *why* the sources would be useful.

Now, considering all these points, look at the next page and try putting this skill into practice.

TIP: Make sure you pick sources that reveal something different, compared to the sources you have already been given. Spend time looking at the different sources in this textbook, and think about the kind of information you can gather from each. For example, you might write: 'I would follow up on the impact of the plague by studying the Bills of Mortality – each week the number of deaths and cause of death were written in these documents.'

TIP: You might then write: 'I would use the Bills of Mortality because this would allow me to look at details about other causes of death, so that I can see the impact of the plague on a city at this time, compared to other causes of death.'

Your challenge is to answer these questions about sources and the historic environment:

1   Describe two features of the streets and buildings in the centre of London in 1666.

2   How useful are **Sources A** and **B** for an enquiry into the impact of the Great Fire of London in 1666? Explain your answer, using both sources and your knowledge of the historical context.

3   How could you find out more about the impact of the Great Fire? Name two sources (other than **Sources A** and **B**) you could use, and explain your reasons. (20)

▼ **SOURCE A** Adapted from the diary of Londoner John Evelyn (1620–1706), who kept a diary from 1640 to 1706. Evelyn did not write as regularly as the other well-known diarist of the time, Samuel Pepys, but his diary covers a much longer period of history.

3 September 1666

'The fire continued because of the wind after a very dry season. I saw the whole south part of the city burning and it was now taking hold of St Paul's church. People were not even trying to save their goods. It burned the churches, public halls, hospitals and monuments, leaping from house to house and street to street devouring houses, furniture, and everything. Here we saw the Thames covered with barges and boats laden with what some had time and courage to save. In the fields people had set up tents to shelter both people and what goods they could get away.

The fire could be seen from 40 miles away. I saw 10,000 houses all in one flame; the fall of towers, houses, and churches, was like a hideous storm, and the air so hot and inflamed that you could not go near it. London was, but is no more!'

▼ **SOURCE B**: A map of the City of London by surveyors John Leake, William Leybourne and four others, to show the extent of the area devastated by the Great Fire of 1666. The white areas near to the river show the parts of London destroyed by the fire. This map was produced in 1667.

The steps below will help you structure your answer. Use the sentence starters to help you begin each point.

1 Describe two features of housing in the centre of London in 1666. (4)

Feature 1:	(1)
Supporting information:	(1)
Feature 2:	(1)
Supporting information:	(1)

2 How useful are **Sources A** and **B** for an enquiry into the impact of the Great Fire of London in 1666? Explain your answer, using both sources and your knowledge of the historical context. (12)

Source A/B

Content:

From the content, I learned that... This is useful because...	(2)

Caption:

The caption tells me... This is useful because...	(1)

Context:

One thing I already know about the impact of the Great Fire is.... This (matches/doesn't match) with what the source says about...	(1)

Conclude:

In conclusion, Source... is... to a study into the impact of the Great fire, because...	(2)

> ⊙ **TIP:** You could copy and complete the sentence starters for each source. Each source is worth 6 marks.

> ⊙ **TIP:** You can pick one of the phrases below that you think fits best in the sentence:
>
>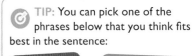
>
> very useful   quite useful
>
> useful in some ways
>
> not very useful

3 How could you find out more about the impact of the Great Fire? Name two sources (other than **Sources A** and **B**) you could use, and explain your reasons (4)

I would find out more about the impact of the Great Fire with this source.... I would use this source because ...	(2)

Another source I would also use is... I would use this source because ...	(2)

> ⊙ **TIP:** It is important that you don't just think of any source – you need to think carefully about the value (or usefulness) of that source to a historian studying the fire.

> ⊙ **TIP:** Explain how the source would help you find out more about the Great Fire.

When Charles II died in 1685, he left 12 children behind. So surely one of them would become king or queen after his death, right? Wrong! Despite having lots of children, none of them were with his wife, the queen. This meant that they weren't allowed, by law, to inherit the throne. So who became monarch after Charles II's death? What happened as a result? And how did it all lead to a revolution?

Objectives

- Discover why Charles II's brother became king.
- Recall the changes that new Catholic King James II made.
- Examine how the monarchy changed back from Catholic to Protestant.

A new king

After the death of Charles II in 1685, his younger brother James became King James II. Just before he became king, James had decided to follow the Catholic religion. However, most people in Britain weren't Catholics – they were Protestants. There hadn't been a Catholic monarch since the time of 'Bloody Mary' over 100 years before. Some people worried that James might make major religious changes that could lead to some sort of religious war. Other people weren't worried at all about the Catholic king. James was quite old and his only children, Mary and Anne, were Protestants. Some thought that King James might die soon and then his eldest daughter, Mary, would take over and everything would carry on as before. But things didn't go to plan…

James makes waves

Soon after James became king he started to make some big changes. This really worried some of the leading politicians in Parliament. Look at the cartoons and see if you can work out why.

In 1687, James decided to rule without Parliament. He was behaving exactly like his father Charles I. Was history going to repeat itself?

James used his power to give lots of the top jobs in the army and in government to Catholics.

King James II's big changes

James built up a large army, even though there were no wars taking place. Could he be planning to use it against Parliament, just like his father (Charles I) had done in the Civil War?

James said in a speech in 1687 that both Catholics and Protestants could worship as they wished. However, he hadn't spoken to Parliament about this at all. Members of Parliament were not happy.

Meanwhile...

In 1687, the same year that James II closed down Parliament, scientist Isaac Newton published his important and influential books commonly known as *Principia*. These texts changed scientific understanding and helped scientists get a much better understanding of physics and the nature of the universe.

A new arrival

In 1688, James's new Catholic wife gave birth to a baby boy. As the baby was male, he pushed past James's daughters to be next in line to the throne. With a Catholic father and mother, it was clear that the baby would be brought up as Catholic too. And when the prince eventually became king after his father's death, his sons would be Catholics, and so on.

This was too much for Parliament. They feared that the country would have Catholic kings for ever more. And Parliament, made up mostly of Protestants, didn't want this – so they decided to do something about it.

Later on...

In 2013, a new UK law put an end to the system where male princes would take priority over their older sisters (known as male primogeniture). So male princes born after 28 October 2011 cannot overtake their older sisters in line to the throne. The new rules also allow members of the Royal Family to marry a Roman Catholic and become king or queen, but a Roman Catholic still cannot become the monarch.

▼ **SOURCE A** A portrait of James II, the first Catholic monarch in over 100 years. This was painted in 1684 by Sir Godfrey Kneller, the leading portrait painter in England at this time.

Over to You

1 Why did none of Charles II's children become king or queen after his death?

2 When James became king, why were some people:
   a worried about this?
   b not worried about this?

Causation

1 Which of James's actions might have worried Parliament the most? Copy the following sentences, placing them in the order you think would have caused most alarm. Write a conclusion explaining your choice of order.
   • He didn't consult Parliament over important matters.
   • He gave all the top jobs to Catholics.
   • He created his own army.
   • His wife gave birth to a son.

2 'Of all the actions taken by James, the one that worried Parliament most was the new army.' How far do you agree with this statement? Use your answers in step 1 to help you. Hint: Reread the story on this page. You will probably disagree with the statement!

Dastardly daughter?

In the summer of 1688, a plot was hatched by some leading Protestants to get rid of Catholic King James II. The plan was for Mary, the king's eldest daughter, and her Protestant husband, William of Orange, to gather a foreign army and fight James – Mary's own father. They would then become joint king and queen. Mary agreed, with the full support of her husband, who was a member of the ruling royal family of the Netherlands.

Fact ✓

Mary refused to be queen unless her husband was made king. William refused to accept any sort of position where his wife was in a higher position. So they really were joint rulers!

Mary and William's army landed in Devon, on the south coast of England, on 5 November 1688, having crossed the sea from the Netherlands. James got an army ready to fight, but John Churchill, one of his key generals, swapped sides and joined Mary and William. James realised that he couldn't beat his daughter's army and fled to France with his wife and son. In fact, there wasn't any fighting at all, but a revolution had taken place, and the ruler had been replaced. Protestants called this the 'Glorious Revolution'.

▼ **SOURCE B** Hampton Court Palace, originally built during the reign of Henry VIII (who took all of his six wives there), was radically updated by William and Mary. They got Sir Christopher Wren to build a beautiful new part to the palace.

Rules for Mary and William

Parliament then invited Mary and William to become joint monarchs, as king and queen. They accepted the offer, but first they had to agree to some conditions. For example, to stop them ruling without Parliament (like James II had done), Mary and William had to agree to involve Parliament in running the country, and to consult Parliament frequently. They were also banned from raising taxes without Parliament's agreement.

The Bill of Rights

One of the first things Parliament made the joint monarchs do was to officially agree to a series of new laws. This is known as the **Bill of Rights**, 1689 (see **C**).

▼ **SOURCE C** An adapted extract of the agreement known as the Bill of Rights, 1689. It was also agreed that Mary's sister (Anne) would become queen after the deaths of Mary and William.

We promise to allow:

- *Parliament to make all the laws*
- *Parliament to decide on taxes*
- *Parliament to share control of the army*
- *Members of Parliament to be free to say what they want*
- *all trials to go ahead without any interference from the king or queen*
- *no Catholic kings or queens ever again.*

Signed William & Mary

A turning point

The Bill of Rights was a turning point in British history. It set up the type of monarchy that we still have today. This means that the country has a monarch, who is the 'head of state', but their powers are clearly defined by Parliament and limited by laws and rules. The laws and rules of a country are called a **constitution**. This is why the British system of government is sometimes called a **constitutional monarchy**.

▼ **INTERPRETATION D** Adapted from an article published in 2018 on the History Channel website.

'The English Bill of Rights has had a long-lasting impact on the role of government in England. It has also influenced laws, documents and ideas in the United States, Canada, Australia, Ireland, New Zealand and other countries. It limited the power of the monarchy, but it also boosted the rights and freedoms of individual citizens. Without the English Bill of Rights, the role of the monarchy might be very different from how it is today. There's no question that this one act greatly affected how the English government operates, and it served as a stepping stone for modern-day democracies.'

Fact ✓

To reward John Churchill for changing sides, William made him Earl of Marlborough. John Churchill was the great-, great-, great-, great-, great-, great-grandfather of Sir Winston Churchill, Britain's prime minister during the Second World War.

▼ **SOURCE E** A gold coin from the time when Mary and William ruled together in 1691.

Over to You .ıl

1 Put the following events in the correct chronological order. You might want to draw a storyboard to illustrate them:
   - William lands in Devon with 12,000 soldiers
   - James flees to France
   - James's wife has a son
   - Important Protestants invite William to invade
   - The leader of James's army joins Mary and William

2 a Why do you think Mary agreed to overthrow her father?

   b William ordered that James should be allowed to escape to France and no attempt should be made to capture him. Why do you think William didn't want to capture James?

   c Suggest a reason why Mary and William chose 5 November as the date to land in England and remove the Catholic king.

3 The Glorious Revolution is sometimes called the 'Bloodless Revolution'. Why do you think it was given this other name?

Significance ⭐

1 What was the Bill of Rights?

2 What impact did the Glorious Revolution have in the late seventeenth century?

3 Read **Interpretation D**. What point is being made here about the importance of the Bill of Rights?

4 Explain the significance of the Bill of Rights.

Mary and William became joint rulers in 1689. But they didn't enjoy an easy reign. There were rebellions in both Ireland and Scotland, which were eventually stopped with great force by William's army. So what exactly happened in Ireland and Scotland? What became of Mary and William? And who ruled after their deaths?

Objectives

- Describe the consequences of the Glorious Revolution.
- Explain the official establishment of the 'United Kingdom'.

Invading Ireland

Many English monarchs had tried to control Ireland. English armies had invaded many times, but the Irish remained determined to keep the English out. After James II had fled to France in 1688, the following year he landed in Ireland and gathered a Catholic army to fight back against his daughter Mary and her husband William. In response, William sent troops to Ireland, and at the Battle of the Boyne in 1690, James's forces were crushed. William took away lots of land from Irish Catholics and gave it to English Protestants. Strict laws were introduced, banning Irish Catholics from teaching, voting or carrying a sword.

Rebellion in Scotland

There was rebellion in Scotland too. Many Scots supported the former king (James II), especially in the mountainous areas called the Highlands. In 1692, in an attempt to settle things, William asked all the important Scottish families (known as clans) to swear an oath of loyalty to him. But one clan – the MacDonalds of Glencoe – missed the deadline for the oath. So William ordered that they all be killed. In total, 38 members of the MacDonald clan were massacred.

William all alone

In 1694, Mary died of smallpox, leaving William to rule alone. William knew that Mary's sister, Anne, would become queen after his death. She was a Protestant, and to ensure that the monarchy would remain in Protestant hands, a new law was passed in 1701 (called the **Act of Settlement**). This stated that the king or queen should always be a Protestant – and this is still the case today. William died in 1702, and Anne became queen.

▼ **INTERPRETATION A** An eighteenth-century image of the Massacre of Glencoe which occurred on 13 February 1692, when 38 members of the MacDonald clan were killed. It is thought that around another 40 women and children later died of cold and hunger, since their homes had been burned during the massacre.

Fact ✓

William was devastated by Mary's death. After she died, he wore her wedding ring and a locket containing some of her hair.

Queen Anne

Anne was the sister of Queen Mary, the daughter of James II, the niece of Charles II and the granddaughter of Charles I – all members of the Stuart family. She gave birth to 17 children, but tragically all of them died before she became queen. However, Parliament knew that the throne would pass to her nearest Protestant relative after her death, rather than her younger brother, who was a Catholic. This was because of the Act of Settlement.

United Kingdom

In order to make the country even more secure, Parliament passed the **Act of Union** in 1707. This meant that England, Wales, and now Scotland were united, with one Parliament based in London. Ireland was also largely under English control by then. So Queen Anne was the first monarch to officially call herself Queen of Great Britain and Ireland.

German George

Queen Anne died in 1714. Her closest Protestant relative was a man called George Louis from Hanover, which is now an area of Germany. Although he didn't speak any English, he became King George I of Great Britain on 1 August 1714. The Stuart family's reign was over, and a new family – the 'Hanoverians' – now ruled. This family (due to the fact that the next three kings after George I were also named 'George') are also called the 'Georgians'.

> ### Over to You
>
> 1 Construct a timeline with the title 'Uniting the United Kingdom'. Mark the following dates on your timeline. Then add a few sentences to explain the importance of each date.
> - 1689
> - 1690
> - 1692
> - 1694
> - 1701
> - 1702
> - 1707
> - 1714
>
> 2 Complete the sentences below with an accurate term:
>   a Charles II was James II's (uncle/father/brother).
>   b James II was Queen Mary's (uncle/father/brother).
>   c James II was Queen Anne's (uncle/father/brother).
>   d Queen Anne was Queen Mary's (sister/mother/niece).
>
> 3 What methods were used to make sure Ireland and Scotland came under English control?
>
> 4 In your own words, explain why a German man became King of Great Britain.

Key Words   Act of Settlement
Act of Union

▼ **SOURCE B** A 1705 portrait of Queen Anne, the last Stuart monarch, painted by Michael Dahl, a Swedish portrait painter who lived and worked in England.

> ### Causation
>
> 1 Define:
>   a the Act of Settlement
>   b the Act of Union.
> 2 Explain why Parliament introduced the Act of Settlement in 1701.

The Battle of Culloden, 1746

What do you think of when you hear the word 'Jacobite'? Is it a unit of computer memory, like a megabyte or a gigabyte? In fact, Jacobite was the name given to a group of people who rebelled against the new monarch, King George I. Why did they rebel? How much of a threat were they? And where did the name 'Jacobite' come from?

Objectives

- Define the word 'Jacobite'.
- Examine the Jacobite Rebellions of 1715 and 1745.
- Explain why 'Bonnie Prince Charlie' was a threat to the Georgians.

After Anne

In 1714, Queen Anne died. She was replaced as monarch by her closest Protestant relative. He was a German named George, who became King George I. But many people weren't happy with this. They wanted Anne's younger half-brother (James Francis) to be king instead. The people who supported James Francis (who was living in France) and the Stuarts were called 'Jacobites' because the Latin for James is *Jacobus*.

The first Jacobite Rebellion, 1715

The reason why James Francis wasn't king in the first place was because he was a Catholic... and the Act of Settlement 1701 banned Catholics from being King or Queen of Great Britain. This was why James Francis's father, James II, was removed from the throne in 1688 and replaced by Protestant rulers, William and Mary. Queen Anne, who followed William and Mary, was a Protestant... and so was King George I.

But James Francis had strong support, particularly in Scotland, and decided to rebel against King George. In 1715, James Francis landed in Peterhead, Scotland and gathered an army. But his army was soon defeated and he fled to Rome, never to return to Britain.

The second Jacobite Rebellion, 1745

Thirty years later, James Francis's son, Charles, tried to take the British throne. By now, George II (only son of George I) was the British king. Charles, known as 'Bonnie Prince Charlie', had been brought up in Rome and had never been to Britain. But when he landed in Scotland in July 1745, on the island of Eriskay, he claimed, 'I am home'!

Bonnie Prince Charlie soon won control of Scotland and headed into England. He reached Derby, 130 miles north of London, but failed to get the support that he had hoped for. As a result, he and his men were forced to march back to Scotland – chased by George II's soldiers.

▼ **MAP A** The Jacobites got as far south as Derby but then had to retreat and fought their last battle against the king's army at Culloden.

The Battle of Culloden, 1746

Eventually, in April 1746, King George's army caught up with Charlie and the Jacobites at Culloden, near Inverness. The Jacobites were outnumbered two to one, poorly armed and half-starving… and were soon beaten by the king's forces. Charlie escaped from the battlefield, but was hunted all over Scotland. Eventually, he escaped to France, dressed as a woman, and never again returned to Britain. He spent another 42 years living unhappily abroad and once said, 'I should have died with my men at Culloden.'

Charlie's defeat at Culloden marked the end of any serious attempt by the Jacobites to restore the Stuart family to the British throne. The era of the Georgians was now firmly established.

▼ **SOURCE C** An eighteenth-century image of the Battle of Culloden. The battle was the last major battle fought on British soil.

▼ **INTERPRETATION B** Charlie was hunted around Scotland for five months. He was eventually rowed in a small boat to the Isle of Skye by a woman called Flora MacDonald. Then he was taken to France. This song, written in the late 1800s, commemorates these events. A 'claymore' is a sword.

'Speed, bonnie boat, like a bird on the wing,
Onward! the sailors cry;
Carry the lad that's born to be king
Over the sea to Skye.
Loud the winds howl, loud the waves roar,
Thunderclouds rend the air;
Baffled our foes stand by the shore,
Follow they will not dare.
Though the waves leap, soft shall ye sleep,
Ocean's a royal bed.
Rocked in the deep, Flora will keep
Watch by your weary head.
Many's the lad fought on that day,
Well the claymore did wield,
When the night came, silently lain
Dead on Culloden's field.
Burned are their homes, exile and death
Scatter the loyal men;
Yet ere the sword cool in the sheath
Charlie will come again.'

Fact ✓

Many people think of Culloden as a battle between Scotland and England. But more Scots fought on the king's side than on Bonnie Prince Charlie's. Charlie was helped by Catholic French soldiers sent by his ally, the King of France.

Over to You 📶

1 What was a Jacobite?

2 What were the similarities and differences between the first and second Jacobite Rebellions?

3 Write a summary of the Battle of Culloden in no more than 100 words. You must explain who fought – and why. Also include why it is viewed as an important battle in British history.

Interpretation Analysis

1 Look at **Interpretation B**. What does the song commemorate?

2 Do you think this interpretation was written by a supporter of Charlie or King George II? Give reasons for your answer.

From Tudor to Georgian times: what changed?

So far, this book has covered around 200 years of British history. We started in Tudor times, and then progressed through the Stuart era. Now we've arrived in Georgian Britain. During the time covered so far, some amazing and lasting changes took place, and altered how people looked at the world.

Objectives

- Define the Enlightenment.
- Discover some of the key discoveries and inventions of the sixteenth to early eighteenth centuries.

c.1536
French army surgeon Ambroise Paré used bandages and soothing ointments (rather than boiling oil) to treat wounds and prevent infection. His famous book *Works on Surgery* (published in 1575) was widely read by English surgeons

1596
Flushing toilet invented by Sir John Harington – but did not become popular for another 200 years!

1609

An Italian, Galileo Galilei, made the first practical telescope and saw planets such as Mars for the first time. However, when he said he could prove that the Earth moved around the Sun, the Church rejected this idea, and made him deny his theory. His work inspired British scientists such as Newton and Halley

1620
British politician and scientist Francis Bacon developed a new way of carrying out scientific experiments. Instead of simply discussing a problem until everyone agreed, Bacon said that if a person wanted to know about the world, they had to study it and experiment – a lot. Bacon's ideas inspired many scientists, including Isaac Newton and Robert Boyle

1628
English doctor William Harvey proved that the heart is a pump and circulates blood around the body. This discovery was a vital stage in the development of surgery and treatment of illness. Medical treatments like blood transfusions and heart surgery would not work without this understanding. Harvey's work developed the theories of others. In fact, many think the first to correctly describe the circulation of the blood was Muslim doctor Ibn al Nafis (1213–1288). However, his books were not read widely and Europeans continued to accept incorrect medical theories until the seventeenth century.

1657
First tea, imported from China, was sold in Britain

1657
Christopher Wren (who later designed St Paul's Cathedral, London) was appointed Professor of Astronomy at Gresham College, London. He had already invented an instrument that wrote in the dark, a weather clock and a new language for the deaf. He met regularly with other scientists and mathematicians. This group would eventually become the Royal Society (see 1662)

1686

Isaac Newton discovered that a force (gravity) pulls an object towards the ground. He realised that gravity is what keeps the moon moving around the Earth. He also improved telescopes, used a prism to show the seven colours of the spectrum, and in 1686 wrote *Principia*, a book that helped scientists understand the universe

1702

World's first daily newspaper, *The Daily Courant*, was published in London

1690

Philosopher John Locke wrote many books and essays about the human mind. He said that a person's experiences in life made them who they were and that a good education is very important. He also said that the rulers of any country should work for the benefit of everyone… and if they didn't, the people should get rid of them

1717

Lady Mary Wortley Montagu experimented with smallpox inoculations (a way of preventing a person getting the disease). After the success of her experiments, King George I even had his own grandchildren inoculated!

1662

The Royal Society was formed, backed by King Charles II. This group of scientists met regularly to discuss their ideas and experiments. This was the first group of its kind in the world and it still meets regularly today. Members included Robert Boyle, Samuel Pepys, Isaac Newton and Christopher Wren

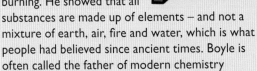

1661

Irish-born Robert Boyle proved that air is essential for both breathing and burning. He showed that all substances are made up of elements – and not a mixture of earth, air, fire and water, which is what people had believed since ancient times. Boyle is often called the father of modern chemistry

Over to You

1 a Choose three developments or inventions from these pages and explain how they made people healthier.

   b Choose another three developments or inventions and explain how they helped improve people's understanding of the world.

   c Do you think we know all there is to know? Or are there lots of things we don't understand about the universe, science and medicine? Explain your answer.

Change and Continuity

1 Write down three things that a person living in 1558 (during Tudor times) might think about the universe, science and medicine.

2 For each thing, say whether someone living 200 years later would still think the same or whether they'd think differently. Write in full sentences and explain yourself clearly.

3 Explain two ways in which knowledge and understanding of the world in 1558 and knowledge and understanding of the world in the 1700s were different.

Fact ✓

The 1600s and 1700s was a time when people observed and explored the world around them and tried new theories and experiments. Some historians said that during this time many became better informed, aware of the world and enlightened, so this period is often called the **Enlightenment**.

The previous two pages took us on a journey from the time when Elizabeth was queen (in the sixteenth century) through the Stuart period (the seventeenth century) and up to the Georgian era. So what was Georgian Britain like?

Society

Like in Tudor and Stuart times, the country is still very divided. Rich people who own lots of land are the politicians and make the laws. Most ordinary people (around eight out of ten) live and work in the countryside, and the vast majority are poor. They rear cattle and sheep and grow enough food to feed themselves and perhaps some extra to sell at market

The relationship between the monarch and Parliament

In Georgian Britain, like Tudor and Stuart times, there is still a monarch – but Parliament creates the laws and controls the country

How united is the United Kingdom?

One monarch, one Parliament for England, Scotland and Wales. Ireland's Parliament is under English control

The main types of communication

As it has always been, people mainly communicate through word of mouth, but printed books and newspapers are more widely available

How do people get around?

Richer men and women still travel by horse and carriage – and the poor walk. There are sedan chairs (early type of taxi) in towns

Popular entertainment

The very rich read books in their own libraries or walk in their landscaped gardens. They still hunt and fish, but they now also go to concerts and the theatre, and play billiards and dice. Poorer people go to the local pub, where they play skittles and cards. During holiday times they continue to go to fairs and gamble on bear-baiting and boxing

What places do Europeans know about?

Eating and drinking

Beer, wine, cheese, meat, bread, more vegetables, potatoes, lemons, melons, apricots, bananas, salad, sugar, syrup, spices, tobacco, knives, forks and spoons. Newer foods include tea, coffee, drinking chocolate, pineapples and coconuts

How many people?

England and Wales = 6.25 million, Scotland = 1.25 million, Ireland = 3.25 million, British settlers overseas = 3.0 million. Total = 13.75 million (including 3 million living abroad)

Science and medicine

People know more about science and the universe – but they still don't know that germs cause disease. Some medical advances, like the prevention of smallpox, but basic operations could result in death because there are no painkillers or germ-free operating rooms

Law and order

Trial by jury continued. Still savage punishments and many executions; prisons used for punishment. Still no police force

How many large towns and cities?

There are over 70 towns with a population of over 2500 people. Some towns will go on to more than double in size in the 1700s.

What about religion?

Most people are Church of England (Protestant)

spent eight years writing the first great dictionary of the English language. There were many great painters such as Thomas Gainsborough and William Hogarth, as well as world renowned composers, such as George Frideric Handel, who came to live in England (from Germany) in 1712.

The Georgians

The Georgian era is named after four of the five kings who ruled after Queen Anne (the last of the Stuarts).

- **George I** (r. 1714–1727) – spoke no English, and left Parliament alone to rule the country. His son took over as king.

- **George II** (r. 1727–1760) – Parliament continued to make laws and hold elections. The king still had to agree with all their proposals before they became law, but Parliament controlled most of the king's money, so they had little trouble getting his support!

- **George III** (r. 1760–1820) – Grandson of George II. Suffered from periods of mental illness and his son (who later became George IV) took over many of his official duties during the last few years of his life.

- **George IV** (r. 1820–1830) – Died without an heir, so the throne passed to the third son of George III, who ruled as William IV. He ruled for seven years until his death, and was succeeded by his young niece (and daughter of the fourth son of George III) – Queen Victoria.

Britain's place in the world

During the Georgian era, Britain's power and influence in the world began to grow:

- The British controlled areas of land in many other countries. Parts of North America, the Caribbean, Africa and India were under British control.

- Britain imported silk, jewels, pottery, ivory and tea from India, and coffee, sugar, tobacco and cod from the Americas. Companies sold these around Britain or they were exported to other customers abroad. Britain was also heavily involved in the slave trade.

- The goods made in Britain, like cloth, pottery and iron, were sold abroad in huge quantities.

How 'arty' was Britain?

The eighteenth century was a great age for the arts. The Georgian monarchs were lovers of culture, particularly of music and architecture. At the same time, there was a growing middle class who enjoyed more wealth, was more educated and looked for cultured hobbies. Daniel Defoe and Jonathan Swift wrote adventure novels, Jane Austen wrote about the middle and upper classes and society, and Samuel Johnson

Fact ✓

In 1735, George II gave the house 10 Downing Street to Sir Robert Walpole, a politician who worked closely with the king. Other politicians teased Walpole for this and called him 'prime minister' as an insult ('prime' means first or favourite). The nickname stuck and Walpole remained prime minister for many years. 10 Downing Street is still home to Britain's prime minister today.

Over to You 📶

1 Prepare a short fact file (100 words or less) on Britain in 1750. Use headings such as 'The population', 'The people in charge', 'Leisure time' and so on.

2 Why did Britain want to take control of land in other parts of the world?

Change and Continuity

1 Create two spider diagrams – one called 'Elizabethan Britain' and another called 'Georgian Britain'. Make brief notes on what you think stayed the same and what changed between the two periods, based on the categories on these pages. Hint: Read the categories carefully – if something is 'still' happening, it means that it stayed the same. You could also review pages 8–9.

2 Explain two ways in which the Elizabethan era and the Georgian era were similar.

⟳ Quick Knowledge Quiz

Choose the correct answer from the three options:

1   In what year did King Charles II die?
   a   1665
   b   1675
   c   1685

2   James II replaced Charles II as king. What was the relationship between the two?
   a   They were cousins
   b   They were brothers
   c   Father and son

3   William and Mary's defeat of James II in 1688–89 is also known by what name?
   a   The Summer Revolt
   b   The Jacobite Rebellion
   c   The Glorious Revolution

4   Which of the following was **not** part of the Bill of Rights?
   a   Parliament is responsible for raising taxes
   b   All trials should be free from any interference from the king or queen
   c   Only Catholics can be the king or queen

5   What is the name of a type of government in which the country still has a king or queen, but their powers are clearly defined by Parliament and limited by laws and rules?
   a   constitutional monarchy
   b   communist state
   c   divine right

6   At which battle in Ireland was James II defeated by the forces of William and Mary?
   a   Battle of Naseby
   b   Battle of the Bulge
   c   Battle of the Boyne

7   What was the name of the act that stated that after Queen Anne's death, the throne would pass to the nearest Protestant relative?
   a   Act of Union
   b   Act of Settlement
   c   Act of Jacobus

8   Queen Anne died in 1714. Her closest Protestant relative was a man called George – but where was he from?
   a.   Flanders, in modern-day Belgium
   b.   Hanover, in modern-day Germany
   c.   Saxony, in modern-day Germany

9   The first Jacobite Rebellion took place in which year?
   a   1715
   b   1745
   c   1760

10   Who led the second Jacobite Rebellion?
   a   Pretty Prince James
   b   Happy Prince Henry
   c   Bonnie Prince Charlie

HOUSES OF PARLIAMENT

DISSOLVED BY THE ORDER OF THE KING

Literacy Focus

Applying key words

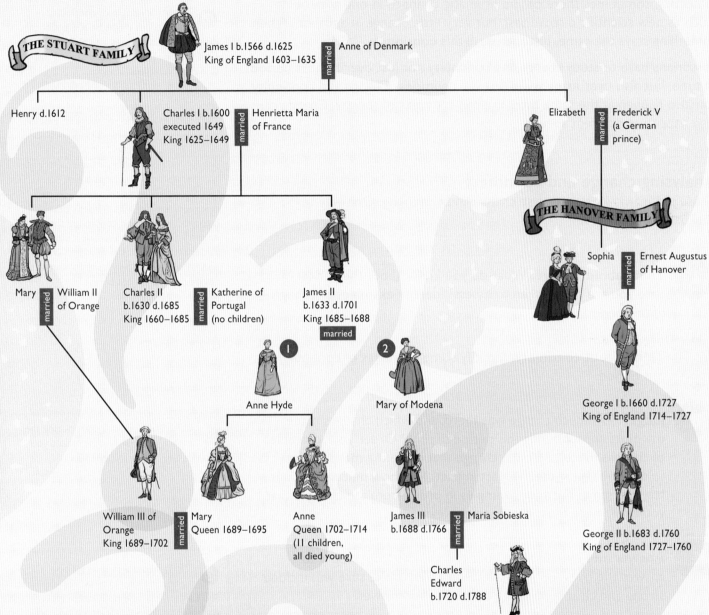

THE STUART FAMILY

James I b.1566 d.1625
King of England 1603–1635 — married — Anne of Denmark

Henry d.1612

Charles I b.1600 executed 1649 King 1625–1649 — married — Henrietta Maria of France

Elizabeth — married — Frederick V (a German prince)

THE HANOVER FAMILY

Mary — married — William II of Orange

Charles II b.1630 d.1685 King 1660–1685 — married — Katherine of Portugal (no children)

James II b.1633 d.1701 King 1685–1688 — married

Sophia — married — Ernest Augustus of Hanover

❶ Anne Hyde

❷ Mary of Modena

George I b.1660 d.1727 King of England 1714–1727

William III of Orange King 1689–1702 — married — Mary Queen 1689–1695

Anne Queen 1702–1714 (11 children, all died young)

James III b.1688 d.1766 — married — Maria Sobieska

George II b.1683 d.1760 King of England 1727–1760

Charles Edward b.1720 d.1788

1   The following words are all related to the family tree. Define each word and explain how it relates to the family tree. The first one has been done for you:

a   execution
Execution means to carry out a death sentence on a condemned person. The execution of King Charles I took place in January 1649 after he was found guilty of being a 'traitor, murderer and a public enemy' by a court assembled by Parliament.

b   Interregnum
c   revolution
d   Restoration
e   constitutional monarchy

In history, sometimes there can be dramatic **changes** in one area of life (such as new scientific discoveries), but very little change in another. When something stays the same, historians call this **continuity**.

Historians have to study change and continuity not just over a short period of time, but also over many years or even centuries. Change and continuity can also happen at the same time, in different areas of society. Change can also happen at different speeds.

Analysing change and continuity

There are many ways to analyse change and continuity. One way to approach this might be:

1 **Think about change:** What do you know about the period of time you are being asked to assess? Identify examples of change in this period.

2 **Think about continuity:** Identify some examples of continuity in this period.

3 **Judge:** How much change was there, and which changes made the most impact during this period of time? Order your examples of changes in step 1 from a change that made the most impact, to the one that made the least impact. And how much did things stay the same? Put your examples in order, from the changes that you think made most impact to the least.

4 **Answer and explain:** Use your top choices from step 3 to answer the question you have been asked. Make sure you include strong and clear supporting details in your answer.

TIP: An example of continuity in Tudor times might be the belief that disease and illness was a punishment from God for sin. This belief had stayed the same for hundreds of years.

TIP: For example, if you were an ordinary farmer or worker, whether you lived in Tudor, Stuart or Georgian times, you would have had very little power and no say in how the country was run. However, if you were a rich landowner in Georgian times, you may have been part of a Parliament that created the laws and controlled the country. This was a dramatic change from Tudor times, when the monarch was in control and really only used Parliament for advice (and to collect taxes).

TIP: When you are considering the impact of something, it means you should think about the effects or consequences that occurred as a result of it.

TIP: It is important to include supporting information. For example, don't simply say 'the population grew' – you must back your statement up with facts and figures.

Now that you have worked through the Tudor and Stuart periods and arrived in the Georgian era, you can consider change and continuity from the mid-1500s to the early 1700s.

Assessment: Change and continuity

Your challenge is to answer this question about change:

In what ways did the lives of British people change, and in what ways did it stay the same between the late Tudor period and the beginning of the Georgian period (c.1550s–c.1700s)? (20)

The steps below will help you structure your answer.

1 **Think about change: review what you know:** What do you already know about the lives of British people from around the 1550s to early 1700s. Identify examples of **change** between the late Tudor period and the beginning of the Georgian period.

1 _____

2 _____

3 _____

2 **Think about continuity:** Identify some examples of **continuity** between the late Tudor period and the beginning of the Georgian period.

1 _____

2 _____

3 _____

3 **Judge:** Look at your list for the bullets in steps 1 and 2. Which areas of life do you think changed the most? And which areas changed the least?

4 **Answer and explain:** Now write your answer and be sure to include clear details and supporting knowledge to back your answer up. The sentence starters below can help you.

There were several areas where the lives of British people changed between the Tudor and Georgian periods. For example...	(5)
Another key area of change was...	(5)
There were several areas where the lives of British people stayed the same between the Tudor and Georgian periods. For example...	(5)
Another area of continuity was...	(5)

TIP: You could think about change and continuity in the following areas:

the relationship between the monarch and Parliament

communication

transport

the United Kingdom

eating and drinking

the population

knowledge of the world

towns and cities

entertainment

religion

science and medicine

society

law and order

TIP: Don't just look at the information on pages 116–119 – look at pages 8–9 and the rest of the textbook to help you compare the two periods.

TIP: You might think that many things must have changed dramatically over the period. But this isn't the case – many things didn't change much at all. For example, the vast division between the lives of the rich and the lives of the poor did not change much during this period.

TIP: Make sure you don't simply say what happened – describe what the situation was like around the 1550s, and then explain what had changed by the early 1700s.

TIP: To show you are thinking deeply about change, you could describe the type and rate of change: was there very little change, or a lot? Did the changes happen very quickly, or slowly?

TIP: Make sure you explain what it was like in the Tudor period – and how it was still the same by the Georgian period.

Most of the goods we buy today are made in factories. But in the 1700s, most goods were hand-made in people's homes, or in small workshops next to their homes. This was known as the **domestic system** ('domestic' describes the home or family). However, in the late 1700s and early 1800s a change took place that would transform the way many goods were made and introduce the world to the idea of 'factories'. How did this happen?

Objectives

- Explain how products were manufactured in Britain before the mid-1700s.
- Examine how and why machines changed the way goods were made in Britain.

It's a family affair!

The domestic system involved the whole family: grandparents, parents and children. The goods that were made included shoes, socks, buttons, lace, hats, gloves, nails, chains and clay pots. One of the most popular goods made in people's homes was woollen cloth. This high-quality material became famous around the world and, as the population increased, was in great demand in Britain, too.

From sheep to shop

In the domestic system a clothier (cloth merchant), for example, bought wool from farmers who had sheared their sheep. The clothier then took the wool to villagers in their houses, who spun it into threads to weave into cloth. The family could work the hours they wanted, as long as they finished the cloth in time. Then the clothier would collect the cloth, pay the family, and take the cloth to a different house to be dyed and made ready for sale.

Money-mad merchants and cash-crazy clothiers

Many cloth merchants made a fortune from the cloth trade. Their profits were made larger by clever inventors who built brilliant machines to speed up the cloth-making process. For example, in 1733, a machine called the 'Flying Shuttle' helped weavers make cloth much more quickly. In 1764, the 'Spinning Jenny' made the production of thread quicker. If more cloth could be made quickly, then more cloth could be sold – which meant more profits!

Meanwhile...

The soft fibres of the cotton plant were brought from British colonies such as India and America. Skilled British spinners would turn this into thread and then expert weavers would weave it into a light and comfortable cloth.

Flying Shuttle

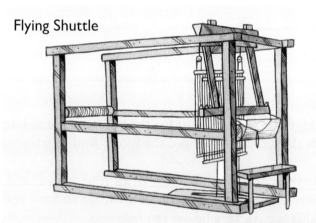

Spinning Jenny

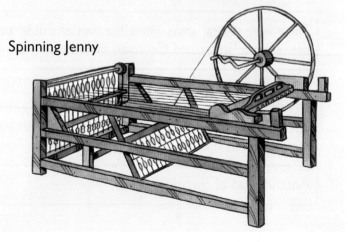

Arkwright and the first factory

Both the 'Flying Shuttle' and 'Spinning Jenny' were small and still allowed the cloth to be produced in homes. However, the next invention changed all that – and the lives of millions of British workers.

The man most responsible for the ending of the domestic system was a former wig maker called Richard Arkwright. In 1769, he invented a machine called the 'Spinning Frame'. It could produce good, strong thread very quickly – but it was so big it couldn't fit in people's homes. Also, the moving parts were so heavy that it couldn't be operated by hand and had to be powered by a waterwheel. Arkwright's solution was to put his huge spinning machines in specially created buildings – known as 'factories' or 'mills'. His first factory opened in 1771 at Cromford in Derbyshire and it was a great success. Look at the diagram below to find out more.

Key Words

domestic system   factory system

3 Arkwright inspired others to invent machines that produced cloth even more quickly and cheaply. In 1779, Samuel Crompton invented the 'Spinning Mule', which produced thread of a higher quality than Arkwright's. In 1785, Edmund Cartwright designed the 'Power Loom', which sped up the weaving process.

4 When working at home, people worked whenever they chose. Now workers had to work when the factory owner told them to.

2 In one week, a machine operator could produce over 60 times more cloth than a whole family working at home – for a fraction of the wages. This meant Arkwright could sell his cloth for a much lower price and make a big profit.

1 All the machines in Arkwright's factory were powered by one waterwheel. The wheel turned all day and night, so the machines (and workers) could work 24 hours a day.

5 The factory owners made huge profits. Arkwright opened lots of factories and made a fortune (over £200 million in today's money).

The death of the domestic system

As more factories were built, millions of people left their villages and went to work in them. Factories guaranteed year-round work and a steady wage. The workers rented rooms and homes, near to the factories, that the owners had built. By the 1820s, it was clear the domestic system was dying out – and was being replaced by the factory system.

> ## Over to You
>
> 1 Define: a the domestic system   b the factory system.
>
> 2 Write a list of advantages and disadvantages of the domestic system for a family of workers.
>
> 3 Richard Arkwright is often called 'the father of the factory'. Do you think this is a suitable nickname? Explain your answer.
>
> 4 Imagine you are a visitor to Cromford, and you have to write a report for someone considering opening a factory. Describe how the factory operates, what is inside it, and who works there. Perhaps include a picture or diagram. Write no more than 150 words.

How did factories create towns?

Eight out of ten people lived in the countryside in the 1750s. Most towns were very small and their biggest buildings would probably have been the church, cathedral or castle. But the new factories changed all this. So how did factories create towns? How were these factories powered? And what did these new towns look like?

Objectives

- Explain how factories caused the population of towns to increase.
- Evaluate the impact of steam power on factories and towns.

The countryside empties

The new factories pulled people into towns from the countryside – with the promise of regular work for all the family and good wages. Factory owners built houses for their workers to rent, and people began to set up shops and inns so the workers could buy food and drink. Soon, roads were being built, along with churches, schools and places of entertainment.

These places needed shopworkers, teachers and nurses, for example – as well as the builders, carpenters and labourers to build them. And all of these people needed more houses. Before long, places that were once tiny villages had grown into large towns – and small towns became huge, overcrowded cities. **Diagram B** shows how the building of a factory could lead to the creation of a large town. **Chart A** shows how some of Britain's towns and cities grew at this time.

▼ **A** This chart shows the approximate increase in population of some towns over 100 years.

	1751	1801	1851
Liverpool	35,000	82,000	376,000
Manchester	45,000	75,000	303,000
Leeds	14,000	53,000	172,000
Bradford	7,000	25,000	105,000
Birmingham	30,000	71,000	233,000

▼ **B** The birth of a town.

Factory

Workers

Houses — Transport — Shops, services

Builders, carpenters, labourers, engineers, drivers, shopkeepers, craftspeople

More houses — More transport — More shops, services — Schools, hospitals

More: cobblers — tailors — teachers — nurses, etc.

▼ **MAP C** These maps show how one town, Bradford, grew in size from 1800 to 1873.

The Bradford branch of the Leeds and Liverpool Canal opened in 1774, making it easier for goods made in Bradford to travel to these two cities.

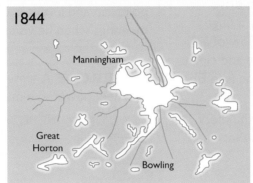

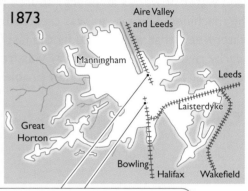

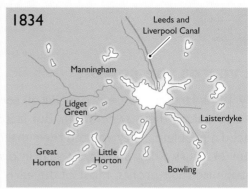

Railway lines linking Bradford to other major cities were built from 1846.

Earlier on... 1665

At the time of the Great Plague (1665), there were only four places in Britain with more than 20,000 people living there – London, Edinburgh, Norwich and Bristol. By 1821, there were over 100 places with a population of 20,000 or more.

▼ **MAP D** Some of Britain's major industrial towns.

Over to You

1 Explain how the building of a factory might lead to the growth of a town.

2 Look at **Chart A** containing figures for the growth of towns between 1751 and 1851.

   a Turn the figures in **Chart A** into a bar chart that represents the growth of each town.

   b What does this chart tell us about the growth of towns?

3 In your own words, explain how Bradford expanded between 1800 and 1873. Use **Map C** and some of the information in the population chart in your explanation.

Knowledge and Understanding

1 Complete the sentences below with an accurate term:

   a Factories promised regular work and wages, so many people left their homes in the _____ to work in them.

   b Between 1751 and 1851 the population of Bradford increased from 7000 to _____ .

   c The _____ Canal linked Bradford to these two fast-growing cities.

   d By the 1870s, Bradford was further linked to other towns by _____ .

I've got the power!

By 1800, factories were producing all sorts of items – and making their owners rich. But factory owners faced a problem. They wanted their machines to run 24 hours a day, 365 days a year in order to maximise their profits. Most of the early factories used water power as an energy source to drive the machines. This power was created by a huge waterwheel that was turned by the fast flow of a nearby river. This type of energy was free and clean, but water power had several key problems (see E).

▼ **SOURCE E** Based on extracts from the diary of John Ward, a Lancashire cotton worker between 1860 and 1864.

29 May 1861: Another very warm day, and this dry weather is much against us as the River Ribble is very low, and in the afternoons our looms go very slow for want of water.

26 November 1861: It was very wet and stormy all night, and the Ribble was so high with the flood that we could not start work until the afternoon.

28 August 1864: There were thirty mills stopped in Blackburn this last week for lack of water, and will not start again until wet weather sets in.

Full steam ahead!

Water power was just not reliable enough. So factory owners turned to a new form of power that scientists had been developing – **steam engines**. These had first been used to pump water out of underground **mines** but they were slow, expensive and kept breaking down. Then, in 1768, a Scottish inventor named James Watt met a businessman called Matthew Boulton at a science club called the Lunar Society in Birmingham. Together they developed a new kind of steam engine that Watt had been working on. It included a new ('sun-and-planet') gear system that turned a wheel just as a river would (see **G**). This new type of steam engine became very popular as soon as factory owners realised they could power the machines in their factories by 'steam power' rather than water power.

> **Fact** ✓
>
> Lunar Society members included scientists, inventors, astronomers, mathematicians, engineers and manufacturers. They met to discuss interesting issues and were committed to using new ideas or developments to improve people's lives. One famous member was US politician and inventor Benjamin Franklin, who attended meetings when he visited Britain.

▼ **SOURCE F** A water wheel in action. This water wheel powered a mill on the River Eye in Gloucester.

Factory fever

The effect on Britain was incredible. Not only was steam power faster and more reliable than water power, it also meant that factories no longer had to be built next to fast-flowing rivers – they could be built anywhere. By 1871, only 3 per cent of factories were using waterwheels. Steam-powered factories started to spring up all over Britain and even more people left the countryside to work in them. Factory towns like Birmingham, Sheffield, Manchester, Bolton and Bradford started to grow and grow. By 1850, Britain's factories produced two-thirds of the world's cotton cloth – even though cotton didn't grow in Britain. Nearly half of the world's hardware (tools, pots, pans and so on) also came from Britain. **Industry** had become **mechanised** and Britain was now known as 'the workshop of the world'. For the first time in British history, more people were now living in towns and cities than in the countryside.

G A steam engine turns a wheel. To do this, coal is burned to turn the water in the boiler into steam. This steam escapes into the cylinder and pushes up the piston – which in turn pushes up one end of the beam. When the piston reaches the top of the cylinder, the steam escapes and the piston and beam are allowed to fall back down. The whole process begins again and the see-saw action of the beam is used to turn the wheel through the 'sun-and-planet' gears.

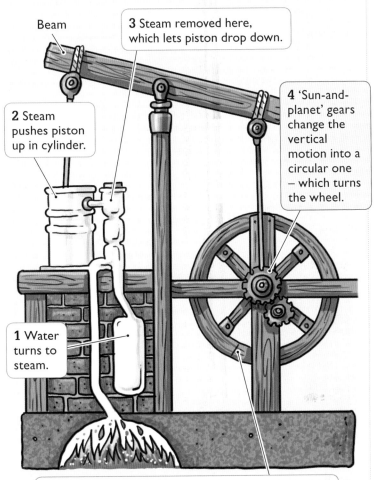

Beam

3 Steam removed here, which lets piston drop down.

4 'Sun-and-planet' gears change the vertical motion into a circular one – which turns the wheel.

2 Steam pushes piston up in cylinder.

1 Water turns to steam.

Wheel attached to belts that drive factory machines.

▼ **SOURCE H** Written by George Weerth, a German writer, living in Bradford in 1840.

'We look in astonishment as our coach drives on. The further we go, the more houses there are, collected along the road. All around we see flames, hissing and rattling. The windows of factories shaking as we go by. The sun darkens as if cloud has blocked it; suddenly it is evening on a bright day! As our horses stop, we see this is a dirty, evil-smelling town.'

Key Words

industry   mechanised
mine   steam engine

▼ **SOURCE I** A picture of factories in Sheffield in the 1800s. The chimneys (sometimes called 'smokestacks') take away the dirty, toxic smoke produced when coal is burned.

Over to You

1 Read **Source E**.
   a What type of power is used in this factory?
   b Name two problems that this type of power caused the factory owner.

2 Look at **G**. Write a sentence to explain the role of the following:
   • coal • piston • sun-and-planet gears
   • beam • boiler • wheel

3 Read **Source H**. Do you think this source was written before or after Britain's industry had become mechanised? Give reasons for your answer.

4 Look at **Source I**.
   a How do you think the mills and factories of Sheffield were powered? Explain your answer.
   b What negative effects does this form of power cause?

Causation

1 Explain why many factory owners introduced steam power.

Britain's early factories were dangerous, harsh places to work. Most factory owners only cared about making a profit, not about providing a safe place to work. There were also no strict government guidelines or laws to control what went on in the early factories. Machines did not have safety guards and workers did not wear protective gear. Noisy, dusty factories made many people deaf and sick. Many factories employed children. What was life like for them?

Objectives

- Examine why so many children worked in factories.
- Describe working conditions in some factories.

Child labour

Poor children didn't go to school, so they would go to work with their parents – even as young as five. Orphans – children without parents – were often sent to work in factories by local authorities. They were known as **pauper apprentices,** and were given food, clothing and a bed in an 'apprentice house'. In return they had to work very hard for the factory owners.

Read the story of Peggy, a pauper apprentice in one of Britain's mills. Would you have been tough enough to survive her life?

1 Work started at 5.30am, Monday to Saturday. Sunday was a 'short day' (4–6 hours of cleaning!). Some children spent years lifting heavy baskets, deforming their bodies.

2 Factory rules were very strict. 6d was about half a day's pay for a woman.

I'm fined if I'm late. My job is to load, unload and carry around those heavy baskets all day. It's exhausting!

Factory rules

1 Late for work – 3d fine. Not let into the factory until breakfast time.
2 Leaving the room without permission – 3d fine.
3 All broken brushes, oil cans, windows, wheels etc. will be paid for by the worker.
4 Talking to another, whistling, singing or swearing – 6d fine.
5 Ill worker who fails to find someone to do their job – 6d fine.

3 Workers weren't just fined or sacked for breaking rules – they were sometimes beaten with sticks or whipped. In one factory in the Midlands, a common punishment was to nail an ear into a wooden bench.

4 There was a short break at 8.00am and another break at lunchtime.

I hardly feel like eating because the dust, heat and smell make me feel sick.

5 A 12-hour working day was common, but at busy times it could be as long as 14 or 15 hours. On average, pauper apprentices like Peggy were smaller and lighter than boys and girls of a similar age who didn't work in factories.

140cm — 45Kg   145cm — 50Kg

6 The children who lived with their parents earned about half the amount that women did, so it was cheaper for factory owners to employ women and children than men.

7 Pauper apprentices worked in shifts – some in the day, the others in the night.

When one group gets in at the end of a shift, the others crawl out of the same filthy beds that we share. We have no spare time to play and meet up with friends.

We will do this until we are 21 — and then get a job as an adult in this factory.

Us pauper apprentices work for no wages but are given food, clothing and shelter. Only the ordinary workers get paid.

Key Words

pauper apprentice

Fact ✓

In 1833, two out of every five accident cases received at Manchester Infirmary (a hospital) were caused by factory machinery.

Fact ✓

In some factories, wages were paid in tokens, which could only be spent at the owner's shop. The quality of goods at the owner's shop might be very poor – but the workers would have no choice but to buy them.

Were all factories the same?

Some employers believed that happy workers were good workers, so they tried to provide decent living and working conditions for their workers. Robert Owen, for example, built good quality houses, schools, shops and parks for his workers in New Lanark, Scotland. He also reduced working hours. Elsewhere, factory owners built good quality villages for their workers at Saltaire (Yorkshire) and Bromborough Pool (Cheshire). But these villages and towns were exceptions, and the vast majority of factories and the towns that surrounded them were dangerous and unhealthy places to live and work.

Meanwhile...

It did not take long for factories to appear in other countries. The first factory in the USA was built in 1790 by Samuel Slater, an English-born businessman who took lots of British ideas to America when he emigrated there. He is referred to as 'Slater the Traitor' by some people in the UK because they think he stole British ideas on machinery design and used them for his own factories in the USA!

Over to You

1 a Write a list of ways in which pauper apprentices like Peggy were treated harshly.

  b Suggest reasons why dangerous, unhealthy and harsh conditions were so common in factories at this time.

  c In what ways did Robert Owen treat his workers differently?

2 a Make a 24-hour timeline for a typical day of your week. Include:
* your sleep time
* times for food, travel, breaks and spare time
* what work you do (a paper round, for example)
* something that a factory boy or girl wouldn't have done – school!

  b Write at least five sentences, each one stating how your day is different from a child's in the early 1800s.

Knowledge and Understanding

1 Describe two features of factory life.

How were factory working conditions improved?

On 4 June 1832, 23-year-old Leeds factory worker Elizabeth Bentley was interviewed by Michael Sadler, a politician who was investigating working conditions. Part of the interview is given below. Sadler's report, published in 1833, shocked the **public**. Soon other investigations and reports followed and working conditions slowly began to change. So what did Elizabeth say? Who else, as well as Sadler, tried to change things? And how did the changes benefit people like Elizabeth Bentley?

Objectives

- Identify why some factory owners were unwilling to improve working conditions.
- Examine key reforms that eventually improved life for Britain's workers.

▼ **SOURCE A** From the Sadler Report, published in 1833, for which 89 people were interviewed. This is adapted from Elizabeth Bentley's interview. She was born in 1809.

Question: What age did you begin work at a factory?
Answer: When I was six years old.
Q: What were your hours of work?
A: As a child I worked from 5am till 9pm.
Q: What if you got tired, or were late, what would they do?
A: Hit us with a strap.
Q: What is the factory like?
A: Dusty. You cannot see each other for dust.
Q: Did this affect your health?
A: Yes; it was so dusty, the dust got up my lungs, and the work was so hard. I got so bad in health, that when I worked, I pulled my bones out of their places.
Q: You are considerably **deformed** because of this?
A: Yes, I am.
Q: How old were you when this happened?
A: I was about 13 years old when it began coming, and it has got worse since.

Were conditions in mines any better?

Elizabeth Bentley worked in a factory – but mines weren't much better. One eight-year-old girl who opened and closed wooden doors (known as 'traps') describes her job in **Source B**.

▼ **SOURCE B** Adapted from an investigation into mine conditions in 1842. Sarah Gooder was asked to describe her working conditions.

'I have to trap without a light and I'm scared. I go at 4am, and come out at 5.30pm. I never go to sleep. Sometimes I sing when I have light, but not in the dark; I dare not sing then. I don't like being in the pit. I am very sleepy when I go sometimes. I would like to be at school far better than in the pit.'

▼ **SOURCE C** An image from the 1842 mines report. 'Trappers' would open and close wooden doors to allow fresh air to flow through the mine. The children pushing the coal carts were known as 'putters'.

Time for change

In the 1800s, many people thought that the government should not interfere with the way factories and mines were run. They believed that it was up to the owners to decide how to run them, and that introducing laws to force owners to spend money on improvements could harm profits. They also argued that reducing the hours that children and women worked might cause money problems for the family.

However, a growing number of people were very concerned about working conditions, especially for children. **Reformers** like Lord Shaftesbury, Richard Oastler, John Fielden and Michael Sadler began to campaign for laws to protect factory and mine workers. Some of these people were motivated by their religious beliefs, while others thought that people might work harder if they were treated better! Some (such as Sadler) collected evidence to prove how bad things were.

Change is coming

After reading the reports, Parliament accepted that it had a duty to look after the more vulnerable people in society. From 1833, new laws (or **Acts**) made changes to the working lives of women and children. Men, it was believed, could look after themselves.

Some factory owners hated the changes. They felt politicians had no right to interfere in their business. But new laws kept being passed and, gradually, they began to protect more and more workers. Inspectors were appointed to enforce the laws and by 1900 factories and mines had become safer and more bearable. They still weren't particularly pleasant places to work, however.

▼ **D** New acts to protect workers.

1833 FACTORY ACT
- No children under nine to work in factories.
- Nine hours of work per day for children aged nine to 13.
- Two hours of school per day.
- Factory inspectors appointed (but there were only four!).

1842 MINES ACT
- No women or children under ten to work down a mine.
- Mine inspectors appointed.

1844 FACTORY ACT
- No women to work more than 12 hours per day.
- Machines to be made safer.

1847 TEN HOUR ACT
- Maximum ten-hour day for all women and workers under 18.

1871 TRADE UNION ACT
- **Trade unions** made legal. Workers all doing the same job (trade) – like railway workers or dockers, for example – were allowed to join together (form a union) to negotiate with their employers for improvements to pay and working conditions. As a last resort, all union members could go on strike.

1878 FACTORY AND WORKSHOPS ACT
- No women to work more than 60 hours per week.
- No children under ten to work.
- Laws on safety, ventilation and mealtimes.

1895 FACTORY ACT
- Children under 13 to work a maximum of 30 hours per week.

Fact ✓

At the time, some people argued that Sadler exaggerated when writing up his investigations. They said he wanted conditions to appear worse than they were, because that would shock people into supporting his campaign.

Over to You

1 a Why did reformers want to change working conditions in factories and mines?

  b Why were some factory owners reluctant to change things?

2 Look at **D**.

  a Write down what you think are three of the most important changes to working conditions between 1833 and 1895.

  b Next to each one, explain why you think it was an important change.

Source Analysis

Read **Source A**.

1 Write down three words or phrases that a reader of this report might feel.

2 Michael Sadler was accused of exaggerating some of the interviews. Does that mean the interviews are not useful to a historian?

3 How could you follow up **Source A** to find out more about factory life in the 1800s?

'Black gold' and the new 'Age of Iron'

The way people lived and worked changed dramatically from the late 1700s. New machines changed the way goods were made, and a large proportion of the population moved from the countryside into the growing towns and cities. 'Black gold' and the iron industry were responsible for many of these changes. But what was 'black gold'? Why was iron so important?

Objectives

- Examine why there was an increase in the demand for coal.
- Outline how iron was produced.
- Describe how iron-making became such an important business.

What is coal?

Coal is a hard, black rock that is buried underground. Specialist workers, called **miners**, get coal out of the ground from mines. Once it is lit, coal burns for a long time – much longer than wood. In the late 1700s, coal was very cheap and used mainly to cook with and heat houses. As the population increased, more coal was needed, and it began to be used to power steam engines in the new factories that were springing up all over the country. Coal was also used in the making of bricks, pottery, glass, beer, sugar, soap and iron.

'Black gold'

By the 1800s, coal was also required to power steam trains and steam ships. The need for more coal meant more money for mine owners. Some mine owners were making so much money from their coal that they began to refer to it as 'black gold'.

▼ **MAP A** The coalfields of Britain in 1800.

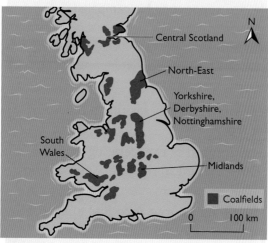

- Central Scotland
- North-East
- Yorkshire, Derbyshire, Nottinghamshire
- South Wales
- Midlands
- ■ Coalfields

0   100 km

A new Iron Age

The eighteenth century saw major advances in the iron industry. Iron had been produced in Britain since Roman times but in the 1700s it began to be used in all areas of life. The army used it for cannons, the navy for 'iron-clad' ships, and the new factories were held up with iron beams and used iron machines that were powered by iron steam engines. Iron was used to make tools, trains and railway tracks, and at home people had fireplaces with iron grates and cooked on iron stoves using iron pans.

How was iron actually made?

1 **Iron ore** – rock containing iron – is dug from the ground.

2 The ore is melted together with limestone (to remove impurities) and charcoal (baked wood) in a furnace. The iron gets so hot it melts and pours out of the bottom of the furnace.

3 Red-hot, liquid iron is poured into casts shaped like pots, pans, pipes, cannons, beams and so on. **Cast iron** is strong but contains air bubbles that can make it brittle.

4 When cast iron is reheated and hammered, the pockets of air are removed and it becomes **wrought iron**. This is purer and stronger, and can be bent into shapes to make chains, tools, furniture, railway tracks and so on.

The kings of Coalbrookdale!

As the population and the number of factories grew, so did the demand for iron. But the producers of iron faced a problem – Britain was running out of forests. Charcoal – made from wood – was needed to make iron. It was possible to use coal, instead of charcoal, but coal contains too much sulphur (a chemical) and makes poor quality iron. Luckily for Britain, a family called the Darbys got involved in the iron industry!

Abraham Darby I (1678–1717): In 1709, he discovered a way of using coal to make iron. Firstly, he heated it to remove the sulphur. This makes something called coke (not the drink!). Cast iron made with coke is much better quality than cast iron made with coal – iron production could continue.

Abraham Darby II (1711–1763): He improved the process invented by his father, removing even more impurities and allowing wrought iron to be made from coke-fired coal.

Abraham Darby III (1750–1789): He decided to show the possibilities of the use of iron by building a magnificent iron bridge. He made the ironworks at Coalbrookdale famous throughout the world.

▼ **SOURCE B** The iron bridge over the River Severn at Coalbrookdale, Shropshire was opened on New Year's Day 1781. The world's first major bridge to be made entirely of cast iron caused a sensation.

Later on...

We now know that coal production and use contributes to climate change. In 2019, the UK used more electricity from renewable sources (wind and solar energy, for example) than from coal for the first time in its history.

Ironbridge – one of the wonders of the world

Writers, artists and rich tourists came from all over the world to see this modern miracle – and Darby charged every one of them to walk across it! It was a fantastic advertisement for what could be achieved with iron, and iron production became one of Britain's most important industries (see **C**). No wonder people began to call the period the 'Age of Iron'.

▼ **C** Iron produced in Britain 1750–1900. After 1856, steel (made from iron ore) started to be produced in Britain too. The figures in the table are in thousands of tons.

	1750	1800	1850	1900
Coal production	5000	11,000	50,000	225,000
Iron production	30	250	2000	9000
Steel production	300	4250	3500	5000

Over to You

1 In no more than three sentences, explain how iron is produced.

2 Explain why the demand for coal and iron increased in the 1700s.

3 a Look at **Chart C**. Draw a bar chart to show how Britain's iron and coal production increased.

   b Write a description to accompany the chart, explaining the increase.

4 Why do you think people were so impressed by the iron bridge at Coalbrookdale?

Significance

To decide if an event or development is historically **significant** or not, you have to assess: a) whether it was important at the time it happened; b) whether it's also important over a long time, perhaps even until now. Let's practise just part a for now.

1 How significant was the coal mining industry for the population of Britain?

The distance between London and Edinburgh is about 650km. If you travelled from one city to the other in the early 1700s, it would have taken you a week by boat or about two weeks by road. By 1900, you could make the same journey in just nine hours. So what changed? How did this shortened journey time become possible?

Objectives

- Outline how changes in industry led to changes in Britain's transport networks.
- Describe what these changes were and how they came about.

Why were transport improvements needed?

A fast, reliable transport system was vital for business and industry from the mid-1700s. Coal had to be taken from mines to factories and towns, cotton had to be moved from ports to factories, and finished goods had to be moved to markets. A fast and reliable postal service was needed too. Many industries used sea- or river-based transport, especially when moving heavy goods like iron or coal – but dozens of towns were miles from the nearest river. In the 1700s and 1800s, a series of developments and inventions completely changed Britain's transport system.

In 1825, the Stockton and Darlington Railway became the first public transport system in the world to use steam **locomotives** (a steam engine that moved wheels along a set of rails or track – often called 'trains'). This was followed in 1830 by the Liverpool and Manchester Railway.

Time for the turnpikes!

In the early 1700s, Britain's roads were in a terrible state and businesses were suffering. The government decided to divide the main road network into sections, and each section was rented out to a group of businesspeople. The group was called a 'turnpike trust' and the first one was set up in 1706. Turnpike trusts promised to improve and maintain their section of road. In return, the trusts were allowed to charge a toll to every person who used their section of road. Much of the cash was used to improve the roads, and specialist engineers went on to create the finest roads Britain had ever seen.

By 1830, there were nearly 1000 turnpike trusts improving over 32,000km of roads, to dramatic effect. It might have taken you two weeks to travel by road from London to Edinburgh in 1745 – but by 1830 you could get there in about 48 hours!

Turnpike roads had gates at the end of each stretch where **toll** keepers collected the money.

TOLLS

Canal mania!

The turnpike trusts had given Britain some excellent roads – but they were still too bumpy for fragile goods like pottery, and too slow for heavy goods like coal and iron ore. So, a new type of transport was developed – **canals**. These were long, narrow, man-made channels of still water, which were ideal for moving heavy and fragile goods, so they soon caught on. By 1830, 6400km of canals had been built and it was possible to travel to every major town and city in England by barge.

Train travel

When steam engines first appeared in the 1700s, inventors soon worked out ways to make them turn wheels. The man credited with building the world's first railway locomotives was a Cornishman called Richard Trevithick. In 1804, to win a bet, his engine pulled ten tons of iron and 70 passengers for 14.5km in Merthyr Tydfil, South Wales. After this, there was a flurry of activity as engineers created lots of different locomotives. By 1900, there were over 32,000km of train track that carried millions of passengers every year. It all had an amazing effect on journey time. The journey between London and Edinburgh that had taken two weeks by road in 1750 now took only nine hours by train.

> The first canal which was 11km long, was completed in 1761. It was built by the Duke of Bridgewater in 1759 and went from his mines in Worsley to the city of Manchester. 'Canal mania' provided work for thousands of 'navvies' (the men who built them) as they all had to be dug out by hand.

Key Words

canal   locomotive   suburb
toll   turnpike road

Meanwhile...

From the 1860s, London even had its own underground railway – or 'Tube' – that took workers from the growing **suburbs** into the city. Other cities around the world soon followed – Budapest, Hungary (opened in 1896), Boston, USA (1897) and Paris, France (1900).

Over to You

1 Write a sentence to explain each of the following:
   a turnpike trust
   b canal
   c locomotive.

2 Each of the following dates is important in transport history:
   - 1825   - 1804   - 1706
   - 1761   - 1830

   Put the dates in chronological order on separate lines in your book. Beside each date, write what happened in that year – and explain why it was important in transport history.

Change

1 Describe how the speed of travel between London and Edinburgh changed between 1750 and 1900.

2 Write a clear and organised summary that analyses the changes in transport between the early 1700s and 1900. Support your summary with examples.

In the eighteenth and nineteenth centuries, the British were very inventive! Some of Britain's greatest inventors and designers created new machines that did things better, faster and for longer. Britain's technology became the envy of the world and Britain was known as 'the workshop of the world'.

Objectives

- Identify some of the achievements of Britain's great inventors, designers and scientists.
- Judge who you think deserves the title 'Greatest Inventor and/or Designer'.

Significance

The next four pages look at seven influential British inventors, designers and scientists. You will decide which of these was the most significant figure during this time. Think about:
- Why were they important *at the time*?
- How did they change things?
- Are they still important *now*?
- Are they more important than any of the other people?

No. 1: James Watt

- Born in Greenock, Scotland, in 1736, and worked as an instrument maker at the University of Glasgow.

- In 1764, Watt repaired an old steam engine. These engines were used mainly in mines to pump out water, but were slow and kept breaking down. He greatly improved the engine, making it faster and more reliable. It used less coal too.

- In 1781, Watt designed a new steam engine that could turn a wheel. Now steam power could be used to drive machinery.

- By 1800, Watt and his business partner Matthew Boulton's factory in Birmingham was producing some of the world's finest steam engines. These steam engines helped develop Britain's industry so Britain became a world power.

▼ **INTERPRETATION B** Adapted from an article on a history website, written by Daniel Rennie (2019).

'James Watt's steam engine not only streamlined travel and manufacturing, but was also a defining development for the Industrial Revolution. Without Watt, the revolution may not have been possible. His very name was honoured as the unit for which we measure the strength of power worldwide: the watt. His contribution to science, especially his steam engine, brought the world from a farming-based society to one centred around technology and invention. Indeed, James Watt is the creator of the modern world of manufacturing.'

▼ **SOURCE A** In 2011, James Watt (right) and Matthew Boulton (left) appeared on a £50 note. The famous steam engine Watt designed and a factory appeared on the note too.

Meanwhile...

The inventors featured on these pages are British – but other important inventors and designers from around the world at this time include Alfred Nobel (from Sweden) who invented dynamite, Thomas Edison (from the USA) who invented a long-lasting, practical electric light bulb, and Jeanne Villepreux-Power (from France) who invented the aquarium so she could study marine life.

No.2: George Stephenson

- Born in Wylam, Northumberland in 1781, his first job at 14 was working at the local coal mine with his father.
- In 1814, he designed his first steam locomotive, the Blücher.
- In 1815, he produced a safety lamp for miners, which could be used safely in areas where methane gas had collected.
- In 1821, he was given the job of designing the Stockton and Darlington Railway. It opened in 1825 and used his locomotives.
- He designed and made locomotives for the first city-to-city line – Liverpool to Manchester – which opened in 1830. His success paved the way for other British railway engineers, helping Britain to become the leader in railways.

▶ **SOURCE C** George Stephenson, with images of his most famous train (the Rocket) and a bridge over the Stockton and Darlington Railway, appeared on British £5 notes between 1990 and 2003.

▼ **INTERPRETATION D** Written by modern historian Bob Fowke, in *Who? What? When? Victorians* (2003).

'Before the coming of the railways, the fastest anyone could travel was the speed of a galloping horse. By the time George Stephenson retired, you could travel from London to Newcastle by train in just nine hours, at an average speed of approximately 28 miles per hour [about 45km]. It was Stephenson, the son of a miner in the Northumberland mines, more than anyone else, who created the British railway system... before he retired in 1845, he had designed most of the railway which connects the major cities of the North of England.'

No. 3: Michael Faraday

- Born in Newington in 1791.
- He worked in a bookshop where he became fascinated by science.
- He was most interested in electricity and magnetism and, in 1831, discovered how to generate electricity.
- His generator worked on the same basic principle that electric power stations work on today.

▼ **SOURCE E**
A British stamp from 1991 showing Faraday.

▼ **INTERPRETATION F** Adapted from the Royal Society of Chemistry website (2019), an organisation set up in 1848 to advance excellence in the chemical sciences.

'[Faraday was] perhaps one of the most influential scientists who ever lived, whose ground-breaking research into the relationship between electricity and magnetism ultimately led to the invention of the electric motor.

One of his most well-known creations, the Faraday cage, is the basis of MRI machines [machines in hospitals that detect medical problems]. He also discovered benzene [a chemical that had many uses before it was linked to ill-health in humans], pioneered research into nanotechnology [looking at things on a very small scale], and gave his name to the Faraday Effect and Faraday's Law.'

Over to You ▪▪▪

1 Complete the following sentences with the correct term:

a In 1781, a new steam engine that could turn a wheel was designed by _____ _____ .

b James Watt and Matthew Boulton's steam engine factory was in _____ .

c George Stephenson designed and made locomotives for the first city-to-city line – the _____ Railway.

d As well as railway engineering, Stephenson also designed a safety lamp for _____ .

e Michael Faraday discovered a way to generate electricity in _____ .

f Faraday's basic idea of generating electricity is one that is still used today in _____ _____ .

2 Look through the great inventors and designers featured so far and make brief notes on:
- why they were important
- how they changed things.

No. 4: Ada Lovelace

- Born in 1815, she studied mathematics and science from the age of four.

- Aged 17, she met inventor and mathematician Charles Babbage, who had designed an enormous mathematical calculating machine.

- She worked out how the machine could be programmed with a code to calculate numbers.

- Some consider Lovelace's plans for a machine to carry out an instruction to be the world's first ever computer program.

▶ **SOURCE G** A model of Babbage's 'calculating machine' constructed in the 1860s. It was for this machine (sometimes called the 'first computer') that Lovelace designed her program. Only part of the machine had been built by the time of Babbage's death in 1871.

▼ **INTERPRETATION H**
Adapted from an article by Terry MacEwen for www.historic-uk.com. He refers to Alan Turing (the famous Second World War code-breaker) who used Lovelace's notes when he was thinking about designs for the first computer.

'Lovelace's influence has continued after her death and is still felt in the world of technology today. She was such a brilliant mathematician and programmer that her notes were actually used by codebreakers in World War Two and in future computer design. It is clear that her legacy lives on even today. She has become such an iconic woman in technology.'

No. 5: Isambard Kingdom Brunel

- Born in Portsmouth in 1806.

- In 1829, aged 23, he designed the Clifton Suspension Bridge in Bristol.

- In 1833, he designed and built the Great Western Railway, said by some to be the best railway ever built. He also built two grand stations – Paddington (London) and Temple Meads (Bristol).

- As a shipbuilder, Brunel designed three huge record-breaking iron ships – *Great Western* (1837), *Great Britain* (1843) and *Great Eastern* (1858). *Great Eastern* was by far the largest ship ever built at the time. It also laid the first underwater communications cable between America and Britain.

- In 2002, BBC TV asked people to vote for 'the Greatest Briton'. In the end, Winston Churchill came first... but Brunel came second.

▼ **INTERPRETATION I** From a website set up by Bristol City Council in 2006 to celebrate Brunel's achievements.

'Brunel's significance today is twofold. First, there is his lasting engineering legacy, visible in the bridges, tunnels, viaducts, buildings and rail routes he left behind. Second, is the example he has set for the engineers and innovators who followed him and who are inspired to translate their creative thought into action.'

▼ **SOURCE J** A 2006 £2 coin, commemorating the birth of Brunel in 1806.

No. 6: Henry Bessemer

- Born near Hitchin, Hertfordshire, in 1813.
- He designed a machine for putting perforations on postage stamps and a new method of producing glass.
- He invented a 'converter', a machine for turning iron into steel – steel is stronger and more durable than iron (see **K**). Soon many of the pots, pans, railway lines and machines that had been made from iron were made from steel instead.
- In 1850, Britain produced 60,000 tons of steel. By 1880, 1.25 million tons were produced each year.
- In America, where his ideas were copied, at least eight cities and towns are named after him.

▼ **INTERPRETATION K** Adapted from a 2013 lecture given to the Royal Society (an organisation set up in 1660 to promote scientific understanding) by a Tata Steel representative. Tata Steel is a large European steel producer.

'Despite modest educational beginnings, Sir Henry Bessemer rose to the highest rank of nineteenth-century industrialists. His lasting legacy resulted from his pioneering and visionary re-engineering of the steelmaking process, which laid the foundations for global mass production of this versatile material, underpinning our modern world.'

▼ **SOURCE L** An illustration of workers using a Bessemer Converter. The huge container is filled with liquid iron. It removes impurities and adds chemicals to make steel.

No. 7: Alexander Graham Bell

- Born in Edinburgh, Scotland, in 1847.
- He worked all his life on making electrical hearing aids for deaf people – his wife was deaf.
- The idea for a telephone – a machine that converts speech into an electrical signal that travels down a wire and is then turned back into sound – came to him while working on designs to help deaf people.
- He invented the telephone in 1876. Lots of people were trying to make telephones at this time and Bell was accused of copying some of the designs of other inventors.

▼ **SOURCE M** An 1877 illustration from an English newspaper explaining Bell's invention.

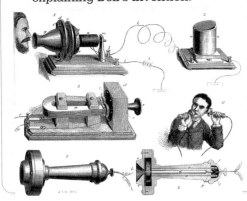

▼ **INTERPRETATION N** Adapted from an article (2003) by John H. Lienhard, author and former Engineering and History professor.

'The telephone is such a huge monument to Bell's inventive genius. But he also developed an early version of the iron lung [a machine that helps people breathe]. He invented the ancestor of the fax machine [a machine that sends instant letters]. He pushed for the use of ethyl alcohol in place of fossil fuels.

He also invented the hydrofoil [a boat that skims quickly over the water on narrow 'feet']. For years it was the fastest thing on water. He left us a legacy of invention that reached far beyond the telephone.'

Over to You

1 Look through the great inventors and designers on these pages and make brief notes on:
- why they were important
- how they changed things.

Significance

To decide if a person is historically significant, you have to assess whether they were important at the time they lived, and whether they are also important over a long time, perhaps even until now.

1 Choose your favourite inventor/designer from pages 138–141. Write a persuasive speech about your choice to convince others that they are significant.
- Mention how important their contribution was at the time.
- Include information about why they are still important now.

So what was the Industrial Revolution?

Historians like to give labels to different periods of time – the 'Stone Age', the 'Norman Conquest', the 'Middle Ages' and the 'Tudor Period' are all good examples. The period of time covered in this chapter also has a label. It is often called the **Industrial Revolution**. Why is it called this? And what caused the Industrial Revolution to take place?

Objectives

- Explain what is meant by the term 'Industrial Revolution'.
- Analyse the causes of the Industrial Revolution.

All change!

Huge changes occurred in the way people worked in the 1700s and 1800s. This was the time when the manufacture of goods moved out of people's homes and into the new steam-powered factories. Machines made things in a fraction of the time it would have taken a person by hand. 'Industrial' is another word for 'work' and '**revolution**' is another word for a dramatic, major change. Certainly then, during this time, industry in Britain had undergone a significant revolution.

Most historians agree that there wasn't just one thing that caused the Industrial Revolution. Instead, several factors all came together at a similar time:

There were more people

As a result of a better understanding of science, medicine and healthcare, the population increased massively in the 1700s and 1800s. All these people needed clothes, shoes, plates, clocks and so on. The factories that produced these goods made a fortune for their owners. Britain changed as factories provided work for the growing population, and made lots of goods for them to buy.

The population was well fed

The growing population needed more food. In the early 1700s, a number of inventions (such as a 'seed drill' that planted seeds in a straight line and covered them back over) helped farmers to produce more. Farms were reorganised as some workers left the countryside and moved to the towns, and new farming methods led to the soil becoming better for growing crops. New ideas about breeding animals led to better quality meat. These improvements in the amount and quality of food improved health and led to an increase in population.

Britain built a huge empire

During this time, Britain built up a vast empire. By the late 1900s, Britain ruled about 450 million people living in 56 colonies all over the world. Britain controlled huge countries such as Canada, India and Australia. Cheap goods, like cotton, were imported to Britain from the colonies; factories turned it into cloth, and sold some of it back to the people in the colonies for enormous profits! The colonies imported vast amounts of iron, steel and pottery made by British companies. Britain also made a fortune from the slave trade that operated within many countries in the British Empire.

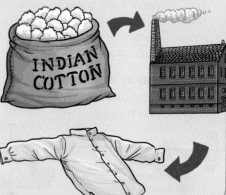

Fact ✓

By 1830, one operator working several factory machines could produce 3500 times more cloth than a person working at home could have done in 1700!

There were some smart businesspeople

Entrepreneurs are businesspeople who are prepared to take risks. They buy **raw materials** (like clay), make it into goods (like teapots) and sell the goods for a profit. At this time, there were large numbers of risk-taking entrepreneurs. Banks were willing to lend them money to put into new businesses, factories and inventions.

Josiah Wedgwood (1730–1795) from Stoke-on-Trent is a good example of a brilliant business person at this time.

He started a world-famous pottery business that used the latest machinery, techniques and business ideas.

There were many brilliant inventors

At this time, some of the world's greatest inventors happened to live in Britain. They created wonderful machines that did things faster than ever before. Steam engines, steam trains, electric generators, telephones and light bulbs are just a few 'British firsts'. Britain changed as it became a world leader in science and technology.

Britain had lots of coal and iron

Britain was rich in some valuable raw materials. By 1850, Britain produced two thirds of the world's coal, half of the world's iron, two thirds of the world's steel and half of the world's cotton cloth! No wonder Britain was sometimes called the 'workshop of the world'.

Key Words   British Empire   entrepreneur
Industrial Revolution   raw material   revolution

▼ **INTERPRETATION A** Adapted from an article on the Newswire website, written by Eric McLamb (2018).

'The Industrial Revolution marked a major turning point in Earth's ecology and humans' relationship with their environment. Relatively overnight, it dramatically changed every aspect of human life and lifestyles. The Industrial Revolution began when machinery started to replace manual labour. Fossil fuels replaced wind, water and wood as energy sources used primarily for the manufacture of textiles and iron making processes. It was the fossil fuel coal that initiated the Industrial Revolution, forever changing the way people would live and use energy. While this propelled human progress to extraordinary levels, it came at extraordinary costs to our environment, and ultimately to the health of all living things.'

Over to You

1 In your own words, explain what 'Industrial Revolution' means.

2 Historians know that big changes, like the Industrial Revolution, have a number of causes. Sometimes the causes of an event are linked. All the following factors were important in creating an 'Industrial Revolution' in Britain. Show how these factors worked together:

> Raw materials   More people   Inventions
>
> Large empire   Entrepreneurs ——①

Key: ① *Entrepreneurs were able to take the new inventions and make them into profitable businesses. This created jobs and wealth.*

a Copy the diagram into your book.
b Draw lines between the factors that you think are connected in some way.
c Give each line a number and, below your diagram, explain the connection between the factors.

To help you get started, one connection has been drawn and explained for you.

Causation

1 'The growth of the British Empire was the main cause of the Industrial Revolution.' How far do you agree with this statement?

Quick Knowledge Quiz

Choose the correct answer from the three options:

1 What name describes the system where people worked in their homes or small workshops making goods, rather than in factories?

  a domestic system
  b home system
  c factory system

2 Who opened their first factory in 1771 at Cromford in Derbyshire?

  a Josiah Wedgwood
  b James Watt
  c Richard Arkwright

3 Which famous society of scientists, inventors, astronomers and engineers met regularly to discuss interesting issues and new ideas?

  a Technology Society
  b Lunar Society
  c Industrial Society

4 What name was given to an orphan who worked in a factory in return for food and a bed?

  a mill overseer
  b factory mule
  c pauper apprentice

5 Published in 1833, what was the name of a report into factory working conditions?

  a Bentley Report
  b Sadler Report
  c Shaftesbury Report

6 Which of the following definitions correctly describes a person who campaigns for change in order to improve something?

  a reformer
  b enforcer
  c refiner

7 What was the surname of the famous family who greatly improved the iron-making process in the 1700s?

  a Sadler
  b Waldron
  c Darby

8 Completed in 1825, what was the name of the first public transport system in the world to use steam locomotives?

  a Liverpool and Manchester Railway
  b London and Edinburgh Railway
  c Stockton and Darlington Railway

9 Which mathematician and scientist is often credited as creating the world's first ever computer program?

  a Michael Faraday
  b Ada Lovelace
  c Isambard Kingdom Brunel

10 James Watt and Matthew Boulton's world-renowned factory for making steam engines was located in which city?

  a London
  b Birmingham
  c Manchester

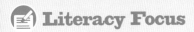 **Literacy Focus**

Writing about historical change

1   Compare the two images below. **Source A** shows Manchester in 1740,
    Source B shows Manchester in around 1850.

   a   Write down at least five adjectives that describe each source.
   b   Make a list of reasons explaining which source shows the earlier
       Manchester and which shows the later Manchester. You can also
       use your answers in step **a**.
   c   Write a paragraph to explain why Manchester changed so much.

▼ **SOURCE A** An engraving of Manchester from 1740.

The South West Prospect of Manchester and Salford

▼ **SOURCE B** An engraving of Manchester from the nineteenth century.

As you know, a **cause** is a reason why something happened. While most historical events have a number of different causes, there is often one cause that is more important than the others.

Historians need to be able to justify *how much* they agree or disagree about the causes of an event. They might respond to a statement that contains a judgement, and argue which cause is the most important.

Responding to statements about causation

This chapter's assessment requires you to think about the causes of the Industrial Revolution.

> 'Britain's entrepreneurs were the main cause of the Industrial Revolution.' How far do you agree with this statement? Explain your answer.

The question asks you to **respond to a statement** about the causes of the Industrial Revolution. The steps below show one way to answer this type of question.

1 **Plan:** Study the statement. Do you agree or disagree with it? What do you know about the topic? What *other* causes led to the event?

2 **Judge:** You need to decide which cause you think was the most important one. List the reasons for your choice.

3 **Answer:** You are asked to respond to the statement, so make sure you answer the question. How far do you agree with the statement? Do you disagree, slightly agree, or strongly agree?

4 **Explain:** Add details/reasons to support your response and explain your view. Use your plan to help you add detail. Try to refer to other reasons when answering the question.

5 **Conclude:** Write a concluding sentence, stating your overall view.

Now, considering all these points, try putting this into practice!

TIP: Entrepreneurs are people who set up new businesses.

TIP: Do you agree a little or a lot (or somewhere in between) with the statement? Think about the *extent* to which you agree that entrepreneurs were the main cause. This means that you also need to think about other causes, and judge which one is the *main* cause.

TIP: Look back at your notes or pages 124–131 of this book to remind yourself how businesspeople contributed to the Industrial Revolution.

TIP: You may not think that one cause was more important than the others. But you can still answer the question – you can argue that several causes are equally important, as long as you can explain your reasons.

TIP: Write why your choice is the *most* important – and why you don't think the others are as important.

TIP: Don't simply write about your choice only. Include other reasons and back them up with factual detail. You might even be able to *link* the causes.

Assessment: Causation

Your challenge is to answer this statement question about causation:

'Britain's entrepreneurs were the main cause of the Industrial Revolution.' How far do you agree with this statement? Explain your answer. (20)

The steps and example sentence starters below will help you structure your answer.

1 **Plan:** Study the statement, which assumes that entrepreneurs (who were prepared to buy raw materials, make these into goods and sell the goods for a profit) were the main cause of the Industrial Revolution. Do you agree? What do you *know* about this?

2 **Judge:** Look at your mind-map. Which of the causes do you think was the *most* important? Try to explain why.

3 **Answer:** Now respond to the statement so you are **directly answering the question**. Remember that the question is asking you the extent to which you agree with the statement.

4 **Explain and conclude:** Sometimes, causes can be linked together, so add any links you can find. For example, would the businesspeople have been able to start their successful businesses without new inventions, or the growing population to sell to?

Finally, add some **details and reasons** to support and explain your view. Try to refer to other causes when answering the question.

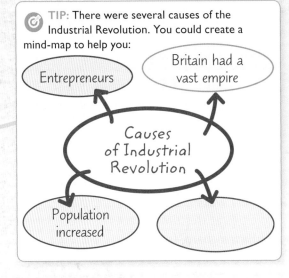

TIP: There were several causes of the Industrial Revolution. You could create a mind-map to help you:

Entrepreneurs

Britain had a vast empire

Causes of Industrial Revolution

Population increased

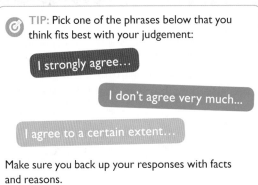

TIP: Pick one of the phrases below that you think fits best with your judgement:

I strongly agree…

I don't agree very much…

I agree to a certain extent…

Make sure you back up your responses with facts and reasons.

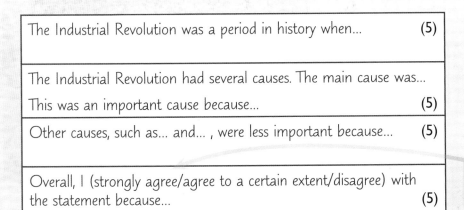

The Industrial Revolution was a period in history when… (5)

The Industrial Revolution had several causes. The main cause was…
This was an important cause because… (5)

Other causes, such as… and… , were less important because… (5)

Overall, I (strongly agree/agree to a certain extent/disagree) with the statement because… (5)

TIP: Remember to conclude your answer. Explain *how far* you agree with the statement.

In 1850, the writer Charles Reade wrote about Sheffield, in the north of England. He described it as 'perhaps the most hideous town in creation'. He reported that black smoke blocked out the sun and 'sparkling streams entered the town, but soon got filthy, full of rubbish, clogged with dirt and bubbling with rotten, foul-smelling gasses'. So what made Sheffield – and many other towns and cities like it – smell so bad? What was it like to live there? And why was there so much disease?

Objectives

- Investigate what life was like for ordinary people in newly expanded industrial towns and cities of the nineteenth century.
- Discover why disease was so common at the time.

A changing nation

Sheffield was no different from many other British towns and cities at this time. Places such as Manchester, Liverpool and Birmingham, for example, were equally as bad. These towns and cities had become horrible places to live because of the factories that had been built there. People flooded in from the countryside to find work, and factory owners then had to build homes for the workers. Houses were built quickly and cheaply, and were crammed close together with narrow alleys between them. Built in **terraces**, the houses were also built **back-to-back** to save space and money.

There was no planning or quality control – some homes were even built without foundations. In 1842, one factory owner went to visit some workers living in a row of newly built houses and found that they had all blown down in a storm the night before.

▼ **SOURCE B** Back-to-back housing at Staithes, Yorkshire in the late 1800s.

▼ **A** A plan of back-to-back housing in Nottingham, 1845.

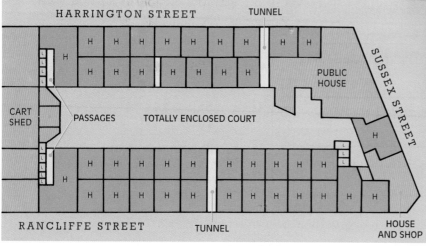

HARRINGTON STREET
TUNNEL
PUBLIC HOUSE
SUSSEX STREET
CART SHED
PASSAGES
TOTALLY ENCLOSED COURT
RANCLIFFE STREET
TUNNEL
HOUSE AND SHOP

| H | HOUSE | L | LAVATORY |

Overcrowding

Almost all factory workers' houses in the largest British towns were crowded; usually five or more people lived in one small room. These rooms were rented from local landlords or factory owners. In 1847, 40 people were found sharing one room in Liverpool!

▼ **SOURCE C** Adapted from a newspaper article written by George Sims, a journalist who believed that the government should improve conditions in crowded towns and cities. The article then appeared in an 1889 book called *How the Poor Live*.

'The other day I visited the room of a widow woman, her daughters of seventeen and sixteen, her sons of fourteen and thirteen, and two younger children. Her miserable apartment was on the street level, and behind it was a common yard. For this room, the widow paid four and sixpence a week; the walls were mouldy and steaming with damp; the boards as you trod upon them made a slushing noise. If we pretend these conditions don't exist, they will continue.'

▼ **INTERPRETATION D** Adapted from historian Simon Mason in *British Social and Economic History* (1990), writing about some of the changes brought on by the Industrial Revolution.

'In these growing towns, overcrowding was probably the biggest single cause of bad conditions. Problems such as slum housing, bad health, poverty, crime and poor working conditions became much more serious. Villages were turned into cities, streams and rivers became open sewers, grey buildings swallowed up fields, cart tracks became roads. Town centres became slum areas squeezed tightly between factories and mills. Well-to-do [richer] citizens left the town centres and built themselves homes in the new suburbs or the country.'

Key Words   back-to-back housing   terrace

Fact ✓

Do you have to share a bedroom? Imagine what it would be like to share your bed with up to six others. A survey in 1839 found that out of 3000 families in Bury, near Manchester, 773 of them slept with three or four to a bed; 209 had five in a bed; 67 had six in a bed; and, in 15 families, seven people slept in one bed.

Later on...

In 1801, only eight towns in England, Wales and Scotland had a population of more than 50,000: Birmingham, Bristol, Edinburgh, Glasgow, Leeds, Liverpool, London and Manchester. By 1900, there were over 60.

Over to You

1 Look at **Plan A** and draw a copy of it.
   a What is missing from the plan of these houses that we would expect to see on a plan for houses today?
   b On your plan, mark which house (or houses) you would least like to live in. Give reasons for your choice.

2 Read **Interpretation D**.
   a How, according to the author, did villages and towns change at this time?
   b How do you think the author knows about the changes that were taking place at this time?

Source Analysis

1 Look at **Source B**. Write a brief description of the picture.
2 Read **Source C**.
   a How many people lived in the one room the writer visited?
   b What is the writer's opinion of the conditions he saw?
3 How useful are **Sources B** and **C** for an enquiry into living conditions at this time?

Why were the towns and cities so filthy?

The disposal of **sewage** was a major problem. None of the houses had toilets indoors, so the best some families could manage was a bucket in the corner of the room. This would be emptied now and again into the street. Sometimes it was stored outside the door until there was enough to sell to a farmer as manure to spread in the fields. Occasionally, there was a street toilet – a deep hole with a wooden shed over it – but this would be shared with 30 or 40 other families. Some streets had a pump that provided water, but often people collected water from the local river, and this would usually be filthy. There were no rubbish collections, litter bins, street cleaners, sewers or fresh running water.

Death in the streets

Sewage trickled down the streets and into nearby rivers. Most families washed themselves in and drank from these same rivers. It was little wonder that disease thrived in towns (see **E**). Unlike today, ordinary people didn't know that germs could cause disease. Far away in laboratories, some scientists and doctors had started to make the connection, but in Britain's streets and slums, people continued to use the filthy water just as they had always done. In 1840, one in every three children died before they reached the age of five. In Britain at this time, the average age of death was 30 – but in some of the larger, dirtier, overcrowded industrial towns, it was much lower. In Leeds, for example, the average age of death for a working-class man was 19 and in Manchester it was 17.

▼ **E** Some of the most common diseases of the 1800s.

Disease	How it was caught	Symptoms	Who it affected
Typhoid	The typhoid germ lives in urine and **faeces**. Sometimes sewage **contaminates** water or food, passing on the germ. This killer disease can also be carried by flies, which land on food.	Headaches, fever, **constipation**... then terrible diarrhoea. A similar disease called typhus was common too, caused by bites from body lice.	Can attack anyone, and killed up to 40% of people who got the disease.
Tuberculosis (TB)	Germs are passed from one person to another in the moisture sprayed when people cough or sneeze. Sometimes called 'consumption'. Another type of TB was caused by infected cows' milk.	Attacks the lungs. Victims cough up blood, lose weight, get a fever, chest pains and shortness of breath.	Can attack anyone. Infected one out of ten people in the 1800s. In 1800, TB caused around 25% of all deaths in London. If you caught it, there was around a 70% chance you would die.
Cholera	Caused by a germ that lives in contaminated water. First arrived in Britain in 1831.	'Cholera' is the Greek word for diarrhoea. As the diarrhoea gets worse, victims can't keep food or water in their bodies. Their bodies turn black and blue, they dehydrate and die – sometimes within 24 hours.	Can attack anyone – and killed 90% of people who got it. In Britain, 32,000 people died from cholera in 1831, 62,000 in 1848, 20,000 in 1854 and 14,000 in 1866. These were known as **epidemics**.

Consequences

1 Define:
   a back-to-back housing
   b contaminated
   c epidemic.

2 Explain two consequences of the rapid growth of towns and cities in the nineteenth century.

▼ **INTERPRETATION F** A modern artist's impression of a typical city street in the 1800s.

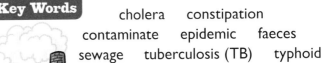

Key Words

cholera   constipation
contaminate   epidemic   faeces
sewage   tuberculosis (TB)   typhoid

Over to You

1 a Make a list of factors about life in towns that might lead to poor health and disease.

  b Make another list of ways the government could improve living conditions.

2 Imagine you were unlucky enough to spend a day looking around streets like the ones on these pages and visiting houses such as the ones featured in **Sources B** and **C** on pages 148–149. Write a letter home to a friend in the countryside describing what you have seen.

  • Explain why industrial towns and cities expanded so quickly in the nineteenth century. (You might want to look at pages 126–129.)

  • Explain what problems this expansion brought with it.

  • Make sure your letter is set out correctly, with an address, date, greeting and sign-off.

KEY

A Drinking in pubs was a favourite pastime. People mostly drank beer but gin was also common.

B Water carriers sold water in the streets (but some people just collected it from the river).

C People used the river to wash their clothes and collect drinking water.

D A water pump, which often pulled up water from the river.

E A dunghill – a large mound of faeces from sewage.

F 'Nightsoilmen' (sewage collectors) taking away sewage to sell.

G Rats, a common sight in nineteenth-century towns.

H A shared street toilet.

I 'Costermongers' hired carts, bought food from local markets and wandered the streets selling door-to-door.

J Crime was common and there was no national police force until the 1850s.

K Families living in one room.

L This family is sick. Cholera was the new killer disease – and death could come quickly, killing many within 24 hours.

M A factory.

N The houses were in poor condition. Landlords cared little about the state of them – and there were no laws to make sure they looked after their properties.

Heroes of public health: Chadwick, Snow, Bazalgette and Nightingale

'Public health' is a phrase used to describe the general health and well-being of ordinary people. In the early 1800s, public health in Britain was in a very poor state. The national average age of death for a working British man, for example, was just 30. In some places, like Liverpool, it was as low as 15. So why were people dying so young? And what was eventually done – and by whom – to improve the state of the nation's health?

Objectives

- Explain why the government was slow to improve public health.
- Evaluate the contribution of Chadwick, Snow, Bazalgette and Nightingale to improving public health.

Stinking cities

Towns and cities grew very quickly in the 1800s. Manchester's population, for example, grew from 45,000 in 1745 to over 300,000 by 1851. New housing was built quickly and cheaply, and nearly all homes lacked basics such as toilets and running water. There were no street cleaners, and no sewers to take away the waste, so rubbish and sewage piled up in the streets and floated in the rivers.

Deadly disease

In these filthy, overcrowded conditions, disease and sickness spread fast. By far the most feared illness was cholera, a killer disease with no known cure. Cholera first arrived in Britain in 1831 and killed around 32,000 people within a year. In some places, where there were severe outbreaks, cemeteries became so full that they had to close (see **A**).

What did the government do?

Special groups called **Boards of Health** were set up by some towns to investigate the cholera outbreaks, but they didn't do much, mainly because they didn't know what caused cholera. They knew that it occurred more often where living conditions were bad and where people were crowded together – but they didn't really know how to deal with it. This was a time, remember, when people didn't know that germs caused disease. And the politicians in London didn't do a great deal either, because many felt it wasn't their job to tell people how to live their lives or ask factory owners and businesspeople to build better housing and facilities.

But cholera kept coming back. After further outbreaks of disease in the 1830s, the government set up an enquiry to investigate conditions in towns and cities. The man in charge was Edwin Chadwick and he sent out inspection teams of doctors all over Britain. What he found out is summed up on the next page.

▼ **SOURCE A** A cholera notice from around 1832 in Dudley, West Midlands. In nearby Bilston, it was said that 'the coffins could not be made fast enough for the dead'.

CHOLERA.

THE

DUDLEY BOARD OF HEALTH,

HEREBY GIVE NOTICE, THAT IN CONSEQUENCE OF THE

Church-yards at Dudley

Being so full, no one who has died of the CHOLERA will be permitted to be buried after *SUNDAY* next, (To-morrow) in either of the Burial Grounds of *St. Thomas's*, or *St. Edmund's*, in this Town.

All Persons who die from CHOLERA, must for the future be buried in the Church-yard at Netherton.

BOARD of HEALTH, DUDLEY.

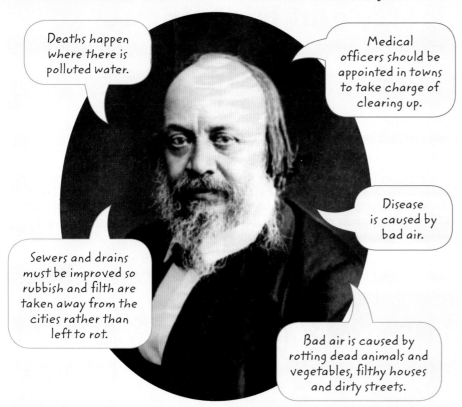

Deaths happen where there is polluted water.

Medical officers should be appointed in towns to take charge of clearing up.

Disease is caused by bad air.

Sewers and drains must be improved so rubbish and filth are taken away from the cities rather than left to rot.

Bad air is caused by rotting dead animals and vegetables, filthy houses and dirty streets.

Key Words   Board of Health
public health

Fact ✓

Britain was not the only place affected by large-scale cholera outbreaks at this time. Russia, Poland, India and China also suffered.

Over to You ..ıl

1 a What is meant by the term 'public health'?

   b In your own words, explain the state of public health in Britain in the early 1800s.

2 a Who was Edwin Chadwick?

   b What was wrong with Chadwick's idea about the cause of disease?

   c Despite getting it wrong about the *cause* of disease, why do you think Chadwick is viewed as an important figure in the fight to improve public health at this time?

3 Why do you think cholera kept coming back, despite a Public Health Act?

The impact of Chadwick's report

Chadwick's report, published in 1842, shocked people. Finally, in 1848 the government passed a new law – the Public Health Act – allowing councils to spend money on cleaning up if they wanted to. Some cities, like Liverpool, made huge improvements, but others didn't bother to do anything… so the filth continued.

Cholera comes back!

Despite clean-up efforts in some places, outbreaks of cholera and other diseases kept happening. In 1848, 62,000 people were killed by cholera, followed by 20,000 in 1854. During the 1854 outbreak a doctor called John Snow decided to work out – once and for all – just what was causing cholera. At this time, there were two main theories about how people caught diseases. John Snow was determined to find out which theory was correct.

THEORY 1:
The miasma theory

Disease is caused by dirty air, known as 'miasma'. Cholera, for example, is carried through the air like a poisonous gas or an infected mist. The stinking, dirty air coming from the filthy towns causes disease.

THEORY 2:
The contagion theory

Disease isn't caused by foul air. It's caused by having personal contact with a sick person, or their clothes or bedding, for example. The sick person is 'contagious' and passes on the disease to someone else.

The John Snow story

By 1854, John Snow (born in York) was a successful London doctor. Snow was a 'contagionist' – he believed that diseases like cholera were passed on by having some sort of contact with an infected person. In 1854, he was able to test his theory.

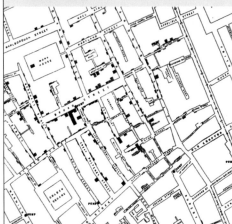

1 In 1854, cholera killed 700 people in a small area of London called Soho. Snow marked on a map where all the victims lived.

He made an amazing discovery – all the victims got their water from the same pump in Broad Street. Those who didn't catch cholera were getting their water from other places.

2 Snow concluded that there must be something wrong with the water and had the pump handle removed.

We'll have to use another pump now!

There were no more deaths – and when Snow investigated further he found a nearby street toilet with a cracked lining. This was leaking sewage into the Broad Street pump's water supply.

3 Snow was right! He proved that cholera wasn't carried by 'bad air'.

The miasma theory is wrong. Cholera is a water-borne disease!

He showed that cholera was carried in water and is passed on through 'contagion' – by coming into contact with a sufferer of cholera or, in this case, drinking water contaminated by a victim's diarrhoea!

Time to act again?

The government now had strong evidence that the filthy state of towns was linked to diseases such as cholera. An engineer named Joseph Bazalgette was asked to draw up plans for an underground sewer system to take away sewage from London's streets. However, these plans were put on hold when the government found out how much it would all cost.

Then, in 1858, a really hot summer caused the stinking River Thames to smell even worse than usual. After several weeks of what people called 'the Great Stink', Bazalgette was given £3 million (about £1 billion today) and told to begin his sewer system straight away.

The sewer king

Bazalgette built 134km of sewers, which could remove 1.9 billion litres of sewage a day. They were finished in 1870 and ended cholera epidemics in London. Other cities soon began building sewer systems.

Soon, Parliament introduced laws to improve the nation's health. For example, it gave councils the power to pull down poor quality housing and insisted pavements be clean and well lit.

The nursing revolution

In the early 1800s, nurses (and the nursing profession) had a bad reputation. Hospital conditions were often terrible, and there was no proper training. But over the next 50 years, nursing was completely reformed – largely due to the work of Florence Nightingale.

Born in 1820, Nightingale trained in Europe as a nurse and returned to run a women's hospital in London. In 1854, she was asked to lead a team of 38 nurses in Turkey to care for British soldiers wounded in the Crimean War. When she arrived, she found horrific conditions – the wounded were poorly fed, unwashed and sleeping in overcrowded, filthy rooms. In these conditions, infectious diseases such as

▼ **SOURCE C** Joseph Bazalgette (top right) at the building of a section of sewer in London, 1862.

Key Words

anaesthetic   antiseptic
surgery   vaccination

typhus and cholera spread quickly. More soldiers in the hospital died from infections and disease than from the war wounds they came in with!

Nightingale and her nurses soon changed things. They set up a kitchen to feed the soldiers properly, cleaned the hospital and got hold of vital supplies for patients.

After the war, Nightingale wrote several books on nursing, set up a nurse training school, and advised the government on hospital design. She also encouraged the setting up of the British Red Cross in 1870, part of a global organisation that continues to help people who are caught up in conflict, or have had to flee their homes. By the time of her death in 1910, there were around 60,000 properly trained nurses in Britain and nursing had become a highly skilled and well-respected medical profession.

Getting healthier

Life expectancy had increased from 30 years in 1800 to 50 years in 1900. Laws had improved public health, and discoveries such as **anaesthetics** and **antiseptics** had made **surgery** safer. A smallpox **vaccination** prevented many deaths, and better training had vastly improved the medical profession.

Meanwhile... 1850s

Mary Seacole (1805–1881) was another nurse who served in the Crimean War. Born in Jamaica, she paid for her own trip to Crimea, where she set up a 'British Hotel' that provided hot food and clean beds for sick soldiers. She also visited battlefields to nurse the wounded.

Over to You

1 a Explain how someone who believed in the miasma theory thought diseases like cholera spread.

   b In what way does someone who believes in contagion think differently?

2 Explain how John Snow proved that cholera was carried in water and is passed on through 'contagion'.

3 What contribution did Florence Nightingale and Mary Seacole make to nursing during the Crimean War?

4 How did Florence Nightingale change the nursing profession?

Later on... TODAY

International Nurses Day is observed around the world each year on 12 May (the anniversary of Florence Nightingale's birth), to mark the contributions that nurses make to society.

Significance

People or events are said to be significant if they make a big impact at the time, change a lot of people's lives and are still important today.

1 Choose one of the four people studied on pages 152–155. Explain their significance to improvements to public health.

How divided was society?

In today's world, most of us make friends with different people, whatever their job, house, income or position. We live in a world where we pride ourselves on the fact that a person's kindness, consideration and personality are far more important than the land they own, the car they drive, the money they earn or the job they do. But in the eighteenth and nineteenth centuries, society was much more divided. How did these divisions affect people's lives?

Objectives

- Examine class divisions in eighteenth- and nineteenth-century society.
- Compare life for the different classes at this time.

In the 1700s and 1800s there were strict divisions in society. These divisions were called 'classes'. Class was based on income, housing, family tradition and social life, and people were divided into three classes: the upper class, the middle class and the working class.

The 'social pyramid'

Most people understood where they 'fitted' into society in the late 1700s and 1800s. The whole system resembled a pyramid, with the rich, upper classes at the top looking down on everyone, and the less wealthy, working classes at the bottom. **Diagram A** illustrates what has been referred to as the 'social pyramid'. Educational opportunities were also related to class – this meant that it was extremely difficult for people in lower classes to get better-paid jobs (see **B**).

▼ **A** The 'social pyramid'.

The very rich
The upper class (About 100,000 people)

Upper middle class
Lower middle class (About 2 million people)

Working class (About 15 million people)

▼ **B** The educational opportunities available to members of the different classes. The term 'middle class' was used from around the mid-1700s to describe people who weren't 'upper class' or 'working class'. The 'middle classes' were professional and business people and included doctors, teachers and bank managers.

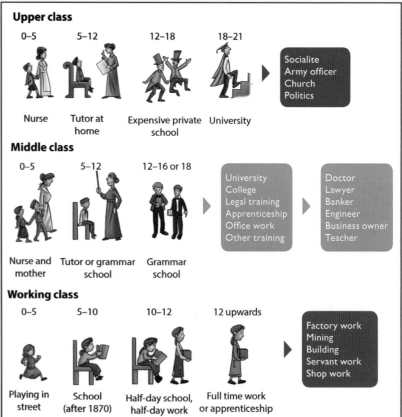

Upper class

| 0–5 | 5–12 | 12–18 | 18–21 | |
| Nurse | Tutor at home | Expensive private school | University | Socialite / Army officer / Church / Politics |

Middle class

| 0–5 | 5–12 | 12–16 or 18 | | |
| Nurse and mother | Tutor or grammar school | Grammar school | University / College / Legal training / Apprenticeship / Office work / Other training | Doctor / Lawyer / Banker / Engineer / Business owner / Teacher |

Working class

| 0–5 | 5–10 | 10–12 | 12 upwards | |
| Playing in street | School (after 1870) | Half-day school, half-day work | Full time work or apprenticeship | Factory work / Mining / Building / Servant work / Shop work |

Where did the different classes live?

Your class often determined the part of town you lived in. Poorer people tended to live in the centre of towns or cities (near factories) while the better-off middle classes lived further out. As you left the overcrowded town, houses would become larger and the occupants would be wealthier – these 'posher' areas were known as the suburbs.

Diagram C illustrates how the inhabitants of a typical town might be divided, while Source D shows the typical diet of two different families living in two different areas.

▼ **C** How the different classes in a typical town might be divided. The upper classes would most likely live in the countryside, well away from the towns, on large family estates.

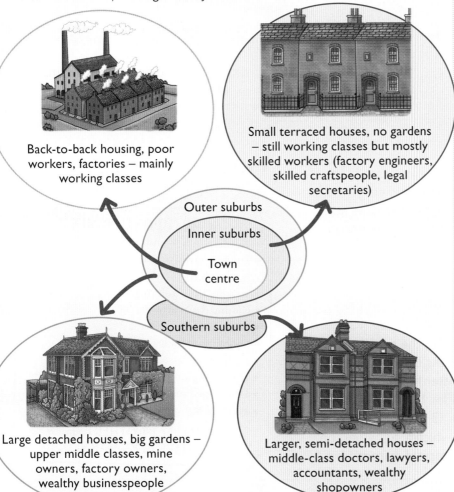

▼ **SOURCE D** In 1899, Seebohm Rowntree (his family made chocolate) interviewed two families in York. He asked them what they ate on a typical Monday. No prizes for guessing which was the richer family and which was the poorer!

FAMILY 1

Breakfast: Porridge, fried bacon, toast, butter, treacle, marmalade, tea and coffee

Dinner: Boiled mutton (sheep), carrots, turnips, potatoes, bread sauce, jam roly-poly pudding and rice pudding

Tea: Bread, teacakes, butter, cake and tea

Supper: Fish, bread, butter, cake, biscuits, cocoa and oranges

FAMILY 2

Breakfast: Bacon, bread and tea
Dinner: Bacon, bread and tea
Tea: Bacon, bread and tea
Supper: Nothing

Over to You

1 Explain what is meant by the word 'class'.

2 Describe the 'social pyramid'.

3 a Why do you think poorer, working-class people lived near the town and city centres?

   b What, and where, were the 'suburbs'?

   c Why did the richer people live in the suburbs?

4   Use all the information on these pages. Imagine you are a researcher in the 1800s, and you have been invited to spend a day with an upper-class family and a day with a poorer family. Write a diary entry for each day, describing your experiences and feelings about your visits. Mention the house you are in, the food you eat, the area of town the house is in and the way each family spends their time.

Similarity and Difference

It is important that you understand that people's lives can be very different even if they live in the same country in the same period of history.

1 Explain two ways in which the life of a working-class person was different from the life of an upper-class person in the 1800s.

Crimes and their punishments are big news. The latest crime figures, the nastiest murder trials and the state of our prisons are always on our TV or computer screens and in the news. It seems like a big part of life today… but crime was a big part of this period too. What was crime like then? Who caught the criminals? How were they punished?

Objectives

- Identify whose role it was to catch criminals in 1800.
- Explain the terms 'capital crime' and 'transportation'.

Keeping law and order

Crime was a huge problem in the late eighteenth and early nineteenth centuries. Many criminals were never caught because there were no police officers or detectives to track them down. That's right – no police force! Instead, catching criminals was still the job of a mixture of people called the watch, magistrates and constables.

Getting caught

If, by some slim chance, a criminal was caught, the punishments were very tough. This was to act as a warning to others. And the punishments were just as harsh no matter how young the criminal was. In 1801, a boy was executed for breaking into a house and stealing a silver spoon – he was 13 years old. In fact, at this time there were over 200 crimes for which a guilty person could be executed. These were known as **capital crimes** (see **A**).

▼ **A** Capital crimes in the 1700s and 1800s, punishable by death.

SOME CAPITAL CRIMES

- Murder, treason and arson
- Theft of anything worth more than 25p (around £15 today)
- Stealing from a shipwreck
- Cutting down growing trees
- Being a pirate
- Shooting a rabbit
- Stealing letters
- Blackening up your face at night
- Damaging Westminster Bridge in London
- Begging without a licence

PLUS ABOUT 180 OTHER CRIMES
YOU HAVE BEEN WARNED!

The watch
The bigger towns set up a watch to patrol the streets at night. The people in the watch, sometimes called 'Charlies', were very poorly paid and were often too old and unfit to get any other type of job.

Magistrates
Each area had a magistrate (also called a Justice of the Peace). Their job was to question suspects and witnesses in a court. They were unpaid volunteers, and could punish criminals however they wanted for minor crimes (like drunken behaviour). For more serious crimes such as murder, the suspect would be sent to a special court with a professional judge and jury.

Constables
Some areas had one or two constables. They helped organise the watch and helped magistrates by trying to catch criminals. They were unpaid volunteers as well, and did the job for a year before someone else took over.

Harsh punishments

The most common type of execution was hanging – and the public enjoyed watching hangings. In fact, a public hanging was a day out for all the family and huge crowds turned up to watch. Some rich people rented houses overlooking the **gallows**, and seats in specially built grandstands fetched high prices (see **B** and **C**). Yet despite the popularity of these hangings, fewer people were hanged than should have been. Courts often took pity on young children or desperate people, even if they had clearly committed a capital crime.

Another common punishment was **transportation** by ship to another place that Britain controlled, such as Australia or Gibraltar. Once there, the prisoner was enslaved for either five, seven or fourteen years, depending on the seriousness of the crime. They would work on the land for settlers, or were sent to build roads or buildings. After this time, they were free to return to Britain. Many never did – they couldn't afford the trip home – and instead settled for a new life abroad. Today, many Australians can trace their ancestors back to criminals transported there in the 1800s.

▼ **SOURCE B** Adapted from the writings of Cesar de Saussure, a Swiss travel writer who lived in England for several years in the 1700s.

'The guilty men are placed on a cart, each with a rope around his neck. A priest would pray with them. Then, the cart was driven off under the gallows. The criminals' friends and relations tugged at the hanging men's feet so that they might die all the sooner.

The bodies and clothes of the dead belong to the executioner; relatives must, if they wish for them, buy them from him, and unclaimed bodies are sold to surgeons for them to experiment on.'

Key Words   capital crime   gallows   transportation

▼ **SOURCE C** An eighteenth-century painting by the famous artist William Hogarth of an execution at Tyburn, London (where Marble Arch stands today).

Over to You

1 a Define: • capital crime • transportation.
   b List three examples of a capital crime in the 1700s and 1800s.
   c Why do you think there were so many capital crimes?
   d Why were fewer people executed than should have been?

2 Look at **Source C**. Write down the numbers – and beside each one, explain what you can see.

3 Read **Source B**.
   a In your own words, describe how criminals were executed.
   b Why do you think some of the criminals' friends pulled down on their feet?

4 How useful are **Sources B** and **C** to a historian studying crime and punishment at this time?

Knowledge and Understanding

1 Who was responsible for catching criminals and putting them on trial at this time?

2 Describe the role of a magistrate in combating crime.

How did the first police force begin?

As Britain's largest city, London had the highest crime rate. But even here there was no police force trained and ready to catch criminals. In 1749, a London magistrate named Henry Fielding decided to do something about the **con artists**, thieves and prostitutes operating near his offices in Bow Street. He gathered six men, gave them handcuffs, a pistol and a stick, and promised to pay them a guinea (£1.05) a week to capture as many criminals as possible. At first, they wore their own clothes, but were later given a uniform. This early police force became known as the **Bow Street Runners**.

Objectives

- Explain the difference between a Bow Street Runner and one of Robert Peel's 'Bobbies'.
- Assess why Peel established Britain's first police force.

Catching the vile villains

In 1763, Henry's brother, John, set up a patrol on horseback to stop robbers on the roads in London. By 1792, seven other areas in London had their own versions of the Bow Street Runners. However, as crime levels kept rising, it was clear that the country needed far more. It needed a proper police force!

A new police force

The man who played a major part in creating Britain's first professional police force was the politician Robert Peel. As the government's Home Secretary, he was responsible for law and order. In 1829, he set up the **Metropolitan Police**. Three thousand men, mainly ex-soldiers, were given a new dark blue uniform, boots, a wooden truncheon, a rattle, a brown coat and a top hat lined with cane and wire. They received 5p a day (not much then, but better than many other jobs) and were expected to walk their 32km 'beat' around London, seven days a week. They had to be under 35 years old, healthy, and able to read and write. Discipline was severe and many early recruits were sacked for drunkenness.

Call the police!

To begin with, many people hated the new police force. Some felt they were a waste of money or spies for the government. Policemen were regularly beaten up in the street and spat at. They were branded 'Peel's bloody gang' and the 'evil blue devils'. But the 'blue devils' did a good job. They were largely well disciplined, good humoured and acted with restraint wherever possible (see **A**). Gradually, the public began to respect and trust them. More criminals were caught, so there was less crime in London too. Soon other towns copied London and, by 1856, every large town had its own policemen.

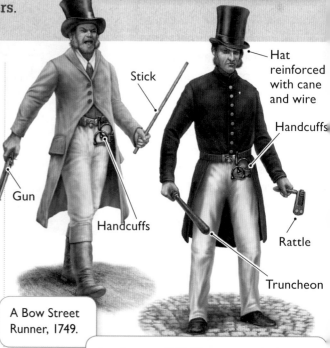

A Bow Street Runner, 1749.

Labels: Stick · Gun · Handcuffs · Hat reinforced with cane and wire · Handcuffs · Rattle · Truncheon

A policeman, 1829. These men soon became known as 'Peelers' or 'Bobbies' after the surname or first name of their founder.

▼ **SOURCE A** Adapted from a list of 'General Instructions' issued to every new police officer in the Metropolitan Police from 1829.

Policemen must:
- prevent crime and disorder
- secure and maintain public respect
- offer individual service and friendship to all members of the public without regard to their wealth or social class
- be friendly and good humoured
- be ready to offer individual sacrifice in protecting and preserving life
- only use physical force when persuasion, advice and warning fail.

Catching criminals

In 1810, the old system of the watch and constables brought 9000 convictions. In 1830, there were 18,000 convictions for major crimes. By 1900, there were 48,000 policemen and 25,000 convictions. The new police force seemed to be getting results.

Fact ✓

Crime levels almost doubled in Britain in the early 1800s. Between 1810 and 1817, there were 35,000 reported crimes. From 1817 to 1824, there were 65,000.

▼ **SOURCE B** London's police record of crimes and criminals, 1837.

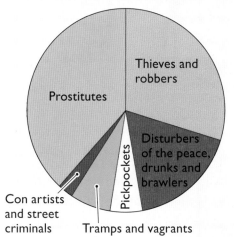

- Thieves and robbers
- Prostitutes
- Con artists and street criminals
- Pickpockets
- Disturbers of the peace, drunks and brawlers
- Tramps and vagrants

Later on... `1915`

Policemen worked shifts seven days a week. Meal breaks didn't exist, so food was carried in a special blue bag and eaten 'on the beat'. Non-uniformed detectives, based at Scotland Yard, appeared in 1842 (after regular policemen messed up a murder hunt) but policewomen didn't appear until August 1915.

Causation

1 Who was Robert Peel?
2 Explain why a police force was set up in the early nineteenth century.

Key Words

Bow Street Runners   con artist   Metropolitan Police

▼ **SOURCE C** A photograph of some of Britain's first 'boys in blue' in London, around 1850.

Over to You

1 Copy out a timeline like the one below.

1740 1750 1760 1770 1780 1790 1800 1810 1820 1830 1840 1850 1860 1870 1890 1900

On the timeline, write in the key events in the history of the Bow Street Runners and the early police forces.

2 a Why do you think the early policemen:
  - carried a truncheon
  - carried a rattle
  - wore a reinforced top hat?
  b Explain why Robert Peel set up Britain's first police force.
  c Why were some people against the police at first?

3  Look at **Sources A** and **C**. Imagine you are looking for a job and you see an advertisement asking for new policemen. Using your knowledge of the type of person Peel was looking for, write a letter to apply, using a formal letter format, and say:
  - why you want the job
  - what qualities you possess
  - why Peel should pick you.

4 a Look at **Source B**. What are the top three crimes in London in 1837?
  b Based on this chart, what inferences might a historian make about London at this time?

Why was Elizabeth Fry on a £5 note?

Look at the banknote on the opposite page. This was the Bank of England's £5 note until it was replaced by a new type of note (featuring Winston Churchill) in 2017. It features a woman named Elizabeth Fry, a prison reformer who spent much of her life trying to improve the state of prisons and the rights and welfare of prisoners. What were prison conditions like? What, exactly, did Fry do? How successful was Fry and other prison reformers?

Objectives

- Describe conditions in prisons in the 1800s.
- Outline the efforts made by Elizabeth Fry and John Howard to improve conditions.

Off to prison

In the early 1800s, a prison visit would have been a very upsetting (and smelly) experience. Because of the lack of proper water supply or sewage systems, visitors used handkerchiefs soaked in vinegar, or nose clips, so they couldn't smell the prisoners. About a quarter of prisoners died each year from disease, and typhus was so common it was nicknamed 'jail fever'.

Meet Charles. It is 1805 – Charles is a 14-year-old boy who was kept in prison awaiting trial for stealing a parcel.

I am cold, dirty and starting to feel ill. My cell is filthy and crowded – and we haven't got enough light, water or proper food. We get porridge and bread every day but it's never enough. And the water we get is so dirty it makes us feel sick to taste it.

We don't get provided with beds either but we can hire them from the jailer at 6p per night. I can't afford one so I sleep on the floor on two old rugs that were left over when another prisoner died. I share my bed with the rats, lice and fleas.

Prison life is tough. We are forced to work on pointless tasks all day long. We pace the treadmill, a sort of large wheel that goes nowhere; we call it the 'everlasting staircase'. Sometimes we have to unpick old ropes and turn them into doormats – I hate this the most because it makes my fingers bleed.

The jailers who run this place don't get paid – they make their money selling us food, beer, tobacco and blankets. Prisoners who can afford it eat and drink well – the rest of us live on local charity.

We get charged for everything – fees for admission (we pay to get into jail!), for release, for food, to have your leg irons removed for a few hours – it's endless!

And if you're found innocent you can't be released until you pay the money you owe. There are some men who have been in here for decades.

Prison heroes

Some people, such as John Howard and Elizabeth Fry, were convinced that prisons should change. In the 1770s, Howard visited hundreds of British prisons to assess conditions. Soon afterwards, he advised Parliament about how to improve conditions – and in 1777, he wrote an influential and widely read book called *The State of Prisons*.

Elizabeth Fry went further. After being appalled by what she saw on a visit to Newgate Prison in 1813, and motivated by her religious beliefs, Fry spent the rest of her life trying to help prisoners. She read to the inmates, taught them to read and write, and helped them tidy their cells. Many of her ideas influenced the 1823 prison reforms in the chart (see **A**).

The government began to take notice of influential people such as Fry and Howard and the prison system began to change. Prisons still remained tough, but conditions improved. By 1900, government figures showed that milder treatment led to fewer people returning to prison after they were released.

A revolution in crime and punishment?

With the new police force catching more criminals, Parliament was persuaded to make punishments less harsh. After 1841, the only hangings were for murder, treason, being a pirate, and burning down a dockyard or an arsenal (where weapons are stored). In 1868, public executions were stopped and transportation was ended. The country seemed to be becoming more civilised!

▼ **A** Key dates of prison reforms in England (1820–1878).

Date	Reform
1820	Whipping of women ended.
1823	Jailers paid wages (so prisoners were not charged for everything). Female prisoners kept separate from male prisoners. Prison doctors, priests and teachers employed. Attempts were to be made to reform prisoners – like teaching them to read and write.
1835	Prison inspectors appointed.
1878	Government took control of all prisons. Before this time, nearly half of all prisons were privately owned, with their owners (and their jailers) trying to make as much money as possible out of the prisoners.

▼ **INTERPRETATION B** The Elizabeth Fry £5 note. Fry is shown reading to female prisoners. This was the last paper £5 note – now they are printed on special plastic.

Over to You

1 a Why was disease so common among prisoners?

  b Why did jailers charge prisoners for the things they wanted?

2 How had prisons improved by 1901? Give examples to support your answer.

Cause and Consequence

1 How did the following people contribute to the improvement of prison life?
   a John Howard
   b Elizabeth Fry

2 Describe two of the methods used by the authorities to improve the prison system in the 1800s.

8.7A Why did the police fail to catch Jack the Ripper?

On 31 August 1888, a poor 43-year-old mother of five children named Mary Ann Nichols was found murdered in Whitechapel, London. She had been killed with a knife. Then, just over a week later, another poor Londoner named Annie Chapman was found dead not far from the first murder. She'd also been killed with a knife. More murders followed, by a killer whose nickname is still known around the world today – 'Jack the Ripper'. How did the murderer get this nickname? How did the police try to catch the murderer? And what does this story tell us about life in Victorian London?

Objectives

- Examine the 'Jack the Ripper' series of murders.
- Analyse the area in London in which the murders took place, and the police investigation.

The killer gets a nickname

It didn't take the police long to realise they had a violent serial killer on their hands. On 27 September 1888, the Central News Agency (a company that searched for news stories and sold them to newspapers) received a letter boasting of the killings and teasing the police for not catching the killer (see **A**). The agency passed the letter onto the police, and within days, gruesome details of the murders appeared in newspapers all over Britain. The press didn't care whether the letter was from the genuine killer or not, they just knew that descriptions of crimes sold papers – and they were happy to print all the details they could. They even began using the name that the writer of the letter had given himself – Jack the Ripper.

Earlier on...

1850s

Tax changes in the 1850s had meant that newspapers could be produced much more cheaply. This resulted in an increase in what we would now call **tabloid** newspapers and magazines. These were cheap to buy and full of the latest gossip and sensational stories. The *Illustrated Police News* (see **B**) is a good example of this, and was the world's first illustrated weekly newspaper.

▼ **SOURCE A** Adapted from 'Jack's' letter received by the Central News Agency on 27 September 1888.

Dear Boss,

I keep on hearing the police have caught me but they haven't. I have laughed when they look so clever and talk about being on the right track. I shan't quit until I get caught. The last job was good work. [...] How can they catch me now? I love my work and want to start again. You'll soon hear of me. I saved some of the red stuff in a ginger beer bottle so I could write to you with it, but it went thick like glue and I can't use it. Red ink is fit enough I hope, ha, ha. [...] My knife's so sharp I want to get to work right away if I get a chance. Good luck.

Yours truly,

Jack the Ripper

Don't mind me giving the nickname

PS They say I'm a doctor now, ha, ha!

More murders

On 30 September, two more women were found murdered. Elizabeth 'Long Liz' Stride and Catherine Eddowes were killed within minutes of each other. A quarter of a mile from her body some graffiti was found, which read: 'The Juwes are not the men that will be blamed for nothing'. However, the policeman in charge of the investigation ordered the evidence on the wall to be cleaned because he feared that local people might attack Jews.

More letters

On the morning of 1 October, the same news agency received another letter boasting of the killings. Experts at the time thought the same person had written both letters – but had no way of knowing if they had been written by the actual killer or not.

▼ **SOURCE B** The *Illustrated Police News* front page on 16 October 1888, reporting the third and fourth victims of Jack the Ripper (Stride and Eddowes).

Key Words   tabloid

On 16 October, the police received yet another letter in an envelope containing a note. Police were unable to tell if the letter came from the same person as the first two letters. However, most detectives at the time felt that different people wrote them.

Murder number five

On 9 November, a fifth woman, Mary Jane Kelly, was murdered. She was the only Ripper victim to be found indoors. Police found Kelly's clothes folded neatly on a chair and her boots in front of the fire.

By mid-November news of the killings had appeared in newspapers as far away as Australia and Mexico. Even Queen Victoria took a keen interest and urged the police to catch the killer quickly.

The killings stop

Mary Jane Kelly is generally considered to be the Ripper's final victim. However, some people think there were other murders that happened both *before* Mary Ann Nichols and *after* Mary Jane Kelly. In fact, reporters and some policemen at the time thought Jack the Ripper might be responsible for as many as 13 deaths. However, the detectives in charge of the case decided to keep the figure at five – Nichols, Chapman, Stride, Eddowes and Kelly.

Over to You

1 a Look at **Source B**. What is shown on this front cover?

  b The *Illustrated Police News* was what we would now call a 'tabloid newspaper' – cheap to buy and full of the latest gossip and sensational stories. Can you suggest reasons why this kind of reporting can misrepresent the truth or harm police investigations?

What was London like in 1888?

London in 1888 was a divided city. The West End was home to wealthier Londoners while the East End was crowded with poor slum housing. Jack the Ripper operated in the East End, in the 'evil square mile'. This area included the districts of Whitechapel, Spitalfields and Aldgate.

The East End was the ideal environment for crime. Smoke and stinking gases from factories and housing choked the narrow streets so badly that, at times, it was impossible to see more than a metre in front of your face. Dark passages and alleyways provided excellent cover for any thief... or murderer. There were many migrant families living in the area who had come to London looking for work from other countries. Migrants were often unfairly blamed for an increase in crime and several people suspected of the murders were from outside Britain.

What did the police do?

The police interviewed over 2000 people, including witnesses who claimed they had seen the victims with 'mysterious-looking' men before their deaths. The police handed out 80,000 leaflets appealing for information and specially trained sniffer dogs were recruited to 'sniff out' any leads. Some policemen dressed up in women's clothing to see if the killer approached them.

The police even took photographs of the victims' eyes in the hope that they might be able to see an image of the last person the victim saw – her murderer. However, in this age before forensic science and fingerprinting, the only really effective way to catch a killer was to see them commit murder or get someone to confess.

▼ **MAP C** A map of the Whitechapel area of London's East End showing where each victim was found. The maze-like streets were full of pubs, houses for rent and cheap 'lodging houses' where a bed in a room cost a few pennies per week.

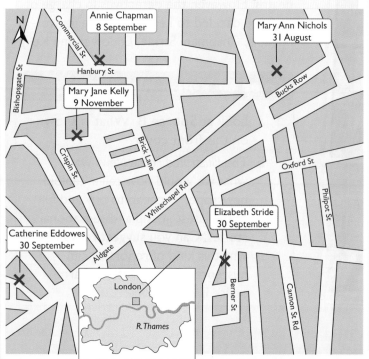

▼ **SOURCE D** A cartoon from *Punch* magazine in September 1888, showing a policeman wearing a blindfold. He is surrounded by criminals who he is trying (unsuccessfully) to catch. It highlights what many people then thought – that the police were very poor at catching criminals.

BLIND-MAN'S BUFF.

The witnesses

For the police, perhaps one of the best chances of finding the killer lay with the witnesses who claimed to have been near one of the murder scenes. The problem with these witness statements was that they often contradicted each other – or were not detailed enough (see **E**).

So who was it?

The Jack the Ripper murder case remained unsolved. Some people at the time believed that the murders were the result of the horrendous city conditions, and that the government didn't care enough about the people living in these conditions to help stop the crimes. The Ripper chose vulnerable victims – they were all very poor, and there is evidence that some were homeless at times and some experienced domestic abuse.

Over the years, many historians have claimed to have worked out who Jack the Ripper really was, but no one has ever proven anything. There have been dozens of suspects, including M. J. Druitt (an English lawyer and teacher), Aaron Kosminski (a Polish barber who lived in Whitechapel at the time), Francis Tumblety (an unqualified American doctor), Severyn Kłosowski (a Polish man, also known as George Chapman, who poisoned three of his partners and was hanged in 1903) and Walter Sickert (an English painter who was fascinated by murder).

Over to You

1 Describe conditions in London's Whitechapel area in the late 1800s.

2 Think carefully about the following pieces of information. For each one, write what it shows about the problems this meant for the police solving the murder:

   a The witness statements rarely agreed on what the murderer looked like.

   b Writing on the wall near to the body of Catherine Eddowes was cleaned off.

   c The murders were committed before forensic science and fingerprinting existed.

   d There was little confidence in the police.

   e Photographs of the victims' eyes were taken because it was believed the last thing the victim saw would be imprinted on their eyes.

   f The area where the murders took place was dark and crowded.

   g The area where the murders took place was occupied by 'lower class' people and had high levels of crime.

3 Using the information in question **2**, write a brief report explaining why you think the Jack the Ripper murders were not solved.

▼ **SOURCE E** From a witness statement, 1888.

'It was very dark. The man was of average height, may have been left or right handed and was wearing a hat. He had his back to me but seemed to be a foreigner. I did not hear him speak and he seemed to disappear into the dark night.'

Fact ✓

In 2020, author Hallie Rubenhold wrote a best-selling book called *The Five* about the lives of the five women killed by Jack the Ripper. She found out more about who these women were and how they came to be living in the East End of London. She also addressed some common myths about them – for example, it is often assumed that all of the women were prostitutes, which is incorrect.

Source Analysis

1 Look at **Source D**. What point is the cartoonist making?

2 How useful is **Source D** for an enquiry into the effectiveness of the police in Whitechapel in 1888?

Quick Knowledge Quiz

Choose the correct answer from the three options:

1   What was the common name for houses that were built quickly and cheaply, and were crammed close together in terraces with narrow alleys between them?

   a   back-to-back
   b   back-to-front
   c   back-to-basics

2   Which disease first appeared in Britain in 1831 and was considered one of the most feared of the age?

   a   smallpox
   b   TB
   c   cholera

3   What was the name of the special groups set up in some towns to investigate cholera outbreaks?

   a   Poor Commissions
   b   Boards of Health
   c   Poverty Action Groups

4   In which year did the government pass a Public Health Act that allowed councils to spend money cleaning up towns if they wanted to?

   a   1842
   b   1848
   c   1854

5   What would a person who believed in 'Miasma Theory' of disease think?

   a   that disease is carried through the air like a poisonous gas or an infected mist
   b   that disease can be passed from one person to another through personal contact
   c   that disease can be a punishment from God

6   What was the name of the doctor who, through careful scientific observation, showed that cholera was carried in water and is passed on through 'contagion'?

   a   Joseph Bazalgette
   b   Edwin Chadwick
   c   John Snow

7   What is meant by the term 'capital crime'?

   a   a crime committed in London
   b   a crime for which a guilty person could be executed
   c   a crime that would result in a large fine

8   What was the name of the Home Secretary who created Britain's first professional police force in 1829?

   a   Robert Owen
   b   Robert Bow-Street
   c   Robert Peel

9   Which famous prison reformer appeared on the Bank of England's £5 note from 2002 until it was replaced by a new type of note in 2017?

   a   Elizabeth Fry
   b   John Howard
   c   Florence Nightingale

10   The Jack the Ripper murders mainly took place in which area?

   a   the Whitechapel area of London's East End
   b   the Digbeth area of Birmingham
   c   the Deansgate area of Manchester

 **Literacy Focus**

Understanding academic texts

▼ **INTERPRETATION A** Adapted from an academic paper published by the Nuffield Trust titled 'Public Health: The vision and the challenge' (1998), by healthcare academics/professors Walter Holland and Susie Stewart. Nuffield Trust is a charity aiming to improve UK healthcare through evidence and analysis.

> Correcting, or the process of putting something right.

'The concept of public health was easy to define in the 1800s and early 1900s. The major threats to life were the result of insanitary conditions such as a foul water supply and defective or absent sewage and waste disposal, inadequate or over-crowded housing, poor and adulterated food and thus poor nutrition, hazardous workplaces and little effective clinical care. Thus what was considered as public health was concerned with rectifying these conditions – largely through legislative and population policies. The tasks of our predecessors entailed identifying the malpractices of landlords, employers, the state and others and persuading these groups that improvements were essential and could lead to improvements in health status and better life expectancy. At the beginning of this century many of these ills had been tackled and we no longer had open sewers or child labour.'

> Conditions that are dirty and dangerous to your health, often because there is a lack of clean water, toilets, drains etc.

> The treatment of patients by properly qualified doctors and nurses.

> The power to make laws.

> The people who came before you.

> Behaviour or conduct by someone professional that is improper, illegal or causes injury.

1 Define 'public health'.

2 Write a short paragraph that summarises what point the authors are trying to make.

3 Give examples of the following from your studies of public health in this book so far:

   a 'insanitary conditions'
   b 'hazardous workplaces'
   c 'little effective clinical care'.

> **TIP:** For example, you could look at pages 148–151 to help you find examples of dirty and dangerous conditions relating to public health.

4 Make a list of ways that 'many of these ills had been tackled'. Hint: How were some of the problems identified in your answer to question 3 tackled? You might also want to name some of the 'predecessors' or people who helped make those changes happen.

   a 'insanitary conditions'
   b 'hazardous workplaces'
   c 'little effective clinical care'.

> **TIP:** For example, you could look at pages 152–155 and 228–231 to help you list how dirty and unhealthy conditions were fixed.

History skill: Significance

How to analyse whether something is significant in History

In History, you will study all sorts of events, developments and people from different periods. Sometimes you will be asked whether an event, a development or a person is **significant**. When you see this word, don't think that this simply means 'important'.

The spider diagram below shows you how to judge how significant something is.

SIG

Special at the time
- Was the event/person/ development important at the time?
- What was its impact? How did it affect people?

Important changes
- Was the event/person/ development important in the long term? Were there long-lasting effects?
- Did it cause important changes?

Going on today
- Is the event/person/ development still important? Is it making an impact today?
- Are they still relevant in today's world?

For this assessment, we are going to think about the significance of Florence Nightingale.

1 **What do you know?** Make a list of facts that you know about the event/person/development.

> **TIP:** Start by looking through your classwork on Florence Nightingale and pages 154–155 of this book to help you. What impact did she have on the health of troops during the Crimean War? What about her impact on nursing in Britain at the time?

2 **Impact at the time:** Consider the impact of the event/person/ development at the time it happened. Make notes on how it changed things.

3 **Long-term impact:** Now think about how the event/person/ development might have had an impact in the longer term. Did some of the changes last for much longer than the time of the event/person/development?

> **TIP:** Think about how the impact of her work continued. Have the things she did made an impact over a long period of time?

4 **Still significant today?** You should also think about our world today. Does the person/event/development still make an impact in the modern world? Remember that the significance of a person, event or development can *change* over time.

> **TIP:** The final paragraph on Florence Nightingale on page 155 will help you consider this.

5 **Conclude:** It is also important to conclude your answer. Sum up your thoughts on the significance of the topic you have been asked to consider – in this case, Florence Nightingale.

Assessment: Significance

Now, considering all the points on the previous page, try putting this into practice with this question:

> Explain the significance of Florence Nightingale in the development of nursing. (20)

The steps below will help you structure your answer. Use the example sentence starters to help you begin each point.

1 What do you know? Start with a brief explanation of who Florence Nightingale is and the reputation of nursing before she made an impact.

> Florence Nightingale was born...
>
> In the early 1800s, the reputation of nursing... (3)

2 Impact at the time: Next, focus on the work of Nightingale at the time – what impact did she have during the Crimean War? And what did she do when she got back to Britain?

> At the time... (4)

3 Long-term impact: Did the work Nightingale change things for a long time afterwards? In other words, did she make a *long-term impact*?

> In the longer term... (4)

4 Still significant today? Is the work of Nightingale began, and the impact she made, still relevant in the modern world?

> Today, Nightingale and her work... (4)

5 Conclude: You are asked to judge the significance of Florence Nightingale in the development of nursing. Is she very significant? Did she make a major impact at the time – and is what she did still relevant in society today?

> In conclusion... (5)

TIP: **Source A** shows Florence Nightingale pictured on a £10 note. What does this tell you about her significance, even in 1992?

▼ **SOURCE A** This £10 note from 1975 to 1992 shows Nightingale caring for soldiers during the Crimean War.

During the 1500s and 1600s, Britain became a powerful trading nation. Goods such as sugar, cotton and tobacco flooded into the country and items made in Britain were shipped abroad. Many British people became rich as a result. But there was a dark side to this trade – the trade in human beings. This was known as the **slave trade**. So how exactly did the slave trade work? How, and why, did it start? And to what extent was Britain involved?

Objectives

- Examine how the slave trade was organised.
- Assess Britain's role in the slave trade.

What is 'trade'?

'Trade' means to buy and sell 'goods'. Goods are things that can be bought and sold – anything from pots and knives, to clothes, horses and homes. And it's possible for people (traders) to make a fortune from 'trading'. Trading had been big business across the world for many thousands of years – but in the eighteenth century, Britain became the world's leading trading nation. British ships carried British goods (like wool, corn and chains) to other countries and sold them. Then traders loaded their ships with goods that were popular in Britain (like tea, sugar, tobacco and cotton) and sold them to the British.

So what was the 'slave trade'?

The slave trade is when human beings are bought and sold, instead of goods. The idea of slavery is a very old one. For thousands of years, people have been captured and enslaved, treated as someone's property and forced to work. From around 1500 onwards, slavery turned into a profitable international business that earned some people millions, while others were forced to move to the other side of the world and live their lives as enslaved people.

Why were people enslaved?

In the 1500s, lots of people left Europe to settle in the newly discovered continents of North and South America. Many were farmers who grew crops that were very popular in Europe – like cotton, tobacco, sugar and coffee – and they sold them for high prices. To begin with, some farmers forced local indigenous people to do the farming for them, but some ran away, and others died out from disease or cruel treatment (see **A**). When they ran out of local enslaved people, the European settlers went to find new ones elsewhere: Africa.

▼ **SOURCE A** An image from 1595 showing Spanish settlers slaughtering or capturing and enslaving indigenous people in South America. At this time, the Spanish built a huge empire in South, Central and the southern part of North America – and slavery was a key feature of this empire.

Earlier on...

c.27BC

From around 27BC to AD476, Romans forced enslaved people (both male and female) to fight in gladiator arenas for entertainment.

The slave trade triangle

Enslaved Africans ended up in North and South America and the Caribbean as a result of a three-legged trading journey known as the slave trade triangle (see **B**).

▼ **B** How the slave trade triangle worked.

Stage 1: A slave trader would leave Europe in a ship. It might be loaded with goods such as pots, alcohol, guns and cloth.

The ship is full of goods that are cheap to buy in Europe, but highly prized in Africa.

Stage 2: The ship would sail to the African coast. The crew might land and kidnap local African men, women and children.

Stage 3: The ship's captain might also meet with local African leaders and swap the goods for prisoners from other local communities who had been captured.

Stage 4: The ship would be loaded with enslaved Africans, who were then taken on a two-month journey across the Atlantic Ocean. This second part of the ship's journey was known as the 'Middle Passage'.

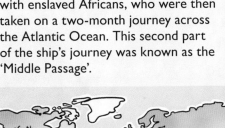

Stage 5: Once the enslaved Africans arrived, they were cleaned, sold and put to work. As well as farming, they might work in houses or mine for gold.

Stage 6: The slave traders then bought a load of sugar, cotton or tobacco and loaded it onto their empty ship. These goods were taken back to Europe and sold for a huge profit.

We will make a fortune selling this!

These goods are so popular back in Europe.

Over to You

1 Define the following:
  a trade
  b enslaved person
  c slave trade

2 Why did European settlers in North and South America and the Caribbean want to enslave people?

3 The slave trade is often referred to as 'triangular trade' or the 'slave trade triangle'. Why do you think it got these names?

Fact ✓

It is estimated that around 12 million people were enslaved and transported from Africa to the Americas and the Caribbean between the 1500s and the early 1800s.

Causation

1 Why was the slave trade so profitable?
2 Write a clear and organised summary that analyses how and why the slave trade triangle operated.

When did the British get involved?

British traders first got involved in the slave trade in 1562. That year, John Hawkins became England's first slave trader when he captured 300 people from Sierra Leone on the west coast of Africa and sold them in the Caribbean. He repeated the journey many times – and other slave traders copied him. These early voyages were the first steps in what would be a highly profitable business for years to come.

Enslaved people on British farms in the Americas and the Caribbean

By the 1600s, thousands of people had left Britain to settle in North and South America and the Caribbean. The settlers were mainly farmers, growing tobacco, cotton and other crops. Historians think that the first enslaved people to work on the British settlers' farms in North America arrived from Africa in 1619 (see **C**).

A royal connection

Britain wasn't the only European nation to get involved in slavery, but it made some of the largest profits. All sorts of people were involved. Queen Elizabeth, for example, was a business partner of John Hawkins. Charles II was a partner in the Royal African Company, a slave trading business that transported 60,000 enslaved Africans between 1680 and 1688. Many of the enslaved people were branded with the letters 'DY' when they were captured – after the man who ran the company, James, Duke of York (Charles II's brother, who later became King James II).

Later on... 1807

It is estimated that Britain transported 3.1 million Africans to the British colonies in North and South America and the Caribbean between 1562 and 1807 (the year when the British slave trade was stopped).

▼ **SOURCE C** A 1901 image of enslaved Africans being brought ashore by Dutch traders to work on a British colony in America in 1619.

▼ **INTERPRETATION D** Adapted from an article by the journalist Mary Murtagh in the newspaper *The Liverpool Echo* in 2007.

'Evidence of Liverpool's slave trade past is all over the city – in its architecture, public buildings and street names. Very few slaves actually passed through Liverpool, but the slave trade made the city rich and powerful, leaving a permanent mark for generations to come. From the grand houses built using slave money to the street names, there are clues everywhere. During the 18th century Liverpool was Britain's main port and formed one corner of the "slave triangle". Ships from the Mersey's shores took at least 1.5 million Africans across the Atlantic to work on plantations in the Caribbean and America's deep South. The city thrived doing ship repairs and importing goods with approximately half of Liverpool's trade linked to slavery. The movers and shakers among slave traders were immortalised with streets named after them.'

Slave trade profits

The British trade in enslaved Africans, between the early 1600s and 1807, generated profits of about £12 million (over £1 billion today). This money helped to make Britain one of the world's richest and most powerful nations. Many of the fine buildings in Liverpool, Bristol and London were built on the profits of slavery (see **D**). In 1785, a well-known British actor, George F. Cooke, said, 'Every brick in the city of Liverpool is cemented with the blood of a slave.' In fact, 20 of Liverpool's mayors between 1787 and 1807 are thought to have been slave traders.

Indeed, many British people played a part in the slave trade – ship owners (who allowed their ships to be used), bankers (who lent them the money), investors (who shared in the profits) and importers (who brought in the goods that enslaved people farmed). Yet Britain's link to slavery goes even further. For example, the world-famous National Gallery in London received its first major donation of paintings from a man who had built up his art collection with money he made from dealing in enslaved people. Several men who ran the Bank of England in the early 1700s were involved in slavery too, and Britain's oldest insurance company (Lloyd's of London) insured some slave ships. Barclays Bank was also started by slave traders.

> ### Fact ✓
>
> Portugal and Britain were the two most active slave-trading countries. It is estimated that between them they accounted for about 70 per cent of all Africans transported to the Americas and Caribbean.

> ### Over to You .ıll
>
> 1 List ways in which Britain was linked to the slave trade. The links could be through the royal family, British cities, slave traders or bankers, for example.
>
> 2 Read **Interpretation D**.
>   a In what way was the city of Liverpool linked to slavery?
>   b How did the people of Liverpool make money from the slave trade at the time?
>
> 3 Look at **Interpretation E**. Do you think the statue should be removed? Or do you think its sign should be updated? Or should the statue be left alone? Write an email/letter to a Bristol newspaper explaining your view.

> ### Fact ✓
>
> Bristol-born Edward Colston was a rich slave trader. When he died he left most of his vast fortune to charity, and many Bristol streets and buildings were named after him.

▼ **INTERPRETATION E** The vandalised statue of Colston which was in the centre of Bristol. This statue was erected in 1895 at a time of great unrest among workers in Bristol, as Colston was viewed as a symbol of unity. The sign on the statue did not mention his slavery connection, but many people thought it should. For many years there were protests calling for the removal of the statue. In June 2020, it was pulled down and pushed into Bristol harbour by protesters.

> ### Interpretation Analysis
>
> Look at **Interpretation E**.
> 1 Who was Edward Colston?
> 2 Why is his statue controversial?
> 3 This statue and its sign give the view that Colston should be remembered as a charitable person, not as a slave trader. Explain why not all historians and commentators have agreed with this interpretation.

It has been estimated that there were around 50,000 slave trade journeys from Africa to North and South America and the Caribbean between the sixteenth and nineteenth centuries. Millions of African men, women and children made a trip of around 4000 miles that lasted between 40 and 70 days. Once at their destination, they were sold and then put to work for the rest of their lives. But what was the journey like? How were the enslaved people sold? What work were enslaved people expected to do?

Objectives

- Examine conditions on a slave ship.
- Compare two ways in which enslaved people were sold.
- Describe life on a plantation.

A slave ship

Slave ships were generally very overcrowded and the men, women and children were kept in appalling conditions. They were given food regularly, but it was usually poor quality. They were also taken up on deck for exercise – remember, slave traders wanted enslaved people to be in acceptable physical condition when they arrived at their destination, so they could fetch the highest prices.

Any enslaved people who died on the journey, or were near death, were thrown in the sea. Some died of dysentery (known as 'the bloody flux'), a nasty form of diarrhoea. Others died of smallpox or heatstroke, or starved themselves to death by refusing to eat. Some died by suicide, by hanging themselves or jumping over the side of the ship. Around 20 per cent of enslaved people might die on the journey – but on some ships, half of them died.

▼ **SOURCE A** An early 1800s plan of a French slave ship, *Vigilante*, which was captured by the British.

Enslaved people were given space of 1.8m length by 0.4m width to lie in.

There was approximately 1.5m between the slave decks.

This plan shows 345 enslaved people on board, but slave ships (depending on their size) could carry anything from 250 to 600 people. We know so much about some slave ships (like the *Vigilante*) because their owners kept detailed records of their journeys. After all, the slave trade made big money – and it was totally legal – so traders treated their job like any other professional business.

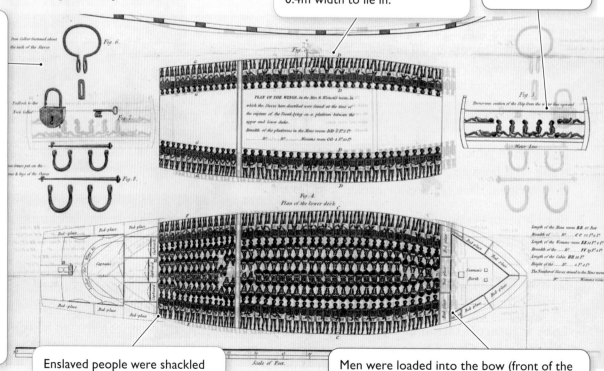

Enslaved people were shackled together in rows, lying either on their backs or on their sides (like spoons).

Men were loaded into the bow (front of the ship), boys in the centre, and women and young girls in the stern (back of the ship).

Selling enslaved people

Before any enslaved people were sold, they were cleaned up. They were washed down with water and given oil to rub into their skin to make them look shinier and healthier. Following this, they were usually sold in one of two ways: **auction** or **scramble**.

Auction: enslaved people were paraded in front of buyers and examined like cattle. They were then made to stand on an auction box and buyers would **bid** for them. They were sold to the person who paid the most. Those who were unhealthy and did not sell were left to die without food or water.

Scramble: buyers would pay the slave trader an agreed amount of money. The buyers would be given a ticket for each person they had bought. Then a bell would sound and the door to the slave cage would be opened. The buyers would rush in and grab the enslaved people they wanted – and give the tickets back to the trader as they left.

▼ **SOURCE B** An image of a slave auction taking place in Virginia, USA, in the 1800s.

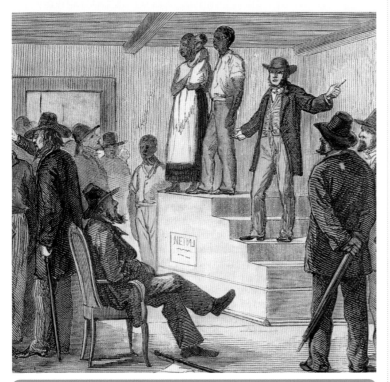

Key Words   auction   bid   scramble

▼ **SOURCE C** Written by Harriet Ann Jacobs in her autobiography *Incidents in the Life of a Slave Girl* (1861). Jacobs was an African-American writer who escaped from slavery and was later freed.

'I saw a mother lead seven children to the auction block. She knew that some of them would be taken from her; but they took all. The children were sold to a slave trader, and the mother was bought by a man in her own town. Before night, her children were all far away. She begged the trader to tell her where he intended to take them; this he refused to do. How could he when he knew he would sell them, one by one, wherever he could command the highest price? I met that mother in the street and her wild, haggard face lives today in my mind. She wrung her hands in anguish and exclaimed, "Gone, all gone! Why don't God kill me?"'

Over to You .ıll

1 Why were so many enslaved people packed aboard the slave ships?

2 Why do you think the enslaved people were chained together for most of the voyage?

3 How and why were enslaved people cleaned up before they were sold?

4 Describe the difference between a slave auction and a slave scramble.

Source Analysis

1 Look at **Source A**. Describe what it shows.

2 Read **Source C**. In your own words, explain what Harriet witnesses.

3 How useful are **Sources A** and **C** to a historian studying the slave trade?

After the sale

Once bought, enslaved people became the personal property of their owner. They were given European names to try to make them forget their past. Then, like cattle, they were **branded** with their owner's initials on their face, chest or back. After this they were made to work.

A life of slavery

Enslaved people were sent to do a variety of jobs in different places – but their lives were always hard. Sometimes enslaved people worked in forests cutting down trees, or on the coast loading and unloading ships or making sails. However, most worked on huge farms, called **plantations**. They were forced to plant, look after and harvest crops that would sell for lots of money in Europe. Sugar was grown in the Caribbean, cotton was grown in North America, tobacco was grown in North and South America, and coffee was grown in South America.

Enslaved people on plantations

Enslaved people would be expected to work for most of their lives. Some worked in the plantation owner's house as cleaners, cooks or servants, but most worked out in the fields. Three- and four-year-olds would work in 'trash gangs' (weeding) or as water-can carriers. As they got older, they would work longer and longer hours out in the fields with the adults. Older people would often do less physical jobs, such as gardening, horse-and-carriage driving, cleaning or nursing. However, hard work (15 or 16 hours a day), a poor diet, harsh punishments and no proper medical attention meant that few enslaved people lived to any great age. Shockingly, the average life expectancy was 26.

Rights of enslaved people

Enslaved people had no legal rights. They weren't allowed to learn to read or write, marry or own property. Some tried to run away, but this was very risky. Teams of 'runaway hunters' scoured the countryside looking for them. Any runaways who were caught were severely punished (see **F** and **G**).

▼ **SOURCE D** This is a branding tool. The new owner of an enslaved person would burn his initials onto their body using a tool like this.

▼ **SOURCE E** A sugar plantation in the Caribbean, 1823. Paintings like this would hang in the homes of proud plantation owners. The man on the horse was probably the plantation

▼ **SOURCE F** Adapted from a 1784 book by James Ramsay, a British doctor working on the British-controlled Caribbean island of St Kitts. He was so shocked by the way enslaved people were treated that he wrote a book that inspired many anti-slavery campaigners.

'The ordinary punishments of slaves are whipping, beating with a stick - sometimes to the breaking of bones - chains, an iron ring around the neck or ankle, or being placed in a dungeon. There have been instances of slitting of ears, breaking of limbs, amputation, and taking out of eyes.'

Rebellion

It was difficult for enslaved people to protest against what was happening to them, but this didn't stop some enslaved people starting rebellions against their harsh lives:

- Antigua 1736 – a plot was discovered to steal gunpowder and blow up most of the British-controlled island's plantation-owning families while they were all at a party. As punishment, 88 enslaved people were put to death.

- Jamaica 1760 – rebels seized guns and took over plantations. It took several months for the British to regain control – and around 400 enslaved people were executed for their role in the rebellion. A few decades earlier, a group of runaway enslaved people (called 'Maroons') had escaped into the mountains where they set up their own settlements. For the next 150 years they fought against the British.

- Saint-Domingue, 1791 – led by a man called Toussaint L'Ouverture, enslaved people took control of this French-controlled Caribbean island. They defeated British and then French troops who were sent to regain control. In 1804, the formerly enslaved people renamed their island Haiti.

- Barbados 1816 – enslaved people burned a quarter of the British-controlled island's sugar crop before the rebellion was stopped.

▼ **SOURCE G** An 1863 photograph of an enslaved person named Gordon who escaped from a plantation in Louisiana, USA, to a place where slavery had been banned. The marks on his back are from punishments by whipping.

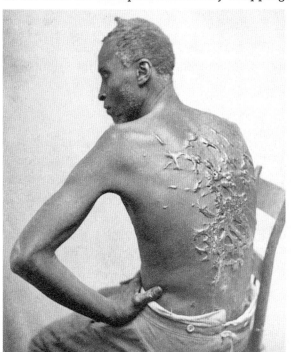

Key Words
branded   plantation

Fact ✓

Enslaved people sometimes rebelled in less violent ways. For example, they spoke their native language whenever possible, pretended to be ill and didn't go to work, or damaged tools or machinery. The slave owners forced the enslaved people to become Christians – but some secretly practised their own religion in private.

Over to You .ıl

1 What sorts of jobs would slaves do:
   a out in the fields?
   b in the plantation owner's house?

2 Look at **Source D**. What was the purpose of this tool?

3 Why do you think enslaved people were given new names?

4 Read **Source F**. Why do you think slave owners treated enslaved people so brutally, especially when they tried to escape?

5 a What effect do you think the revolt in Saint-Domingue would have had on slave owners in other countries? Explain your answer carefully.
   b Why do you think Haiti is a very special island to many Africans, even today?

Source Analysis

1 Look at **Source E**. Describe what it shows.

2 The working conditions in the painting don't appear to be that bad. What could explain this?

3 Give two things you can infer from **Source E** about slavery in the early nineteenth century.

Why was slavery abolished?

In 1807, the British Parliament **abolished** the slave trade in the British Empire. In other words, it made it illegal to buy and sell enslaved people – but people were still allowed to keep the enslaved people they already owned. In 1833, Parliament banned slave ownership too. So why did Parliament do this? Why was slavery – which made so much money for so many people – banned? And what were the most important factors that played a part in ending slavery?

Objectives

- Discover when both slave trading and slave ownership ended in Britain.
- Outline the different factors that contributed to the abolition of slavery.
- Assess the different factors that led to the abolition of slavery.

The beginning of the end

Britain had been involved in the slave trade since the mid-1500s. It was originally legal to make money from it and all sorts of people – including members of the royal family – were involved. But some people felt slavery was wrong – and by the late 1700s a campaign had begun to ban the slave trade. This **anti-slavery** group was very important – but was slavery banned just because of this group, or were there other reasons why it ended? Your challenge is to look through the following factors very carefully and try to form your own thoughts on what might answer the question 'Why was slavery abolished?'

▶ **SOURCE A** In 2007, a special edition £2 coin was made to commemorate the abolition of the slave trade. Have you ever seen one of these coins?

Factor No.1: Slavery wasn't making as much money as it used to

Some people have argued that the decision to get rid of slavery was made easier for Parliament because the slave trade was making less money than it used to. In the 1770s, the price of sugar dropped. Many British plantations in the Caribbean couldn't make a profit and closed down. And with fewer plantations, fewer enslaved people were needed. In 1771, plantation owners in Barbados bought 2728 enslaved people from Africa. The following year they bought none. So with fewer people making enormous profits, there were fewer people to argue in *favour* of keeping the slave trade. Also, some people claimed that enslaved people didn't work as hard as people who got paid for their work. They said enslaved people had no reason to work as hard as possible because they didn't get any rewards or bonuses (see **B**).

▼ **SOURCE B** Adapted from what the famous Scottish **economist** Adam Smith wrote about slavery in 1776 in his book *The Wealth of Nations*.

'The work done by slaves, though it appears to cost only their maintenance [food and shelter], is in the end the most expensive of any. A person who can gain no property can have no other interest but to eat as much and to work as little as possible. Whatever work he does can be squeezed out of him by violence only.'

Factor No.2: Enslaved people helped end slavery

Other people have argued that it was the actions of enslaved people themselves that led to the end of slavery. In 1791, the enslaved people on the French colony Saint-Domingue (in the Caribbean) rebelled, killed many of the plantation owners and set fire to the sugar-cane fields. Led by the inspirational formerly enslaved person Toussaint L'Ouverture, they kept control of the island despite attacks from both French and British soldiers.

In 1804, the island was renamed Haiti, and the people there declared independence and outlawed slavery. Plantation owners throughout the Caribbean were terrified that the rebellion would spread and that their crops would soon be in flames. A common **racist** view at the time was that Africans were inferior to Europeans and that their natural position was to be following orders and doing simple, manual work. What had happened in Haiti had proved to many people that this argument was wrong.

▼ **SOURCE C** An illustration of Toussaint L'Ouverture, by French artist Louis Bombled (1862–1927).

Key Words

abolish   anti-slavery
economist   racist

Later on...

To guarantee against another invasion by the French army, and to compensate the French slave owners, in 1825 the government in Haiti agreed to pay $21 billion (in today's money) to the French government. It took Haiti 122 years (until 1947) to pay it all.

Over to You

1 Write a sentence explaining what the word 'abolish' means.

2 What's the difference between the anti-slavery law passed in 1807 and the one passed in 1833?

3 Look at **Source C**.
   a Who was Toussaint L'Ouverture?
   b Choose three words or phrases from this list that you might use to describe Toussaint L'Ouverture in this image:

   leader   weak   strong

   powerless   in control

   disorganised   powerful

   threatening

   c Explain why you have chosen these words.
   d How might the plantation owners in Saint-Domingue and other places react if they saw this image?

Factor No.3: The racists were proved wrong

All sorts of people – doctors, businessmen, lawyers – thought that slavery was perfectly acceptable.

But enslaved people who lived in Britain, brought here by slave traders, got a chance to prove these attitudes wrong. In Britain, there were originally no laws that said slavery was illegal, but there were no laws to say it was legal either. So some enslaved people, helped by anti-slavery lawyers, went to court to claim their freedom. More and more judges, impressed by their arguments, allowed them to go free.

One formerly enslaved person, Olaudah Equiano, campaigned tirelessly to convince British people that the slave trade was wrong. He had been taken from his home in Africa to Barbados aged 11. He worked as a servant to a ship's captain, travelled widely, and learned to read and write while in England. He was then taken to North America and sold once more but, through incredible hard work and patience, he bought his freedom and moved back to Britain, where he wrote his life story. This was widely read and turned many people in Britain against slavery. The fact that he was clearly intelligent and articulate made a nonsense out of the claims that Africans were inferior and only suited to manual work.

▼ **SOURCE D** Adapted from a letter published in *Gentleman's Magazine*, April 1789, a popular monthly magazine founded in London in 1731. At this time, articles in the magazine were often in favour of slavery. The term 'negro' was used at the time to describe black people, but it is considered offensive today.

'The negroes of Africa, when they are in Africa, are useless. They never improve themselves or learn about art or science. The only way to improve them is to make them useful and happy by making them work hard.'

▼ **INTERPRETATION E** Adapted from historian Paul Turner, writing in *The Changing Face of Britain and its Empire* (2009).

'So why did many people believe that slave trading was acceptable? Some slave traders actually believed that the slaves had a better standard of life than in their own country as a free person. Traders at the time simply did not have the same moral standards as today. They saw nothing wrong with trading in people. In fact, being a slave trader was a "respectable" occupation, not one that was looked down on.'

▼ **SOURCE F** From Olaudah Equiano's bestselling 1789 autobiography. He toured Britain raising awareness of the slave trade, and his tales of cruelty changed many people's attitudes. With another formerly enslaved person, Ottobah Cugoano, he formed a group called the 'Sons of Africa' and met MPs to persuade them to abolish slavery.

Fact ✓

Enslaved people could earn small amounts of money in some areas of America. If they saved enough, they could buy their freedom from their owners.

Factor No.4: The anti-slavery campaigners

Some people believe it was the actions of some Europeans that had most impact on the ending of slavery. Granville Sharp, for example, helped formerly enslaved people in court cases against their old masters and helped bring the injustice of slavery to public attention. In 1787, a group of strict Christians formed the Society for the Abolition of the Slave Trade. This group, including Sharp and a man named Thomas Clarkson, collected evidence of the horrors of the slave trade and the treatment that enslaved people faced. The campaigners, who believed that slavery went against Christ's teachings, used this evidence to collect signatures from the public on huge petitions. They also convinced the politician William Wilberforce to make speeches against slavery in Parliament. Between 1789 and 1806, Wilberforce made many long speeches in Parliament calling for a law to end the slave trade.

▼ **SOURCE G** Adapted from a speech made to Parliament by William Wilberforce in 1796.

'The grand object of my parliamentary existence is the abolition of the slave trade. Before this great cause all others dwindle in my eyes. If it pleases God to honour me so far, may I be the instrument of stopping such a course of wickedness and cruelty as never before disgraced a Christian country.'

▶ **SOURCE H** The pottery manufacturer Josiah Wedgwood was an anti-slavery supporter. In 1787, he began producing medallions to convince people that slavery was wrong. Over 200,000 were made and the logo 'Am I not a man and a brother?' appeared on plates, bracelets and brooches.

The end of slavery

Eventually, after years of campaigning, Parliament abolished the slave trade in the British Empire in 1807. But this didn't mean *owning* enslaved people was banned. So, the campaign to end slavery completely continued. Famous campaigners at this time included Mary Prince, a formerly enslaved person who became the first black woman to write an autobiography, and Elizabeth Heyrick, who encouraged other women to set up anti-slavery groups around Britain (there were over 70 women's groups in the 1820s). Finally, in 1833, Parliament passed the Slavery Abolition Act, giving all enslaved people in the British Empire their freedom.

Fact ✓

When slave ownership ended in the British Empire in 1833, the government paid out £20 million to former slave owners for their 'loss of property'. The Bishop of Exeter, for example, received over £12,000 for the loss of 665 enslaved people he owned with his business partners in the Caribbean.

Over to You ..ıl

1 Read **Source D** and **Interpretation E**. Do they help explain the slave trade and the way enslaved people were treated? Explain your answer.

2 Look at **Source H**. Design your own medallion that campaigns for the abolition of slavery. Remember to include an eye-catching image and slogan.

Causation

1 Write down three reasons why slavery was abolished. Under each, write down all the evidence you can find on pages 180–183 to support the reason.

2 'The main reason for the abolition of slavery was that slavery wasn't making money any more.' How far do you agree with this statement? Hint: You don't have to agree with the statement, as long as you can explain why you think another reason is more important.

Have you been learning?

Quick Knowledge Quiz

Choose the correct answer from the three options:

1   The part of the slave trade triangle where enslaved people were taken on a two-month journey across the Atlantic Ocean is commonly known by what name?

   a   Middle Passage
   b   Second Half
   c   Pacific Passage

2   Which of the following goods were regularly produced in the Americas and the Caribbean for transport back to Europe?

   a   wool, coal and pottery
   b   cotton, sugar and tobacco
   c   rice, iron and steel

3   Who is commonly referred to as Britain's first slave trader?

   a   John Hawkins
   b   Francis Drake
   c   the Duke of York

4   King Charles II was a partner in which slave trading company?

   a   the Royal African Company
   b   the Royal Society
   c   the Slavery Association

5   As well as London, which two English ports made vast fortunes from the slave trade?

   a   Hartlepool and Brighton
   b   Ipswich and Grimsby
   c   Bristol and Liverpool

6   Enslaved people were usually sold in one of two ways: auction or scramble. What was a scramble?

   a   Enslaved people were sold to the person who offered the highest price
   b   A price was agreed before the buyers rushed into a cage to grab the person they wanted
   c   Enslaved people were labelled with individual prices and buyers purchased the ones they wanted

7   What was the name of the huge farms where many enslaved people worked and lived?

   a   plantations
   b   empires
   c   smallholdings

8   After a successful revolt by the enslaved people living there, a new name was given to the island of Saint-Domingue. What was the island's new name?

   a   Dominican Republic
   b   Barbados
   c   Haiti

9   The British government abolished slave trading in which year?

   a   1789
   b   1807
   c   1833

10   Which formerly enslaved person wrote a bestselling autobiography in 1789 that massively raised awareness of the cruelty of the slave trade?

   a   Mary Prince
   b   Olaudah Equiano
   c   Toussaint L'Ouverture

Literacy Focus

Note-taking

Note-taking is a vital skill. To do it successfully, you must pick out all the important (key) words in a sentence. The important words are those that are vital to the meaning (and your understanding) of the sentence. For example, in the sentences:

> British traders first got involved in the slave trade in 1562. That year, John Hawkins became England's first slave trader when he captured and enslaved 300 people from Sierra Leone on the west coast of Africa and sold them in the Caribbean. Britain wasn't the only European nation to get involved in slavery, but it made some of the largest profits. All sorts of people were involved. Queen Elizabeth, for example, was a business partner of John Hawkins.

… the important words and phrases are: 1562; England's 1st slave trader; John Hawkins; 300 enslaved people; Sierra Leone; west coast; Africa; sold in Caribbean; Q. Elizabeth partnered with Hawkins

The original sentences were over 50 words long – but the shortened version is fewer than 30 words long and contains abbreviations. Note-taking like this will help your understanding of events – and provides you with a great revision exercise.

1 Write down the important words in the following sentences. These important words are your notes.

a Traders leave Britain and other European ports, headed for Africa, with ships full of goods such as alcohol, guns and cloth. These goods are old and cheap to buy in Europe, but are highly prized in Africa.

b Traders trade these goods with local African leaders in return for prisoners from other local African communities, who have already been captured to sell; they also kidnap Africans. The ships are loaded with the enslaved people and sail across the Atlantic. This part of the slave triangle is known as the 'Middle Passage'.

c In the Americas, the enslaved people are sold to plantation owners and farmers. The profits are used to buy goods such as sugar, cotton or tobacco. These are loaded onto the ships, which sail back to British or European ports to be sold at great profit.

> **TIP:** Sometimes, it can be really helpful to use a simple image when you create your notes. Using a simple drawing with a brief description can make the information stick in your memory a little better! Look at the map below for an example.

▼ **A** The slave trade triangle.

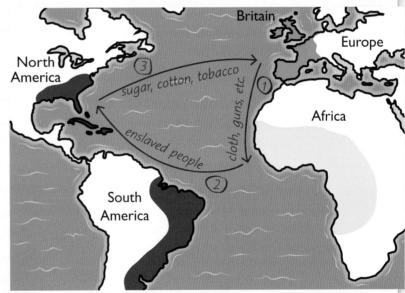

History skill: Causation

Historians use the term 'causes' – or reasons – to describe the things that made events happen. When historians try to work out different causes of historical events, they need to be able to justify *why* they think one cause (or reason) is more important than another.

Comparing different causes or reasons

This chapter's assessment asks you to compare the different causes of a historical event – in this case, the causes of the abolition of the slave trade.

> Which of the following was the more important reason why the slave trade was abolished in the British Empire in 1807:
>
> • the efforts of the enslaved people themselves, and formerly enslaved people
>
> • the anti-slavery campaign in Britain?
>
> Explain your answer with reference to both reasons.

The question asks you to compare two reasons, judge which one is more important, and explain your decision. The steps below show one way to answer this type of question.

1 **Plan:** Look at the two bullet points. Make some brief notes on each of them. For each point, try to note why this reason was more important than the other.

> **TIP:** Look back on your work on the abolition of the slave trade (pages 180–183). Pay particular attention to the two reasons listed.

2 **Judge:** Once you have thought about the two bullet points, you need to decide: Which do you think was the more important reason? What supporting information or details can you provide to back up your choice?

3 **Answer:** You are asked to decide which bullet point was more important, so make sure you answer the question. Introduce your argument when you start writing your answer.

4 **Explain and conclude:** You now need to add details to support your decision and explain why you are taking this view. Use your plan to help you add supporting information. Remember to write about *both* bullet points in your answer – try to explain what each point is about, before comparing one to the other. Then, after considering the impact of each reason, it is important to conclude and explain your choice.

> **TIP:** The question says 'explain your answer with reference to *both*', so don't forget to do this!

Now, considering all these points, try putting this into practice!

Assessment: Causation

Your challenge is to answer this question comparing different causes or reasons:

> Which of the following was the more important reason why the slave trade was abolished in the British Empire in 1807:
> - the efforts of the enslaved people themselves, and formerly enslaved people
> - the anti-slavery campaign in Britain?
>
> Explain your answer with reference to both reasons. (20)

The steps and example sentence starters below will help you structure your answer.

1 **Plan:** Look at the two bullet points, which are about the causes of the abolition of the slave trade. Make some brief notes on each of them. For each point, try to note why this reason was more important than the other.

2 **Judge:** Which do you think was the more important reason? What supporting information or details can you provide to back up your choice?

> **TIP:** Do you think that the efforts of enslaved and formerly enslaved people helped end the slave trade more than the anti-slavery campaigners? Or vice versa? Why do you think this?

3 **Answer:** You are asked to decide which bullet point was more important, so make sure you answer the question. Introduce your argument when you start writing your answer.

> The slave trade was abolished in…
> When looking at the reasons for the abolition of the slave trade, I think that… was a more important reason than… (5)

> **TIP:** Remember to write about *both* bullet points in your answer. You might also try to link the bullet points in some way – for example, some formerly enslaved people actually became involved with the anti-slavery campaign movement. Examples are Olaudah Equiano and Mary Prince.

4 **Explain and conclude:** Add details to support your decision and explain why you are taking this view. Then, after considering the impact of each reason, it is important to come to a conclusion and explain your choice.

> **TIP:** Add details here about how the efforts of the enslaved and formerly enslaved people contributed to the end of the slave trade.

> On the one hand, the efforts of the enslaved and formerly enslaved people was a key reason why the slave trade was abolished… (5)
> On the other hand, the anti-slavery campaign in Britain… (5)
> To conclude… was the more important reason for the abolition, because… (5)

> **TIP:** Add details here about how the efforts of the anti-slavery campaign contributed to the end of the slave trade.

> **TIP:** You are being asked to write down your judgement here. This is where it might be possible to link the bullet points – did one bullet point help out the other – if so, do you think that makes it more important – or not?

Britain versus France... in North America

In the 1600s, settlers from lots of different European countries sailed to the newly discovered continent of North America. People from Spain, France, Britain, the Netherlands, Sweden and Finland all arrived hoping to start a new life and make their fortune. But there were more British and French settlers than any others so, as you'd expect, they tried to grab the most land. And when both Britain and France wanted the same piece of land, can you guess what happened? That's right – they went to war. So where did the British and the French clash? Who won the war? And what impact did the fighting have on each country?

Objectives

- Outline where European settlement occurred in North America.
- Explain how Britain came to dominate the continent.

Land grab

The British grabbed lots of land, stretching over 1600km, along the east coast of North America. The settlers split themselves up into separate areas, or colonies, and farmed the land – growing cotton, tobacco, corn, oats, potatoes, wheat and barley. The French occupied a lot of land in the northern part of North America (now known as Canada) and inland around the Mississippi and St Lawrence rivers.

Both the French and the British were well armed, and built forts to guard their land. The Spanish had claimed land in North America too, in the south of the continent (see **A**).

▼ **MAP A** A map showing how land in North America was roughly divided up by European settlers in the 1600s and early 1700s.

French territory

Quebec
A large, important town in French territory. Founded by the French in 1608.

Great Lakes/St Lawrence River
Settlements nearby such as Quebec, Montreal and Detroit contained French farmers, traders and fishermen.

New Orleans/Louisiana area
Lots of French settlers here.

French forts
A string of forts stretched from French territory in the south up to the north.

Spanish territory

The Spanish had controlled this land for a long time, but were probably unwilling to go north as they believed there was no gold there.

Florida
A Spanish colony.

British territory/colonies

Hudson Bay
A few hundred British hunters lived in this vast area.

New England
British farmers, fishermen and shipbuilders.

Middle colonies
The Dutch settled here but in the 1600s the British took their land. Still, a large Dutch population mixed with the British. Lots of farmers, traders and businesspeople. A growing number of rich towns.

Southern colonies
Richer British farmers with huge estates growing cotton and tobacco. Slaves brought over from Africa to work on the farms.

British territory
French territory
Spanish territory
× French forts and settlements

N

0   500km

How did the settlers get the land?

When the European settlers went to America, indigenous people were already living there. There was conflict – many tribal nations (communities of indigenous peoples), such as the Iroquois, saw the settlers as invaders, while the settlers felt they had a right to live wherever they wanted (see **B**). In the British-controlled areas of North America, for example, the settlers usually drove local indigenous communities away and destroyed the forests so they could farm the land. Indigenous communities then moved further inland onto the vast plains.

On the warpath

By the mid-1700s, tension had increased between Britain and France in North America – and it was beginning to look like the two countries might soon fight each other. The French wanted the rich farmland that the British had developed near the east coast, and the British wanted to expand into French land so they could set up more farms. In 1754, the French built a new fort very close to British territory. The consequences of this led to a war known as the Seven Years War. Read through the story over the next few pages to see what happened.

▼ **INTERPRETATION B** Adapted from an article called 'The making of a nation – American history' on an educational website, written by Steve Ember, an author and broadcaster, in 2012.

'Perhaps the most serious was the difference in the way that the American Indians and the Europeans thought about land. This difference created problems that would not be solved during the next several hundred years.

Owning land was extremely important to the European settlers. Land meant wealth and power. Many of the settlers who came to North America could never have owned land back home in Europe. They were too poor. When they arrived in the new world, they discovered that no one seemed to own the huge amounts of land. For many, it was a dream come true.

On the other hand, the American Indians believed that no one could own land. They believed, however, that anyone could use it to live on and grow crops. They might hunt on one area of land for some time, but again they would move on. They hunted only what they could eat, so populations of animals could continue to increase. They did not understand that the settlers were going to keep the land. To them, it was like trying to own the air, or the clouds. As the years passed, more settlers arrived, and took more land. They cut down trees. They built fences to keep people and animals out. They demanded that the American Indians stay off their land.'

Meanwhile... 1750s

The British did not just fight the French in America – there was lots of fighting in other places too, including India and Canada. This was a time of major expansion for the British Empire. Robert Clive defeated French forces in India and gained land they had occupied, while General Wolfe defeated the French in Canada, which led to the surrender of Canada (New France) to the British.

Earlier on... 1492

People lived in the Americas long before the arrival of Christopher Columbus in 1492 and European settlers. The first people to live in a land are called indigenous people, which means they were the original settlers. The indigenous people of the Americas are often called American Indians (in the USA) and First Nations (in Canada).

Over to You

1 Why do you think settlers from European nations were so eager to settle in North America?

2 Look at **Map A**. In your own words, describe how the land in North America was divided up between different European countries.

3 Read **Interpretation B**.
   a According to this interpretation, what differences were there between the way Europeans and American Indians viewed land ownership?
   b Does this view help explain why there was conflict between American Indians and European settlers?

The Seven Years War officially started in 1756 during the reign of King George II – but in North America, the build-up began in 1754. It is important to note that it wasn't just a conflict between Britain and France – other countries took sides. For example, Britain was supported by the states of Prussia and Hanover (now in modern-day Germany) while France had help from Austria, Russia and Sweden. Spain (with France) and Portugal (with Britain) were later drawn into the conflict too.

Meanwhile...

1756–1763

Conflict took place in many areas of the world where the countries involved had land, such as in the Caribbean, Africa and India. For these reasons, some historians (including Winston Churchill) have called the Seven Years War the 'first world war'.

1 In 1754, the newly built French fort, Fort Duquesne, directly threatened British territory.

◻ French territory
▦ British territory
▲ French settlement
● French territory
△ British fort

Hudson Bay
Quebec
Montreal
Fort William Henry
Fort Oswego
Fort Duquesne ▲
New Orleans
Florida
Atlantic Ocean
N

2 A British army tried to capture Fort Duquesne, but was defeated. The defeated British army was led by a young George Washington who later became the first President of the United States.

3 The French then captured two British forts (Oswego and William Henry). The French were now set for an all-out attack on British territory. War was officially declared in May 1756.

4 Meanwhile, British Prime Minister William Pitt had sent lots of troops to North America to defend British territory. The troops arrived just in time.

5 In 1758, the British forts of Oswego and William Henry were recaptured, and the French Fort Duquesne was captured too (it was renamed 'Fort Pitt' in the Prime Minister's honour). The French were no longer a threat to British territory, so the British went on the attack!

6 In September 1759, the British decided to attack the French city of Quebec. The French thought the city was impossible to attack. But James Wolfe, a talented young general leading the British, had a plan!

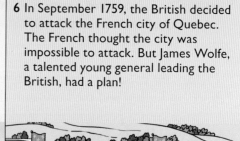

7 Under cover of darkness, James Wolfe led 5000 men in rowing boats down the St Lawrence River. They silently climbed the steep cliffs to launch a surprise dawn raid on the French (see **C**).

8 Soon the British captured all the French forts and settlements, including Montreal. The British captured Quebec, but Wolfe was wounded and died soon after. The French commander, Montcalm, was also killed.

A peace treaty, signed in Paris in 1763 (called the Treaty of Paris), gave French land in North America to Britain. The French lost New Orleans (to Spain) also. Britain also gained French territory in the Caribbean, and took Florida from the Spanish.

Peace of Paris 1763
FRENCH LOSE   BRITAIN WIN

▼ **INTERPRETATION C** This image was published in 1797 in London. It shows British soldiers, in red, climbing the steep cliffs to capture Quebec.

A real victory?

Although Britain defeated France and took over its land in North America, the French were always looking for revenge against the British – and they soon got their chance! Twelve years later, the people who lived in America decided they no longer wanted to be part of Britain. They decided that, despite being British and speaking English, they wanted to break free from British rule, run the country themselves and not pay taxes to Britain. In short, they wanted their **independence**, so the British sent over troops to control these rebels. And guess which country was only too happy to help the rebels fight the British troops? That's right, France!

Over to You

1 Describe the role played in the war by:
   a George Washington
   b William Pitt
   c James Wolfe.

2 What was agreed at the Treaty of Paris in 1763?

3 Write a narrative account of the Seven Years War analysing the British conquest of North America between 1756 and 1763.

▼ **INTERPRETATION D** Adapted from an article in *The Economist*, July 2014.

'Like the First World War, this global conflict reshaped the globe. Indeed, it is the reason why the modern world is an English-speaking one. As a colonial power, France was mainly destroyed. All of North America east of the Mississippi became British, save the city of New Orleans, which became Spanish. And the foundations of British rule in India were laid as well. As for George Washington, he ended up leading a rebel army of North American colonists who decided that they would rather go it alone. The conflict he started in 1754 was the first true world war, though it is not generally referred to as such.'

Interpretation Analysis

Study **Interpretation D**.

1 Why do some people refer to the Seven Years War as the 'first world war'?

2 How does the interpretation support the view that the Seven Years War was a major global conflict like the First World War?

In what way is the execution of a French king linked to Britain?

Source A is a French engraving from 1793. The man's head has been cut off by a **guillotine** – a tall frame with a heavy, sharp blade that drops down when it is released. Guillotines were used many hundreds of times during this period of French history, and Source A shows it being used on a French king, Louis XVI. So why did he have his head chopped off? What events led up to this moment? How is a war between Britain and France in North America linked to this event?

Objectives

- Recall why the French Revolution took place.
- Discover how the war in North America between Britain and France was connected to the French Revolution.

Britain versus France – and then America

For seven years, between 1756 and 1763, Britain and France were at war over who should control North America. Britain won the Seven Years War, but the French wanted revenge!

In 1775, the people who lived in some of the American east coast settlements (who were officially British) decided they no longer wanted to be part of Britain. They saw themselves as 'Americans' and were fed up with British controls and laws. They had to pay taxes to Britain, but they didn't have an MP in Parliament to represent their views, so they felt these taxes were unfair. On 4 July 1776, the British colonies in America issued a Declaration of Independence. They said that they were free from British control and would no longer take orders from the British Parliament. The British sent troops over to fight these American 'rebels'. This is known as the American War of Independence. The French helped the rebels, sending troops and supplies. Against all odds, the rebels (helped by France) beat the British. In 1781, the British surrendered and left the Americans to rule themselves. In 1783, the area officially became known as the United States of America.

Impact on France

The French were on the winning side in the war, but the war cost them a fortune. As a result, the French king increased taxes to pay for it. The poor French people were furious.

▼ **SOURCE A** An engraving titled 'The French Revolution' by Pierre Berthault, showing the execution of King Louis XVI in 1793.

Also, the ordinary French citizens had seen how the Americans had got rid of their British rulers and set up their own government. This inspired them. So in 1789, the unhappy, hungry and poor French people began a rebellion against the king and all his rich followers. This became the French Revolution.

The French Revolution

There were riots all over France as local people took control of different areas. King Louis XVI had little choice but to give up some of his powers, and the country was run by a National Assembly (a sort of Parliament). The new rulers famously published a list of rights that they believed people should have (see **B**).

▼ **SOURCE B** Adapted from some of the ideas contained in the **Declaration of the Rights of Man**. But the rights only applied to men – it was many years until women got equal rights. Several countries (as well as the United Nations when creating the Universal Declaration of Human Rights, 1948) have used this list when deciding how their countries should be run.

- All men are born and remain free and equal in rights.
- Governments should always try to preserve these rights.
- No one should be punished except by laws set up before the offence was committed.
- Every man is presumed innocent until proven guilty.
- No one should be picked on for his opinions or religious beliefs.
- Every citizen may speak, write and print freely.
- Taxation should be fair and based on what people can afford to pay.
- No one can have their property taken away for no good reason.

War and execution

Thousands of rich French people fled to other European countries. They urged other countries to help them end the revolution. Meanwhile, the French government called for a worldwide revolution. The rulers of Britain, Austria, Prussia (now part of Germany), the Netherlands and Spain were afraid that the revolution might spread to their countries – and soon a war broke out between France and these nations.

Meanwhile, many of the wealthy French people who stayed in France were killed by the revolutionaries in what became known as the **Reign of Terror** (September 1793–July 1794). In a move that astonished (and worried) many of Europe's leaders, the French even executed King Louis XVI and his wife, Marie Antoinette, in 1793.

Fact ✓

Around 17,000 people were officially executed in France, including over 2500 in Paris, during the Reign of Terror. Many more died in prison.

▼ **SOURCE C** A British cartoon by James Gillray from 1792 titled 'A little Parisian soup', commenting on the massacres of the wealthy and royal French people by the revolutionaries.

Over to You

1 Look at **Source A**.
   a Describe what's happening in the picture.
   b Why were many ordinary French citizens so angry with the king and his wealthy supporters?

2 a What was the Declaration of the Rights of Man?
   b Why has this declaration been seen as so significant in the years since it was written?

3 In your own words, explain how the execution of a French king is linked to Britain.

Source Analysis

1 Look at **Source C**. Can you see:
   a the rich victims of the massacres
   b the sharp-toothed revolutionaries eating the rich
   c a bag containing the crown and other royal jewels
   d a picture of a headless Louis XVI (labelled 'Lewis le Grand'), drawn on the wall of the poor French person's home?

2 Describe what you think the cartoonist felt about the revolutionaries.

3 How useful is this source for an enquiry into British reactions to the French Revolution?

The French Revolution of 1789 saw the execution of France's leading royals and many other wealthy French people. Other European leaders didn't want a similar revolution to happen in their countries – and tensions increased across Europe. These tensions eventually led to war between France and several other European nations. They became known as the French Revolutionary Wars, and later, the Napoleonic Wars. So which countries dominated the wars? Who were the key leaders? And how was the battle of Trafalgar fought?

Objectives

- Examine Napoleon's career.
- Explain how successful Nelson's tactics were.
- Recognise the importance of the Battle of Trafalgar.

The wars did not go well for France's enemies. The French had a strong army and a brilliant leader, named Napoleon Bonaparte (see box). By 1796, Napoleon's forces had taken control of large parts of Europe. Only Britain, with its large navy, was unbeaten. But Dutch and Spanish forces then joined France against the British, combining their naval forces into one huge force. They met the British navy in battle in October 1805.

Attacking Britain

Napoleon's forces needed to defeat the British navy in order to get across the English Channel to invade Britain. The British commander given the job of preventing this was Vice Admiral Horatio Nelson (see **A**). He was already a national hero (and as popular as a famous footballer or pop star today) because of previous naval victories against the French. But he knew that if he was to make Britain safe from France, he needed to completely destroy the French navy and gain control of the seas.

What was Nelson's plan?

The traditional way of fighting at sea at this time was for ships to sail alongside each other, firing their cannons. They tried to get close enough for soldiers to jump onto enemy ships and fight hand-to-hand. Battles often ended in a draw or with no clear winner. To avoid this, Nelson came up with a plan that he hoped would defeat his enemies. His plan became known as 'Nelson's touch'. When he told his captains of his idea, he claimed, 'It was like an electric shock, some shed tears, all approved.'

Napoleon Bonaparte

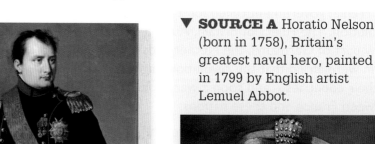

Born: 1769

Early career: Attended military school, joined army aged 16.

Military career: Quickly promoted. In 1796, Napoleon reorganised (then led) a French army that beat Austrian forces in Italy. After unsuccessfully leading a French army in Egypt, Napoleon returned to Paris in 1799.

Leader of France: On his return he saw food shortages, problems in the government, and little money left for war. He took leadership of France in November 1799. He introduced some new laws and systems that France still uses today. As he became stronger and won more victories, he placed his relatives on the thrones of the Netherlands, Italy and Spain.

Title: Known as 'First Consul', but in 1804 he crowned himself emperor. As emperor, it was his ambition to unite Europe. The wars fought by the French at this time are referred to as the Napoleonic Wars.

▼ **SOURCE A** Horatio Nelson (born in 1758), Britain's greatest naval hero, painted in 1799 by English artist Lemuel Abbot.

Traditional attack (old)

France and Spain had more ships than Nelson – so he knew he needed a new tactic!

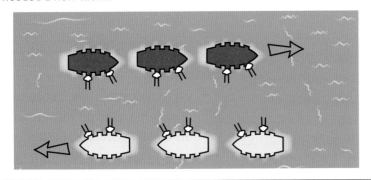

Nelson's touch (new)

Nelson planned to break the enemy line at a 90° angle. This would allow his ships to fire through the length of the enemy ships – without them firing back.

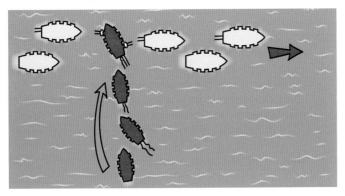

▼ **INTERPRETATION B** Nelson's victory was commemorated in London with Trafalgar Square and Nelson's Column. Constructed in the 1840s, four bronze lions were made from captured French cannons and placed at the base of a column with a statue of Nelson on top.

The Battle of Trafalgar

The two sides met on 21 October 1805, near Cape Trafalgar just off the Spanish coast. The British ships attacked in two different places, and caused colossal damage. However, amid scenes of fierce fighting on board HMS *Victory*, Nelson was injured by French gunshot. Despite this, French ships started to surrender and, at 4.15pm, the injured Nelson was told that the battle had been won. He replied, 'Now I am satisfied. Thank God, I have done my duty.' By 4.30pm, Nelson was dead.

The cost of victory

Of 27 British ships, none were sunk! Of 33 French and Spanish ships, 15 were sunk, blown up or run ashore, eight were captured and only ten got back to France. Around 1700 British and 7000 French and Spanish sailors were killed or wounded. With Napoleon's navy destroyed, he couldn't invade Britain – but he still remained a threat.

The importance of Trafalgar

As the years passed, British people began to see Nelson's victory over Napoleon's navies as increasingly important. Not only had it removed the threat of French invasion, it also enabled Britain to become richer and more powerful. Having control of the seas meant that Britain could trade with countries such as India and China safely and without competition.

Over to You

1 a What is a 'national hero'? Use a modern example in your answer if you wish.

  b Why do you think Horatio Nelson is regarded as a national hero in Britain?

2 a What was 'Nelson's touch'? Use only 20 words – and a diagram if you like – in your description.

  b Was 'Nelson's touch' a success or not?

3 a How did Nelson die?

  b How were Nelson and the Battle of Trafalgar commemorated?

  c Why do you think some historians view the victory at Trafalgar as a key moment in British history?

Waterloo: Napoleon's last stand

By 1811, Napoleon Bonaparte and his siblings ruled much of Europe between them. In 1812, Napoleon invaded Russia, but was driven back by the freezing Russian winter. Following this defeat, Napoleon was forced to **abdicate**, giving up his position as France's emperor, and was **exiled** to the island of Elba in the Mediterranean Sea. But he managed to escape in 1815, return to Paris and raise a new army. He marched his soldiers to Belgium where he fought a famous battle in Waterloo against the Duke of Wellington, leader of a huge army of British, Prussian, Dutch and Belgian troops. Napoleon lost. But was it Wellington's leadership that won the day? Did Napoleon cause his own downfall?

Objectives

- Discover why the Battle of Waterloo was so important in the Napoleonic wars.
- Judge whether Wellington's brilliance or Napoleon's mistakes contributed to the outcome of the battle.

Napoleon's defeat at Waterloo in June 1815 meant that the French domination of Europe was finally over. Never again did Napoleon take to the battlefield. But ever since the battle, historians have argued over whether it was Wellington's brilliance or Napoleon's mistakes that caused the French defeat. Look through boxes A to I, consider the evidence and decide for yourself.

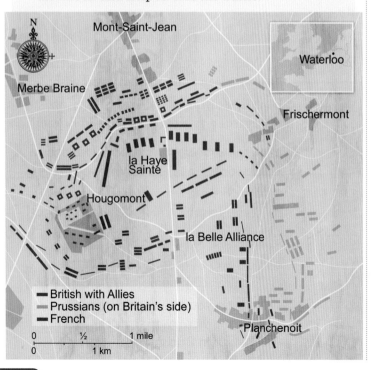

▼ **MAP A** The formation at the start of the Battle of Waterloo. The Prussians arrived in the afternoon and helped win the battle.

Mont-Saint-Jean
Waterloo
Merbe Braine
Frischermont
la Haye Sainte
Hougomont
la Belle Alliance
Planchenoit

— British with Allies
— Prussians (on Britain's side)
— French

0   ½   1 mile
0   1 km

A Wellington investigated what the land around the battlefield was like before the battle began. He realised how important the farmhouses in the middle of the battlefield would be and got some of his best soldiers to defend them. These farmhouses were an important line of defence because they shielded the soldiers and provided cover. The French attacked them many times but failed to occupy them.

B It rained heavily the night before the battle. The wet ground made movement slow and difficult but Napoleon still ordered the attack to go ahead.

C Wellington spread his infantry in lines just two men deep – this allowed all the soldiers to fire their muskets at the same time.

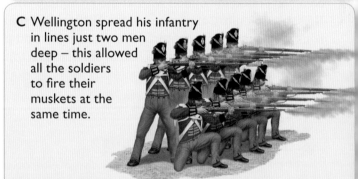

D When Wellington's infantry came under heavy fire from French **artillery**, he ordered them to move behind a ridge and lie down in long grass. This caused the French to think they were retreating and allowed the British soldiers to wipe out the French as they came over the ridge.

E Many people say that Napoleon wasn't his usual energetic and inspirational self at Waterloo. He even left the battlefield for a lie down for a short time because he felt ill. He put Marshal Ney in charge – who made some poor decisions.

F The French infantry advanced in narrow columns that were just six men wide but many rows deep. This meant that only those at the front could fight and most of the men in the column couldn't fire their muskets.

G Napoleon put all of his artillery in one place – at the front of his army. This meant they could deliver devastating firepower but couldn't reach all areas of the battlefield.

H Wellington inspired his troops by putting himself in the thick of the action and only narrowly avoided being killed several times.

▼ **INTERPRETATION B** A painting from the late nineteenth century showing Wellington at Waterloo.

I The Prussian army was rapidly marching to join Wellington's soldiers. Napoleon sent 30,000 men from the battlefield to try to stop the Prussian advance. They failed and the Prussians were soon at Waterloo, attacking Napoleon.

▶ **SOURCE C** A breastplate from the Battle of Waterloo, damaged by a cannonball.

Later on... `1821`

After the Battle of Waterloo, Napoleon was captured and sent into exile again, this time on St Helena, a tiny island in the middle of the Atlantic Ocean. He remained there until he died in 1821.

Over to You   .ıll

1 Read through each piece of evidence (A–I) to assess why Wellington won the Battle of Waterloo.

  a Make a table with two columns – the first one titled 'Wellington's brilliance' and the second one 'Napoleon's mistakes'. Where does each piece of evidence belong? Write a brief description of the evidence in the correct column.

  b Based on your work in step **a**, do you think 'Wellington's brilliance' or 'Napoleon's mistakes' was the most decisive factor in the outcome of the battle?

  c Are there any other factors, apart from Wellington's brilliance or Napoleon's mistakes, that might have affected the outcome of the battle?

Causation

1 How important were Napoleon's mistakes in the French defeat at the Battle of Waterloo? In your answer you should discuss the importance of Napoleon's mistakes alongside other factors in order to reach a judgement. Hint: Use your answer in the 'Over to You' questions to help you consider the different factors.

⟳ Quick Knowledge Quiz

Choose the correct answer from the three options:

1 In which year did the Seven Years War begin?

   a   1754
   b   1756
   c   1758

2 Which British army general famously led a group of 5000 men in capturing the French-held city of Quebec?

   a   William Henry
   b   George Washington
   c   James Wolfe

3 Which 1763 treaty gave French land in North America to Britain?

   a   Treaty of London
   b   Treaty of Quebec
   c   Treaty of Paris

4 The conflict, following the rebellion of the North American colonies against British rule, is known by what name?

   a   the American War of Independence
   b   the French Revolution
   c   the War of the Worlds

5 What is the name of the tall frame in which a heavy, sharp blade is placed, used to execute people during the French Revolution?

   a   the guillotine
   b   the rack
   c   the gallows

6 Which French king was executed during the French Revolution?

   a   Louis XVI
   b   Napoleon Bonaparte
   c   Charles I

7 Who led the British navy during the Battle of Trafalgar?

   a   Horatio Nelson
   b   Duke of Wellington
   c   William Pitt

8 In which year was the British victory at the Battle of Trafalgar?

   a   1799
   b   1805
   c   1815

9 In 1812, Napoleon made an unsuccessful attempt to invade and defeat which country?

   a   France
   b   Russia
   c   Sweden

10 In which country did the Battle of Waterloo take place?

   a   Belgium
   b   Russia
   c   France

 **Literacy Focus**

Writing in detail: adding adjectives

When writing historically, it's really important that you give detailed descriptions. One way to add detail and improve the quality of your writing is to use adjectives. An adjective is a word that describes a noun. For example, the *intelligent* commander considered a *new* tactic.

Adjectives can add extra detail to your writing. For example, they can give you extra information about:

- the size or weight of something (large, tiny, heavy)

- the colour or brightness of something (dull, blue, shiny)

- the condition of something (worn, new, used)

- the mood or intelligence of a person (smart, angry, ill)

- the shape of something (low, deep, steep)

- the sound of something (deafening, melodic, harsh)

- the time of something (rapid, young, early).

They can also tell you about other qualities of a noun – what something is made from, what it tastes or smells like, what its shape is like or what you, personally, think about it.

Look at the paragraph below:

> In September 1759, the British decided to attack the city of Quebec. The French thought the city was impossible to attack. But James Wolfe, a general leading the British, had a plan. Under cover of darkness, he led 5000 men in rowing boats down the St Lawrence River. Then they climbed the cliffs to launch a raid on the French.

This paragraph is simply a collection of short, sharp sentences. Look at the paragraph below to see how adjectives have improved it.

> In September 1759, the British decided to attack the *strategically important French* city of Quebec. The French thought the city was an *impregnable* fortress that was impossible to attack. But James Wolfe, a *talented young* general leading the British, had a *cunning* plan. Under the *dark* night sky, he led 5000 men in rowing boats down the St Lawrence River. Then they climbed the *steep* cliffs to launch a *surprise* raid on the French.

1 Now it's your turn. Add adjectives to improve the quality of this paragraph:

> In June 1815, at Waterloo, Napoleon's forces were defeated by the Duke of Wellington, leader of British, Prussian, Dutch and Belgian troops. Wellington used a variety of tactics. For example, Wellington investigated the land around the battlefield before the battle. He realised it would be important to control the farmhouses in the middle of the battlefield and got soldiers to defend them. These farmhouses were a line of defence that shielded the soldiers and provided cover. The French attacked them many times but failed to occupy them. Also, when Wellington's infantry came under fire from artillery, he ordered them to move behind a ridge and lie down in grass. This caused the French to think they were retreating and allowed the soldiers to wipe the French out as they came over the ridge.

A consequence is a result or impact of an event or development. A good historian needs to be able to explain the consequences of an event in order to judge how important the event was, and assess its impact.

Explaining consequences

Here is one way to answer a question on consequences. Imagine you have been asked:

> Explain the importance of the French Revolution for relations between Britain and France.

TIP: This is the *main* topic you are asked to think about.

TIP: The *last part of the question* contains the other thing you need to consider. So, you should not simply think about the French Revolution – but think about its *impact on* the relationship between Britain and France.

1 **Plan:** What do you know about the main topic? A good way to start would be to make some brief notes on the topic itself.

TIP: For example, you might write these notes about the French Revolution:
- The French Revolution began in 1789 when poor French people rebelled against the French King (Louis XVI) and all his rich followers.
- Thousands of rich French people fled to other European countries. They urged other countries to help them end the revolution in France.

2 **Importance:** It's now time to think about the importance (or consequences) of the main topic *for the last part of the question*. After all, this is what the question is asking you to explain.

TIP: For example, you might write about these consequences of the revolution *for British-French relations*:
- The rich French people who left France after the revolution started, had urged other countries to help them end the French Revolution.
- The rulers of Britain, Austria, and others were afraid that the revolution might spread to their countries – and soon a war broke out between France (led by Napoleon Bonaparte) and these nations, including Britain.
- In 1805, the British Navy beat the French at the Battle of Trafalgar.

TIP: Remember, don't just write about whether the French Revolution was important or not – make sure you say whether it was important *for British-French relations*!

3 **Explain and conclude:** Complete your answer with some concluding thoughts. After all, the question asks you to 'explain' the importance. Was the main topic 'very important' or 'quite important' for the last part of the question?

TIP: For example, you might write:
- The French Revolution was very important for the relationship between Britain and France. As a result of the fear in Britain caused by the revolution, Britain was drawn into a war with France known as the....
- As a consequence of these wars, Britain and France...

Now, considering all these points, try putting this into practice!

Assessment: Consequences

Your challenge is to answer this question about consequences:

> Explain the following:
>
> - the importance of the treaty, signed in Paris (1763), for Britain's position in North America
>
> - the importance of the Battle of Trafalgar for relations between Britain and France. **(20)**

Steps 1–3 and the example sentence starters below will help you structure your answer for each bullet point. You will need to repeat steps 1–3 for the second bullet point. Each bullet point is worth 10 marks.

1 **Plan:** Take each bullet point individually. First, work through your whole answer to the question relating to the treaty that was signed in Paris in 1763 – and *then* deal with the Battle of Trafalgar afterwards. So what do you know about the treaty that was signed in Paris in 1763?

> In 1763, a treaty was signed in Paris between...
>
> It was signed to end the...
>
> This war...   (2)

> **TIP:** This shows your background knowledge of the main topic.

2 **Importance:** Now it's time to think about the consequences of this treaty on Britain's position in North America.

> The treaty gave Britain...
>
> For example...   (4)

> **TIP:** Don't forget to write about the importance (or consequence) of the treaty *for Britain's position in North America*!

3 **Explain and conclude:** What are your concluding thoughts? How important was this treaty for Britain's position in North America?

> I think the treaty was (somewhat/very) important for Britain's position in North America because...   (4)

Now work through the steps again to help you answer the second bullet point – how important was the Battle of Trafalgar for relations between Britain and France?

11.1 The development of the British Empire

An empire is a collection of areas of land (or whole countries) that are ruled over by one leading or 'mother' country. The places controlled by the mother country are usually called colonies. More than 100 years ago, Britain ruled the largest empire the world had ever known. Britain ruled over 450 million people living in 56 colonies around the world. So why did Britain want such a large empire? And how did it get its empire?

Objectives

- Define the words 'empire' and 'colony'.
- Explain how and why Britain gained an empire.

▼ **MAP A** By 1900, Britain's empire contained a quarter of the world's population and covered a quarter of the Earth's total land area.

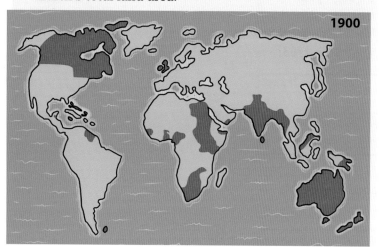

1900

So why did Britain want an empire?

The four main reasons why Britain wanted an empire were:

1 to get valuable raw materials and riches (such as diamonds, gold, spices, sugar and tea that were found in other countries)

2 so it could sell goods to the people in the colonies and make money

3 to become a more powerful country

4 because it thought it was the right thing to do.

▼ **INTERPRETATION B** From a History textbook by Bea Stimpson (2000).

'The colonies had to purchase all their manufactured goods from Britain. This gave Britain a guaranteed market for its manufacturers.'

▼ **INTERPRETATION C** Adapted from a section titled 'Attitudes of Empire' on a BBC revision webpage about 'The British Empire through Time' (last updated 2019).

'Many British people at the time thought that they were doing the right thing by taking the British government and Christianity to the rest of the world. The British generally felt that the way they lived their lives was the right way. They believed that colonising various countries was a means of helping others to become like Britain and therefore improve.'

▼ **INTERPRETATION D** From the historian Paul Turner in *The Changing Face of Britain and its Empire* (2009).

'Many goods were of interest to the Europeans, most specifically silk, calico, dyes, saltpeter [to preserve meat], cotton, pepper, cardamom, other spices and tea. India, the Europeans believed, would be easy to exploit.'

▼ **INTERPRETATION E** Written by historian John Child in *Reform, Expansion, Trade and Industry* (1992).

'The British government used the army and navy to take over land to prevent countries like France and Germany getting it first. This happened in Africa and New Zealand. Some places, like Gibraltar, were taken as naval bases.'

So how did Britain get its empire?

War

If Britain won a war against another country, it could often take over any land the other country owned around the world. For example, when Britain won the Seven Years War (1756–1763) against France, land previously conquered by France in America and India became part of the British Empire. British victories in war were also how Canada and islands in the Caribbean such as Tobago and St Lucia became part of the empire too.

Discovery

Occasionally, explorers would find land and just claim it for Britain. That happened in 1770 when Captain James Cook sailed to Australia. To strengthen the claim that the land belonged to Britain, British settlers who went there built colonies. The people who already lived there (the indigenous people) were ignored and Australia became part of the British Empire.

Settlers

Sometimes British people would go to another part of the world and start to live there. They might be looking for new business opportunities or a chance to own land, or be running away from the ill-treatment they received in their home country as a result of their religion. This is how large parts of the American east coast became part of the British Empire in the 1600s and 1700s.

Trade

When British companies went to trade in some places, they slowly took over large areas. The British government sometimes sent soldiers to support the companies by keeping order, guarding trading settlements and controlling the local people. This happened in India and parts of Africa for many years from the 1600s.

Fact ✓

In the 1880s, so many European countries competed to grab as much of the African continent as they could that it became known as the 'Scramble for Africa'.

A long process?

As you can see, Britain got its empire in different ways. Sometimes it took over areas quickly, but often things took a lot longer. For example, the British first went to India to trade in the early 1600s, but it took until the mid-1800s before India officially became part of the British Empire during Queen Victoria's reign.

Meanwhile...

1500s

Another great empire was at its most powerful during the time when the British Empire was just beginning to grow. The Ottoman Empire ruled over much of south-east Europe, parts of Central Europe, parts of Eastern Europe, North Africa and the Middle East. It reached its peak during the reign of Suleiman the Magnificent, who ruled from 1520 to 1566.

Later on...

1839

In China, British merchants traded Chinese tea, silk and porcelain for goods such as wool and opium (a drug). Before long, many people there became addicted to opium, so the Chinese tried to stop sales of the drug. In 1839, the Chinese seized over 20,000 chests of opium from British traders, which started the first of two Opium Wars.

Over to You ▪▪▪

1 Test your understanding by explaining the following: empire, mother country, colony.

2 Look at **Map A**. Describe the British Empire in 1900. Think about the number, size and location of the colonies.

3 Study **Interpretations B** to **E**.
   a Can you match each one with the four reasons why Britain wanted an empire (see page 202)?
   b In your own words, explain why Britain wanted an empire. You must use a quotation from each of **Interpretations B, C, D** and **E** in your answer.

Knowledge and Understanding

1 Describe two methods used by the British to gain an empire.

11.2 What was India like before the British arrived?

At one point there were over 50 colonies in the British Empire. They were dotted all over the world and made the empire the largest the world had ever known. One of the largest places in Britain's empire was India. It was the colony that many Britons were most proud of, calling it the 'jewel in the crown' of the empire. So why was India so attractive to the British?

Objectives

- Describe what India was like before the British took over.
- Examine why India was such a rich prize for a conquering nation.

Incredible India

India today is an independent country. It's the seventh largest country in the world – and the second most populated. Modern India, located in Asia, borders Pakistan, China, Bangladesh and Nepal. The maps show India today compared with India around 1500, before many Europeans began to settle there.

Conquest

People from several different parts of the world had previously settled in India, or tried to conquer it. The Persians and Iranians settled there in ancient times. Alexander the Great (a Greek) invaded it – and so did Genghis Khan (from east Asia). The Chinese went to India in pursuit of knowledge and to visit the ancient Indian universities. The Mughals, from Central Asia, invaded in the 1500s and then, in the 1600s, came the French, the Dutch, the Danes, the Portuguese… and also the British!

Raw materials

India is rich in natural resources – iron ore, copper, gold, silver, gemstones, spices, tea and timber. This meant that any country that made strong trade links with India could potentially become rich and powerful. Any country that managed to take control over India could become even more so.

A divided nation?

Three of the world's major religions – Hinduism, Buddhism and Sikhism – originated in India (see **C, D** and **E**). Other religions have since arrived there too. At various times throughout India's history, science, technology, engineering, art, literature, mathematics, astronomy and religion have flourished there.

Before many European nations began to sail to India to trade in the 1500s, India was divided into lots of kingdoms (see **A**). Most were run by Hindu princes. Occasionally the kingdoms would go to war against each other – but there were long peaceful periods too. But in the early 1500s, the Mughals, who were Muslims, invaded India and took control. Within decades, the great Mughal emperor, Akbar, had managed to unite

▼ **MAPS A & B** By the sixteenth century, India was divided into lots of kingdoms, but under the main control of one particular group – the Mughals.

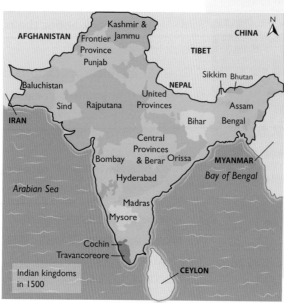

Indian kingdoms in 1500

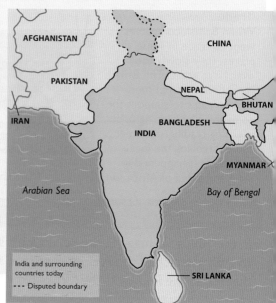

India and surrounding countries today
--- Disputed boundary

▼ **SOURCE C** Brihadeeswarar Hindu Temple in Thanjavur, India. It was built in the eleventh century.

▼ **SOURCE D** Mahabodhi Buddhist Temple in Bodh Gaya, India. It was built in the fifth or sixth century.

▼ **SOURCE E** The Golden Temple in Amritsar, India – the holiest place of worship for Sikhs, originally built in the late 1500s.

▼ **SOURCE F** The Taj Mahal, India, built by Akbar's grandson, Emperor Shah Jahan, between 1632 and 1648 in memory of his third wife.

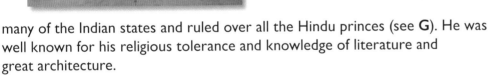

▶ **SOURCE G** Drawing of Akbar the Great, who ruled the Mughal Empire (including nearly all of India) between 1556 and 1605.

many of the Indian states and ruled over all the Hindu princes (see **G**). He was well known for his religious tolerance and knowledge of literature and great architecture.

The Mughal emperors mainly ruled peacefully. However, Akbar's great-grandson, Aurangzeb, was a very strict Muslim who was intolerant of India's other religions. As wars over control and land broke out all over India, the Mughals eventually lost control of the country by the early 1700s. It was exactly this time, when much of India was at war, that European nations became very interested in controlling the country.

Here come the Europeans

Several European nations saw the conflict in India as an opportunity to increase their own influence there. Many nations, but mainly the Dutch, French and British, realised that by helping certain Indian princes – with weapons and soldiers, for example – they could affect the outcomes of the wars as they wanted. Then, when the kingdom they helped was successful, they could demand rewards from the prince – perhaps land or goods. European countries could even fight against the Indian princes and take their lands for themselves.

Over to You

1 Plan a slideshow presentation, poster or video presentation called 'What was India like before the British took control?' Include details of India's eventful history and rich culture, and explain why European nations took an interest in it. Include text, images and/or film clips. Use no more than 100 words in total.

In 1497, a Portuguese explorer named Vasco da Gama discovered how to get to India from Europe by sea. Soon, many European countries were sending ships to India to trade. At first the ships simply reached an Indian port, traded their goods with local traders for silk, spices, cotton or tea, and brought these home to sell for a big profit. After a few years, and with the permission of Indian rulers, the traders began to set up permanent trading stations. These were large warehouses surrounded by huge fences and guarded by men with guns. So who ran the trading stations and how did they work?

Objectives

- Examine how trading works.
- Discover the importance of the Battle of Plassey.

Which countries?

Britain, France and the Netherlands were the main countries with trading stations in India in the early years, but Denmark and Portugal traded there too (see **B**).

The East India Company

The British trading stations in India were all run by the East India Company (EIC). Set up in 1600, it sent ships all over the world for many years. The ships left Britain full of cheap British goods, and traded them for goods such as fine china, silk, coffee and spices in countries as far away as Japan, China and, of course, India. Then they brought these goods back to Britain to sell at high prices. The businesspeople in charge of the Company, and the kings and queens to whom they paid taxes, all made a fortune from this trade (see **C**).

Later on... `1900s`

India later became not just a valuable source of goods, but also of *people* for Britain. Britain could not always find enough people to help control its growing empire, so it trained and paid local Indian people to become soldiers and fight for them. Indian soldiers would go on to play an important role for Britain and its allies in the First and Second World Wars.

▼ **SOURCE A** A painting of the British trading station at Bombay, run by the East India Company, in 1731.

▼ **MAP B** European settlements and trading ports in India by the mid-1700s – and the nations that founded them.

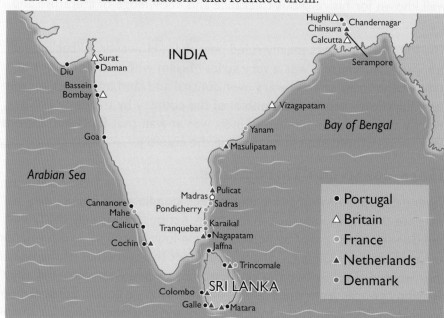

- Portugal
- △ Britain
- ○ France
- ▲ Netherlands
- ● Denmark

▼ C How businesspeople made a fortune from trade.

Stage 1: A group of rich businesspeople got together to buy (or rent) a ship.

Well there she is!

The first of many voyages I hope.

I hope she doesn't sink!

Stage 2: They loaded the ship with goods wanted in India – guns, ammunition, swords, tools, buttons and shoes.

Most of these goods are old and second hand!

But they are in high demand over there.

Stage 3: They sailed to India (or perhaps China or Japan).

Britain

Africa

India

I feel seasick

Stage 4: They unloaded the goods at a trading station – and traded them for things that are cheap and easy to get in India but hard to get in Britain.

Stage 5: They sailed back to Britain with a fully loaded ship.

Britain

I'm still seasick

Africa

India

Stage 6: They sold the foreign goods in Britain – for far more than they paid for the British goods they traded them for.

What a great way to make money.

The East India Company is the only British company allowed to trade in India.

Let's do it again!

The fighting begins

The East India Company first set up trading posts in Surat (1612), Madras (1639) and Bombay (1668). In the 1700s, the Company began to take more Indian land. It had its own army and navy, and used them against the rulers of India. At the Battle of Plassey in 1757, for example, Robert Clive (known as 'Clive of India') led around 3000 Company soldiers (2200 of whom were local Indians) and defeated a much larger Indian army (perhaps as large as 40,000) led by Prince Sirajud-Daulah. The Indian prince was supported by a number of French troops because, at this time, Britain was at war with France in the Seven Years War (see pages 188–191). This victory was an important one for Britain: it was able to expand more into India, increasing trade and military power. It continued to fight against France (and the Netherlands) and take over their trading posts and settlements in Asia too.

The Company expands

Over the following decades, various Indian rulers were either beaten in battle or played off against each other, so that more of India came under British rule. In the late 1700s, Britain lost control of its colonies in North America when it lost the American War of Independence. India was viewed as an ideal replacement for the 'lost' American colonies. By the mid-1850s, most of India was controlled by the British – but a major rebellion that shocked the world was just around the corner.

Over to You

1 a List the European countries that set up trading stations in India in the 1600s.

b Why were these countries so interested in India?

2 a What was the East India Company?

b Explain how the company gradually took control of most of India.

Change

'Turning points' in history are points of great change, leaving things different from how they were before.

1 'The Battle of Plassey was a turning point in the British control of India.' How far do you agree?

11.4 Indian mutiny... or war of independence?

By the 1850s, most of India was ruled by the British. The East India Company had gradually taken more and more land, and many Britons who worked for the Company lived in great luxury in India and made huge fortunes. To help 'protect' them – and to make sure things ran smoothly – the Company used its own British soldiers. It also employed local Indians as soldiers. However, on 10 May 1857, Indian soldiers (called 'Sepoys') working for the British in Meerut, northern India, shot dead a number of British soldiers. Soon there was fierce fighting between the British and Sepoys across northern India. This is known as the Indian Mutiny – or the War of Independence! So what caused the uprising? How did the British respond? And why does the same event have different names?

Objectives

- Examine the causes and consequences of events in India in 1857–1858.
- Compare different interpretations of the events of 1857–1858.

Suffering Sepoys

By the 1850s, the British Army in India was made up of around 200,000 Sepoys (mainly Hindus and Muslims) and 40,000 British. Many Sepoys felt that they weren't treated very well, had little hope of promotion, and were often the first to be sent to the most dangerous places. Some Sepoys also felt that they were being pressured into converting to Christianity.

New guns and ammunition

The conflict in India started as a result of what the Sepoys saw as a lack of cultural understanding by the British. In January 1857, each Indian soldier was given a new rifle that used bullets and gunpowder kept in a container (called a 'cartridge'). The cartridge was covered in grease to make it easier to slide the bullets down the gun barrel. Loading the gun quickly involved biting the top off the cartridge with your teeth. However, it was rumoured that the grease was made from animal fat, probably (but not definitely) a mixture of pork and beef fat – the worst possible mixture for Hindus and Muslims. Hindus don't eat beef because cows are viewed as sacred, and Muslims are forbidden from eating pork.

Fact ✓

By the early 1800s, the British government had gradually taken increasing control of the East India Company – and by the 1850s, the EIC was managing India on behalf of the British government.

▼ **SOURCE A** Indian Sepoys in the British Army taking orders from a British Army officer, painted by British artist Richard Simkin in 1885.

Rebellion!

The Sepoys' objections to the new cartridges were largely ignored. And when 85 Sepoys refused to use the cartridges, they were arrested and sent to jail for ten years. Days later, other Sepoys rioted in support of them. Many local Indian leaders, unhappy with British interference in India, joined the Sepoys – and soon the whole of northern India was engulfed in conflict.

India at war

There were major battles between British troops and Sepoys in Delhi, Cawnpore and Lucknow and both sides acted brutally. The conflict lasted around 18 months and it ended in July 1858 when the British, helped by Indian soldiers who remained loyal, defeated the Sepoys. Revenge was violent, bloody and swift (see **B**).

▼ **INTERPRETATION B** A Russian illustration from the 1880s showing the brutal punishment of rebel Sepoys, who have been strapped to a cannon about to be fired. Many other Sepoys were hanged.

The end... and after

The conflict shocked the British. Many people were taken aback by the ferocity of feeling that had been shown against the British in India.

After the rebellion, the British government took over full responsibility for running India from the East India Company. A new government department, the India Office, was set up in 1858, and a viceroy was put in charge of India on behalf of Queen Victoria.

Before the rebellion, the British policy in India was to introduce British ideas about religion and education – which threatened the Hindu, Muslim and Sikh ways of life. After 1858, the British tried to interfere less with religious matters, and started to allow Indians more say in the running of India by allowing them jobs in local government. However, by 1900, nine out of ten jobs running the country were still done by Britons.

What's in a name?

At the time in Britain – and often also today – this event was known as the 'Indian Mutiny' or the 'Sepoy Rebellion'. However, Indians and Pakistanis today refer to it as the 'First War of Independence' or the 'Great Rebellion'. It is seen as the first episode in the great struggle against the British for a free India. On the Indian government website, the rebellion is covered in a section entitled the 'Indian Freedom Struggle'.

Key Words   mutiny   Sepoy   viceroy

Later on...

In 2007, the Indian and Pakistani governments celebrated the 150th anniversary of the rebellion of 1857 with special events and ceremonies.

▼ **INTERPRETATION C** An extract from the official website of the Indian government, created in 2005 (and updated in 2014) to celebrate the 'Indian Freedom Struggle'.

'The Hindus, Muslims and Sikhs and all other brave sons of India fought shoulder to shoulder to throw out the British.'

Over to You

1 What was a Sepoy?

2 List the causes of the 1857 rebellion. Try to divide them into 'short-term' and 'long-term'.

3 Look at **Interpretation B**. Why do you think the punishments were so brutal?

4 How did the British change the way India was governed as a result of the events of 1857–1858?

5 a Why do you think British politicians at the time called the events of 1857 the 'Indian Mutiny'?

   b Why do you think Indians today call the same event the 'First War of Independence'?

Consequences

1 Explain two consequences of the Indian Mutiny/Indian War of Independence of 1857–1858.

India was the richest and one of the largest of all the countries in Britain's empire. In the 1850s a viceroy, appointed by the British, was put directly in charge of the country and ran it on behalf of Queen Victoria. The Queen even gave herself an extra title and started calling herself 'Empress of India' as well as 'Queen of Great Britain and Ireland'. India was a colony that many British people treasured most – even calling it 'the jewel in the crown'. What was it like for Indians at the time of the British rule? And what was it like for Britons living there, and at home?

Objectives

- Identify a variety of viewpoints on the British takeover of India.

Study the following sources and interpretations carefully: they give a fascinating range of insights into British rule in India.

Fact ✓

The term 'British Raj' was used to describe the period of British rule in India between 1858 and 1947. The word 'raj' is Hindi for 'rule'.

▼ **SOURCE A** A drawing by English artist E. K. Johnson in 1881. Many Britons living in India enjoyed a lifestyle that was far more luxurious than the one they had at home.

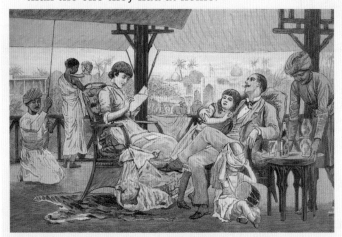

▼ **INTERPRETATION C** Adapted from *Pax Britannica* by historian Jan Morris (1968).

'Ceylon [once a part of India, but now Sri Lanka] was united under British rule in 1815. Over the next 80 years the British built 2300 miles [3700 km] of road and 2900 miles [4700 km] of railway in India. The land used for farming increased from 400,000 acres [160,000 ha] to 3.2 million acres [1.3 million ha], the schools from 170 to 2900, the hospitals from 0 to 65.'

▼ **SOURCE B** The British built thousands of kilometres of railway over India. This railway station was built in Bombay (now Mumbai) in 1897. It was known as Victoria Station until 1996, when it was renamed after a seventeenth-century Hindu king, Chhatrapati Shivaji.

▶ **SOURCE D** George Curzon (pictured with his wife after a hunting expedition in 1905) was Viceroy of India from 1898 to 1905. He is remembered negatively by some for dividing up Hindu and Muslim areas and angering locals, but positively by others for building schools, setting up a national irrigation system to help relieve famine, and rebuilding many old Indian buildings. It was Curzon who restored the Taj Mahal after it had started to decay.

▼ **INTERPRETATION E** A quote from the first Prime Minister of India, Jawaharlal Nehru, in conversation with a leading politician in the British government, Lord Swinton, in *c.*1955.

'After every other Viceroy has been forgotten, Curzon will be remembered because he restored all that was beautiful in India.'

▼ **SOURCE F** Adapted from an essay written in the late 1800s by Florence Nightingale, the famous British nurse, about British attitudes towards Indian famines. There were several famines in the late 1800s and the British, including Curzon, were often accused of not doing enough to help. A famine in 1899–1900 killed up to 6 million Indians.

'We do not care enough to stop them dying slow and terrible deaths from things we could easily stop. We have taken their land, and we rule it, for our good, not theirs.'

Meanwhile...

British control of India made a huge impact on Britain itself. British factories used cotton brought in from India – and Indian goods were sold to other countries. This created many jobs and vast fortunes were made by British traders, businesspeople and factory owners.

Changing a nation

The issue of British control and influence in India has always been controversial and has often been interpreted differently. Some argue that India benefited from British influence in some ways. By 1900, the British had built thousands of kilometres of roads, as well as many schools, hospitals, factories and railways. They also introduced a new legal system and helped settle ancient feuds between rival areas and regions… whether the Indians wanted these things or not!

However, it has been argued that the roads and railways were only built to allow British traders to move their goods more quickly. British customs were forced on the people and local traditions, culture and religions tended to be ignored. Indian workers were often exploited, the county's raw materials were taken back to Britain, and native lands were seized. If there was ever any resistance, the British Army usually came down very hard on the rebels.

▼ **SOURCE G** Written by Mohandas K. Gandhi in *Indian Home Rule* (1910).

'India has become impoverished [poor] by their [Britain's] government. They take away our money from year to year. The most important jobs are reserved for themselves. We are kept in a state of slavery. They behave insolently [insultingly] towards us and disregard our feelings…'

Later on... 1947

By the late 1800s, many Indians started to believe that India should be free from British control. Mohandas K. Gandhi (1869–1948) was a famous Indian political leader who inspired Indians to be proud of their country and to resist British rule without using violence. India eventually became independent of Britain in 1947.

Over to You

1 Write a sentence or two explaining the terms:
   a Empress of India
   b British Raj.

2 Make two lists, one of all the positive things that British rule brought to India and one of all the negative things about British rule. For each positive and negative thing, write where you got your information from.

3 'It is not clear cut whether British rule in India was a good thing or a bad thing.' Discuss this statement with a partner or as a group. What issues do you face when thinking about whether you agree or disagree with the statement?

Interpretation Analysis

1 Study **Interpretation E**. Who is Nehru?

2 Give two things you can infer about Nehru's opinion of British rule in India. Hint: What point do you think Nehru was making about many of the viceroys?

3 Suggest one reason why the author of **Interpretation E** might have this view about Curzon.

Quick Knowledge Quiz

Choose the correct answer from the three options:

1   Which of these terms correctly defines 'a collection of areas of land (or even countries) that are ruled over and controlled by one leading or "mother" country'?

   a   a colony

   b   an empire

   c   a viceroy

2   Which three religions originated in India?

   a   Hinduism, Buddhism and Sikhism

   b   Hinduism, Christianity and Islam

   c   Judaism, Hinduism and Buddhism

3   Who ruled much of India between the early sixteenth century and the mid-nineteenth century?

   a   the Crusaders

   b   the British

   c   the Mughals

4   Shah Jahan, an Indian emperor who reigned from 1628 to 1658, built which beautiful building in memory of his wife?

   a   Victoria Station, Mumbai

   b   the Taj Mahal

   c   the Golden Temple

5   Which Portuguese explorer discovered how to get to India from Europe by sea in 1497?

   a   Vasco da Gama

   b   Christopher Columbus

   c   George Nathaniel Curzon

6   What was the name of the British trading company that first set up trading posts in India in the 1600s?

   a   East India Company

   b   West India Company

   c   Indian Trade Company

7   Which 1757 battle saw the British defeat a much larger Indian army and expand more and more into India?

   a   Battle of Waterloo

   b   Battle of Madras

   c   Battle of Plassey

8   An Indian soldier working in the British army was known by what title?

   a   Sepoy

   b   Viceroy

   c   Sapper

9   The Indian Mutiny/First War of Independence began in which year?

   a   1757

   b   1816

   c   1857

10   What was the term used to describe the period of British rule in India between 1858 and 1947?

   a   British Raj

   b   Pax Britannica

   c   Hope and Glory

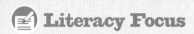

Literacy Focus

Writing in detail

1 Look at the paragraph below. It is a very basic answer to the question:

'Describe what India was like in the 1500s, before Europeans arrived.'

> Give examples of these natural resources. How might these resources affect India?

> Can you add detail about these kingdoms? Add detail about the Hindu princes, the Mughal emperors, conflict and peace.

> India was a large country that had many natural resources. The people who lived there followed different religions. India was divided into kingdoms.

> Over the centuries, what has flourished in India? Think about India's history – science, technology, engineering etc.

> Which religions were followed? Remember, India is the birthplace of three of the world's major religions.

The answer does not contain many specific, factual details. Rewrite the paragraph to include more detail – adding names, examples and facts where possible. It might be a good idea to re-read pages 204–205 before you start this task.

Defining key words and terms

As a historian, it is important that you can quickly recognise and define key terms and words. You should also be able to describe them at length.

1 Complete the sentences below with an accurate term.

    a Some of the most common goods traded with India by the Europeans were…

    b The British trading stations in India were all run by the…

    c The first British trading station set up by the East India Company was in 1612 in…

    d In 1757, Clive of India defeated a combined Indian and French force at the Battle of…

2 Write two definitions for each of the following words, terms, events and people:

    a For the first one, use no more than ten words.

    b The second definition can be more detailed, using up to 30 words.

    The first one has been done for you:

- British Empire

    a *Land Britain controlled around the world (6 words)*

    b *The land or even countries that were ruled over and controlled by Britain – the 'mother' country. Examples include Australia, New Zealand and India. (24 words)*

- colony
- Empress of India
- Raj
- Battle of Plassey
- viceroy
- Indian Mutiny
- Sepoy

Historians study different kinds of evidence to help them understand the past:

Source: This is evidence from the period you are studying. Sources provide information historians need to create 'interpretations'.

Interpretation: This is evidence that is created much later than the period you are studying. Interpretations are produced by people with a particular opinion about an event in the past. For example, a historian could write an interpretation to share his or her view about a particular moment in history. Or a person (non-historian) might paint a picture, make a movie or write a story that shows a particular viewpoint after the events have happened.

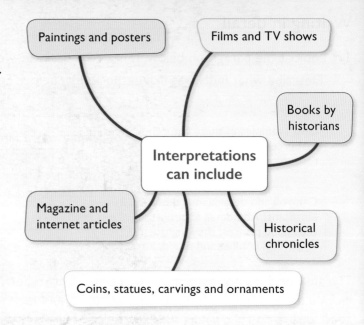

Paintings and posters

Films and TV shows

Books by historians

Interpretations can include

Magazine and internet articles

Historical chronicles

Coins, statues, carvings and ornaments

Comparing interpretations

When analysing different interpretations, a good historian should firstly work out what is being said, or what message the person who created the interpretation is trying to get across, before comparing the different interpretations.

Here is one way to compare two interpretations.

1 **What is the main difference?** For each interpretation, think about the **content** and understand what the person is saying and/or showing. Then, **compare** them: find the ways in which the content is different.

2 **Suggest why they give different views:** Can you provide a reason *why* the two people who made the interpretations might have different opinions about the topic?

3 **Judge how far you agree.** This is about how much (or to what extent) you agree with an interpretation. You should use information from both interpretations and your own knowledge to help you judge and explain your answer.

TIP: You could approach this question in different ways – you could think about:
- what the interpretations focus on
- what you know already about the topic
- the writers' backgrounds. Look at the captions: what do they tell you about why the two interpretations might show different opinions?

TIP: You could pick one of the phrases below that you think fits best with your judgement of how much you agree with the opinion in the interpretation:

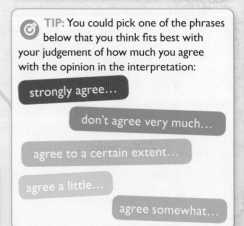

strongly agree...

don't agree very much...

agree to a certain extent...

agree a little...

agree somewhat...

TIP: It's ok if you agree with one interpretation more than the other – just make sure that you explain why.

TIP: What do you know about the topic – in this case, about the impact of British control on India? Look at your notes or pages 206–211 to help you.

Imagine you have been asked:

Key Words   interpretation

1   Interpretations **A** and **B** give different views on the impact of the British Empire on India. What is the main difference between the views?

2   Suggest one reason the interpretations give different views about the impact of British Empire on India.

3   How far do you agree with **Interpretation A** about the impact of the British Empire on India? Explain your answer, using both interpretations and your own knowledge of the historical context.

TIP: When answering assessment questions, especially the ones worth lots of marks, it is important to think carefully about spelling, punctuation and grammar.

▼ **INTERPRETATION A** Adapted from a book called *The Case for India* written by Will Durant, an American historian/philosopher, while on a visit to India in 1931. On his travels, he was shocked by the devastating poverty he saw which he thought was a result of British involvement in India. Later, he supported the idea that India should be free of British rule and become an independent nation.

'The building of 30,000 miles (48,000 km) of railways could have brought wealth to India. But these railways were built not for India but for the British themselves; for the British army and British trade. Trade via the sea is dominated by the British even more than on land. The Indians are not allowed to organize sea trade of their own; all Indian goods must be carried in British ships… I have seen a great people starving to death before my eyes, and I am convinced that this is not due to over-population, but to the most criminal exploitation of one nation by another in all recorded history. Britain has year by year been bleeding India to the point of death.'

You should always read about the writer carefully. Here, the writer (Will Durant) has clearly been affected by what he has seen in India – and this is reflected in what he has written.

Different views: Here, Durant is clear about why he thinks the British built so many miles of railway.

Content: Durant is talking about the starvation he has seen. Does this back up what you have learned? Were there famines in India?

Judge: Durant clearly thinks that the British have used India to get what they want. This is where you might agree – or disagree.

▼ **INTERPRETATION B** Adapted from a 2003 online article by Niall Ferguson called 'Why we ruled the world'. Ferguson is a British historian who is known for his views in defence of the British empire.

Maps showing the British Empire hung in schools all over the country. But the extent of Britain's empire could be seen not only in the world's atlases. Britain was also the world's banker, investing immense sums around the world... the fact remains that no organisation in history did more to promote trade than the British Empire. And no organisation did more to promote fair systems of law, order and government around the world. For much (though certainly not all) of its history, the British Empire made sure that the colonies were ruled fairly. There therefore seems a possible argument that empire enhanced global welfare – in other words, it was a Good Thing.

Information about the writer often helps you understand why they might have the opinions they have!

Content: Are Ferguson's views of the British Empire positive or negative?

Different views: What impression of the empire do you get from what Ferguson has written here?

Different views: In what ways is this view of the empire different to Interpretation A?

11 Assessment: Interpretation analysis

Your challenge now is to answer this question about analysing interpretations:

> 1 **Interpretations C** and **D** give different views on the impact of British control of India. What is the main difference between the views?
>
> 2 Suggest one reason **Interpretations C** and **D** give different views about the impact of British control of the British Empire.
>
> 3 How far do you agree with **Interpretation C** about the impact of British control of the British Empire? Explain your answer, using both interpretations and your own knowledge of the historical context. **(20)**

TIP: In your answer, you should include details from both interpretations.

TIP: It is important to read the caption to find out more about the author. Think why Attlee might say positive things about the British government.

▼ **INTERPRETATION C** Clement Attlee, British Prime Minister at the time, in a speech in the House of Commons in relation to the independence of India (10 July 1947). (Adapted).

'The history of our connection in India begins with the East India Company. In the earlier days we were concerned mainly with trade providing opportunities for making fortunes. But, as time went on, there was an increasing appreciation of the responsibility which fell to the British. The British government in India became more deeply concerned with the well-being of the people of India, who are divided by race, language and religion. Looking back, we may well be proud of what the British have done in India. There have, of course, been failures, but our rule in India will stand comparison with that of any other nation which has been charged with the ruling of a people so different from themselves.'

TIP: Does this back up what you know about the early relationship between India and Britain?

TIP: How does he describe the way Britain treated India? Is he being mainly supportive – or not?

▼ **INTERPRETATION D** Adapted from an article published in a British newspaper in 2017 called *'But what about the railways ...?' The myth of Britain's gifts to India*, written by Shashi Tharoor, an Indian politician and writer. Tharoor has written many books on India and its history.

TIP: Think why Tharoor might have these opinions.

The British ran government, tax collection, and law and order. Indians were excluded from all of these... The death of an Indian at British hands was always an accident, but any crime by an Indian against a British person was always dealt with severely... The construction of the Indian Railways is often pointed out as a benefit of British rule, but the railways were created for Britain's benefit. British investors made huge amounts of money when the railways were built, and they were used mainly to transport Indian resources – coal, cotton and so on – to ports for the British to ship home to use in their factories.

British rule exploited India and meant ruin to millions, ending lifestyles that had flourished for many years. In 1600, when the East India Company was established, Britain was producing just 1.8% of all the world's goods and services [known as GDP], while India was generating some 23%. By 1940, after nearly two centuries of British rule, Britain accounted for nearly 10% of world GDP, while India had been reduced to a poor "third-world" country.

The India the British entered was a thriving society: that was why the East India Company was interested in it in the first place. Far from being backward, pre-colonial India exported high quality manufactured goods much sought after by Britain's fashionable society.'

TIP: How does he describe the way Britain treated India? Is he mainly being critical – or not?

TIP: Think how this interpretation differs from **Interpretation C**.

The steps and sentence starters below will help you structure your answer.

1 **What is the main difference?** For each interpretation, think about the **content** and try to understand what the person is saying and/or showing. Then, **compare** them: find the ways in which the content is different.

> A main difference is that Interpretation C... (2)
>
> However, in Interpretation D... (2)

TIP: You can quote the interpretation if you like, but make sure you use your own words as well to explain.

2 **Suggest why they give different views.** Can you suggest a reason *why* the two people who made the interpretations might have different opinions about the topic?

> One reason the authors have different views is...
> The writer of Interpretation C... (2)
>
> However, the writer of Interpretation D... (2)

3 **Judge how far you agree:** You should use information from both interpretations and your own knowledge to help you judge and explain your answer.

TIP: What do you know about the topic – in this case, about the impact of British control on the British Empire? Look at your notes/pages 206–211 to help you.

> Interpretation C says that... I (agree/don't agree) with this opinion about the impact of British control in India, because... (3)
>
> Interpretation D offers a different view of this when it says... (2)
>
> Interpretation C also says that... I (agree/don't agree) with this opinion about the impact of British control in India, because... (3)
>
> Interpretation D offers a different view of this when it says... (2)
>
> To conclude... (2)

TIP: What do you know from what you have studied about this? Does the interpretation back up what you know, or not? You are using your own knowledge here.

TIP: This is where you sum up 'how far' you agree. Do you agree 'fully' or 'partly' for example. Explain why you think this.

1848: How close was a British revolution?

On 10 April 1848, a meeting was planned at Kennington Common, London. Half a million people were expected to attend, and they all wanted big changes to the way the country was ruled. There had already been revolutions in Paris, Berlin and other major European cities – and the government was worried that the same might happen in Britain. So what happened? What changes did people want? And just how close was a British revolution in 1848?

Objectives

- Recall how and why people fought for improved rights.
- Judge how successful they were.
- Examine events such as the Swing Riots, the Peterloo Massacre and the Kennington Common meeting.

Protest and violence

When people are unhappy with their lives, they often join together to **protest**. This might mean meeting in large numbers and listening to speeches and new ideas, or marching and demanding that the government improve their lives. Sometimes people protest peacefully, but sometimes they turn to violence (you might remember the Peasants' Revolt of 1381).

There were lots of issues that angered ordinary people in the early 1800s – high food prices, unemployment, poor working conditions and voting rights, for example. These issues often became the focus of violent protests or reactions. In fact, between 1790 and 1840, there were around 700 large **riots** in Britain.

St Peter's Field massacre

In August 1819, a large crowd gathered at St Peter's Field in Manchester. At this time, only a small number of wealthy men could vote in elections and many ordinary people, who weren't allowed to vote, thought this was unfair. They knew that if they could vote, the politicians might try to sort out issues like high food prices and poor working conditions. So a huge meeting was planned and thousands of people attended. Whole families came, some carrying flags saying 'Votes for all'. But local magistrates sent in soldiers on horseback to stop the meeting, saying it was against the law. Armed with swords, they rode into the crowd. Eleven people were killed and over 400 injured.

Impact of the massacre

The events at St Peter's Field shocked the nation. People started to call it the Peterloo Massacre, a sarcastic reference to the famous Battle of Waterloo when the British defeated the French in 1815. The government took steps to restrict people meeting. New laws were introduced (known as the Six Acts) that banned meetings of over 50 people, tightened up gun laws, and gave courts more powers to search homes and put people on trial without a jury.

▼ **SOURCE A** An 1819 cartoon by political cartoonist George Cruikshank, showing the Peterloo massacre. The soldiers are shown as butchers armed with axes attacking women and children. One soldier is shown saying 'Chop 'em down my brave boys…'

▼ **INTERPRETATION B** Adapted from a 2007 letter written to the *Guardian* newspaper by the historian Michael Bush.

'The massacre was carried out on the authority of the town council. And the event - in showing how crowds could be controlled by small numbers of troops - delayed the establishment of democracy by over 50 years. It was a humiliating defeat for the power of the people and one from which it had great difficulty in making a recovery.'

The Luddites

A few years earlier, in 1811, groups of workers in the north went into factories and smashed up the new machinery that was taking over people's jobs. They were supposedly led by Ned Ludd, who lived secretly in Sherwood Forest, Nottingham – but no one ever found him! This is why they were called the 'Luddites'. The gangs caused lots of damage, so in 1812, the government made machine-smashing a crime punishable by death.

▼ **C** The relationship between the price of corn (a raw ingredient of bread) per quarter (an old type of measurement) and the occurrence of riots in Britain in the early 1800s.

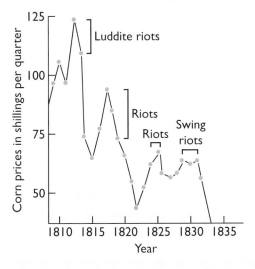

The Swing Rioters

In the 1830s, workers in the countryside attacked new farm machines because they were being used to do their work. Fields were set on fire, farmhouses burned and barns smashed up. They were called the 'Swing Rioters' because they said they were led by Captain Swing – but no one ever found him either!

Earlier on... 1789

The French Revolution of 1789 had spread ideas of equal rights – as a result, people in Britain with no right to vote began to protest.

Over to You

1 What did the Luddites and Swing Rioters have in common and how were they different?

2   Look at **Chart C**. What does this source tell us about one of the reasons for protest in the 1800s?

3 Look at **Source A**. Do you think the cartoonist supported the protesters or the soldiers? Explain your answer.

Reasons for protest

The right to vote in elections had been one of the biggest issues driving the protests in the 1800s. So what was wrong with the British voting system at this time? Look at the cartoons to find out more.

> There are around 16 million people in Britain, and only about 500,000 can vote. And they're all rich property owners!

> I live in Manchester – and Manchester doesn't even have any politicians to represent us in Parliament. Nor has Birmingham or Sheffield.

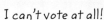

> Some tiny villages have MPs. These are called 'rotten boroughs'. Appleby, a small village in Cumbria, has one voter, yet they still have an MP! How ridiculous is that, when huge towns like Manchester have no MPs?

> I can't vote at all!

Interpretation Analysis ⭐

1 Look at **Interpretation B**. In your own words, what is the author saying about the massacre?

2 Suggest one reason why the author might feel the massacre was a 'humiliating defeat' for ordinary people.

Reform at last

By 1830, thousands of people had been protesting about the British voting system for many years. These people saw change as a chance for a better life. But politicians worried that a protest might turn into a large riot, and that the rioters might become strong enough to take over the country by force. These MPs realised that reform was needed and introduced a new system of voting (see **D**).

▼ **SOURCE D** Adapted from the main points of the first Reform Act.

The Reform Act, 1832
- More people allowed to vote – increase in voters from 450,000 to 800,000
- Some big towns like Manchester and Birmingham given MPs for the first time
- Some of the old 'rotten boroughs' removed

Most people were bitterly disappointed with the new voting laws, because they still didn't have the vote! You still had to own property to vote, so only one in five men could vote, and no women.

In 1836, a new campaign group was formed. Most members simply wanted more change – but others wanted to take over the country and change it by force. They issued a list of six things they wanted (see **E**). The list was called the 'People's Charter' – so the group was known as the **Chartists**. The government soon saw the Chartists as a major threat.

How did the Chartists try to change things?

The Chartists knew that trying to get Parliament to change the voting laws was going to be difficult. So they held huge meetings in big cities such as Birmingham and Leeds to show the government that a vast number of people agreed with them. In 1839, they drew up a **petition**, with over a million signatures (it was nearly 5km long!) of those who supported their ideas. It was sent to Parliament – but it was rejected. In Newport, South Wales, there were even violent clashes between Chartists and government soldiers which resulted in the deaths of 20 Chartists.

In 1842, another petition was organised, this time containing three million signatures. Yet again, Parliament ignored it. Some Chartist leaders started to talk about taking the country over and forcing the changes.

▼ **SOURCE E** Adapted from the list of what the Chartists wanted. Votes for women did not make it onto the list.

The six points of the People's Charter
1 Every man of 21 years of age or over should be allowed to vote.
2 Voting should be done in secret.
3 Anyone should be allowed to become an MP, not only those who own property.
4 MPs should be paid and then ordinary people can afford to become MPs.
5 Voting districts (constituencies) should have an equal number of voters.
6 There should be an election every year.

Fact ✓

Women played an active role in the Chartist movement too – the Birmingham Charter Association, for example, had over 3000 female members – and around one third of those who signed the Chartist petitions were women.

One more try

In 1848, a third petition was organised with six million signatures! The Chartists planned a massive meeting of over half a million people on Kennington Common, London, before marching to Parliament. The government was worried – was this the start of a revolution? Plans were drawn up to defend London and Queen Victoria was moved to safety. But the meeting was a flop. It rained heavily and only around 20,000 Chartists turned up.

The petition turned out to be a flop too. It was found to contain just over two million names, many of them fakes. Little was heard of the Chartists again. They had failed – or had they?

▼ **SOURCE F** A rare photograph of the Chartist meeting on Kennington Common, April 1848.

A success story?

For a few days in 1848, the government had feared the Chartists, who had shown that working people were powerful (and potentially threatening) if they came together. While a proper revolution didn't happen, the Chartists did draw attention to the problems of working-class people and showed that there were national issues that politicians must deal with. In fact, of their six original demands, all but one (Point 6) later became law.

Power to the people

The changes to voting continued after the Chartist movement. The Second Reform Act (1867) gave the vote to every man who owned a house (one in three men), and the Third Reform Act (1884) gave even more working people the vote. In 1872, the Ballot Act said that men could vote by putting their ballot paper in a ballot box. This stopped people bribing and bullying voters. Many more changes followed.

▼ **G** Reforms to Britain's voting system. Campaigns for women to be allowed to vote started in the 1860s, but it took until 1928 for all adults to get equal voting rights.

Electoral reforms

1832: First Reform Act
1858: Any man over 21 allowed to become an MP, whether they owned property or not.
1867: Second Reform Act (one man in three could now vote).
1872: Ballot Act (voting now done in secret).
1884: Third Reform Act (two out of every three men could now vote).
1885: Voting districts (constituencies) to have equal numbers of voters.
1911: MPs paid.
1918: All men over 21 and many women over 30 could vote.
1928: Vote for everyone over 21.
1969: Vote for everyone over 18.

Key Words

Chartist   petition

▼ **INTERPRETATION H**
Historian Bea Stimpson, writing in *The World of Empire, Industry and Trade* (2000).

'Despite internal squabbles and the unfortunate ending, [Chartism] did give the working classes a sense of solidarity [togetherness] and purpose. This had been the first nationwide movement of working class protest, and people had become more politically educated.'

Over to You

1 Why do you think ordinary people were so keen to get the vote in the early 1800s?

2 a Make a list of things that were wrong or unfair about the voting system before 1832.

 b Some people call the first Reform Act (1832) a success. Others call it a failure. Why do you think there are two views about it?

3 a Who were the Chartists?

 b Write a sentence or two to support the following statements. Can you use **Interpretation H** to help you?

 • 'The Chartists were a short-term failure.'

 • 'In the long term, the Chartist movement was important in the history of British democracy.'

Revolution, Industry and Empire: Britain 1558–1901   **221**

Was this an age of improvement for women?

In 1832, Joseph Thomson tried to sell his wife at auction for 50 shillings (£2.50). Unbelievably, he managed to sell her for 20 shillings (£1.00) and a dog! Today, we are shocked by his actions… but at the time this was viewed by many as an acceptable thing to do. Mr Thomson could treat his wife as his property, and do whatever he wanted with her. In today's world, where men and women have equal rights by law, it is hard to imagine women's place in society at that time. When did things start to change?

Objectives

- Assess the position of women in the eighteenth and nineteenth centuries.
- Evaluate the importance of the Match Girls' Strike of 1888.

▼ **SOURCE A** Joseph Thomson speaking at an auction in Carlisle in 1832 (adapted).

'Gentlemen, I offer my wife, Mary Anne Thomson, whom I mean to sell to the highest bidder. It is her wish as well as mine to part forever. She has been a snake to me. I took her for my comfort but she has turned into a curse, a tormentor and a daily devil. However, she has a bright and sunny side. She can read novels, milk cows, make butter and shout at our maid. She cannot make rum, gin or whisky, but she is a good judge from long experience in tasting them.'

▼ **INTERPRETATION B** Historian J. F. Aylett writing in *The Suffragettes and After* (1988).

'[In 1800], once married, her husband owned her… that was the law of the land. A wife's duty was to obey her husband. If she did not, he could beat her. A wife's duty was to please her husband; if she did not he might take a mistress. Either way, there was almost nothing she could do about it. An Act of Parliament was necessary to end a marriage. It could cost £2000 and only two women ever did it. It was quite different for the man. He could spend all "her" money and she could not stop him. If he got into debt, her possessions could be taken to pay off the debts… even her clothes!'

A man's world?

In the nineteenth century, women from all classes of British society, both rich and poor, depended on men. While poorer women's lives were harder (they had to work for a start), all women were second-class citizens with few rights. It was difficult for women to change this because the country was controlled by men. All MPs were men, only men could vote, and men had all the powerful jobs.

Campaigning women

Many women did not accept their position in society. Writer Caroline Norton, for example, who wanted to divorce her cruel husband in the 1830s, began a campaign to allow her to do this. Several politicians helped her and their efforts led to the Custody of Infants Act of 1839 (see **C**). Norton, along with activist Barbara Bodichon, were influential in the passing of the Marriage and Divorce Act of 1857. Women were also active members of the Chartist movement (see pages 220–221), and middle-class women such as Josephine Butler and Emily Davies campaigned for women's voting rights and better educational opportunities.

Gradually, changes began to happen. In 1847, women could no longer work more than ten hours a day in a factory. Women such as Frances Buss and Dorothea Beale opened girls' schools and campaigned for girls to have as good an education as boys. As more women became educated, they got jobs as typists, nurses, teachers and shop assistants. By 1900, the position of women had improved, but one of the biggest issues still remained – women still couldn't vote or become MPs. This issue would not change until the twentieth century.

▼ **C** Some of the key legal rights gained by women in the 1800s.

1839	If a man left his wife she was allowed to keep all the children under the age of seven.
1849	Bedford College became the first higher education college for women. It became part of the University of London in 1900.
1857	A wife could divorce a husband who was cruel or had left her, but only if he had also cheated on her. Women who divorced their husbands gained some legal rights to property.
1870	A wife who earned money was allowed to keep it for herself, rather than giving it to her husband. Girls between five and thirteen were given the same right to go to school as boys.
1876	Women could go to medical schools.
1882	A wife could own property and do what she liked with it.
1886	A husband would have to support his wife if he left her.
1894	All women could now vote in local council elections.

▼ **SOURCE D** An 1867 cartoon titled 'Success in Life: Role reversal and the modern professional woman'. The cartoon is referring to Elizabeth Garrett Anderson, who had recently become the first woman in Britain to qualify as a doctor. Can you see the young boy holding a doll; the girl riding a horse; the husband pouring tea for his wife?

Fact ✓

In 1865, Elizabeth Garrett Anderson became the first woman in Britain to qualify as a doctor – she was also the country's first female mayor and magistrate.

Over to You ▂▃▅

1 Read **Source A**.
   a What words does Joseph Thomson use to insult his wife?
   b What does he say are her good points?
   c What shocks you about this source?

2 a Explain what the word 'sexist' means today.
   b Make a list of sexist laws, rules and regulations that were in force in Britain in the early 1800s.
   c Why do you think these laws were in force?

3 Describe the role played in the changes to women's rights and their position in society by two of the following:
   • Caroline Norton   • Josephine Butler
   • Barbara Bodichon   • Emily Davies
   • Frances Buss   • Dorothea Beale

4 Look at **Source D**.
   a Who was Elizabeth Garrett Anderson?
   b What is meant by the term 'role reversal?
   c The cartoon is mocking Elizabeth Garrett Anderson's achievement. How do you know?

Change

1 Look at **Chart C**. Write down three changes to women's rights in the 1800s.

2 In what ways did the lives of women change in the 1800s?

Case study: The match girls

Not everyone was happy about women making a stand against unfair and sexist treatment. The case of the match girls shows this. Look at the four characters below. Then, read about the Match Girls' Strike in 1888 and try to imagine what each of the characters might feel about this event.

A match girl, who worked in the Bryant & May factory

A dockworker who worked on London's docks loading and unloading ships

A politician

Mr William Bryant, one of the owners of the Bryant & May factory

Who were the match girls?

In the 1800s, one of the largest producers of matches was the Bryant & May factory in London – and the vast majority of workers were women. At that time, the bit of a match that burst into flame was made from white phosphorus, which is an explosive – and poisonous – chemical. The fumes from white phosphorus could rot the teeth and cause them to drop out after a few months. The disease could spread to the jawbone too, and rot it away. Sometimes an infected person's jaw had to be completely removed, and in some cases the poison caused death.

More side effects

About 1400 match girls worked in the Bryant & May factory and many had nasty skin diseases. The factory didn't have sinks for workers to wash their hands, so the phosphorus burnt their skin and got into the food they ate. Some workers lost their hair and others shone in the dark because phosphorus is luminous. And they only earned a low weekly wage, which was reduced even further by the amount of fines the workers had to pay for breaking ridiculous rules. For example, a worker could be fined for simply leaving a match on a bench.

▼ **SOURCE E** A drawing of match making at the Bryant & May factory in East London, about 1880.

'White slavery'

In 1888, a women's rights campaigner and journalist, Annie Besant, interviewed some of the women in the factory. She published what she found out in an article called 'White Slavery in London'. As you'd expect, the factory owners weren't happy. They sacked the women who spoke to Besant and forced the others to sign a document saying that the conditions in the factory were good. One woman who refused to sign was sacked.

▶ **SOURCE F**
A photograph of Annie Besant, taken in 1889. Besant supported a number of workers' demonstrations for better working conditions, campaigned for better women's rights, and supported the idea of India, one of Britain's colonies, being allowed to rule itself.

A strike in a match factory

Besant helped the workers to organise a **strike**. She also held public meetings and raised money to give to the striking women. Many newspapers took the women's side and within two weeks the women had been promised better pay and conditions and an end to the numerous fines, so they went back to work.

▼ **SOURCE G** Factory workers on strike outside the Bryant & May factory (July 1888). Besant got them lots of publicity and encouraged them to walk around the West End of London (a richer area).

More strikes

The Match Girls' Strike was the first time in Britain that a group of factory workers succeeded in striking for better working conditions and pay. It inspired other workers across the country. A year later, in 1889, the London dockworkers, who earned even less than the match girls, went on strike. And after a long and bitter strike, they got a pay rise too!

▼ **INTERPRETATION H** Adapted from *Men, Movements and Myself* (1936), by Henry Snell, a politician and campaigner. Here, he is writing about the Match Girls' Strike.

'These courageous girls had neither funds nor leaders, and they appealed to Mrs Besant to advise and lead them. It was a wise and most excellent inspiration. Money was quickly subscribed for their support and, within a fortnight, the employers agreed to their demands. The number affected was quite small, but the match girls' strike had an influence upon the minds of the workers which entitles it to be regarded as one of the most important events in the history of workers' rights in any country.'

Key Words   strike

▼ **INTERPRETATION I** From historian J. F. Aylett in *In Search of History* (1985).

'In less than a fortnight, the girls were promised better conditions. The fines were ended and box-fillers given a nine per cent pay rise. It was a milestone in union history and other victories soon followed. In 1889, the gas workers demanded – and got – an eight-hour day. Later that year, the London dockers went on strike… they also won.'

Over to You

1 What is white phosphorus?

2 Describe the effects of white phosphorus poisoning.

3 a Why do you think Annie Besant used the title 'White Slavery in London' for her article about the match girls?

   b Can you suggest why it was hard for unskilled workers, like the match girls, to go on strike?

   c Explain the part played by Besant in the improvement of conditions for the match girls.

4 Look at the four characters on page 224. For each one, write down one or two things that they might feel about:
   • the Bryant & May factory
   • Annie Besant
   • the results of the strike.

5   Design a campaign poster in support of the striking match girls. Include as many facts about the factory conditions as you can, and what needs to be done. Include one or two images and a headline.

Interpretation Analysis ⭐

1 Study **Interpretations H** and **I**. They give slightly different views on the Match Girls' Strike and its impact on workers' rights. What is the main similarity between the two views?

2 What is the main difference between the views?

In 1841, a group of boys told an investigation into people's lives that they'd never heard of London, and thought the Queen's name was Albert! Few had heard of Jesus – 'Does 'e work down our pit?' asked one young miner. These boys were being serious, and they could not read, write or do simple sums. Something had to change. So what did the government do?

Objectives

- Describe what life was like in a Victorian schoolroom.
- Explain how and why schools changed in the 1800s.

Time for school

In the early 1800s, there were no government-run schools. Nor were there any laws that said children had to go to school. Sons of wealthy parents were sent to public (fee-paying) schools to learn Latin, Greek, Literature, History, Geography, Science and Sport. Daughters of rich parents were mostly educated at home. It was assumed that girls would get married and have lots of children – so they learned to play the piano and sing in order to entertain their husbands' guests.

For children from poorer families, about six children in ten (both boys *and* girls) were getting some very basic teaching. The Factory Act of 1833, for example, said that children who worked in factories should get two hours of education a day – but this was done very badly (or not at all) in many factories. Instead, some youngsters went to a **dame school** for an hour or more a week. Run by a local woman in her front room, a child might learn to count and say the alphabet in return for a few pennies. If this was too expensive, and for many it was, parents could send their children to a **ragged school**. First set up in 1844 for orphans and very poor children, these places often had 300 students in one room with one teacher! Sometimes the teacher would only teach the older pupils in the room, who would then go off and teach the younger or weaker pupils. However, many children stayed away from school altogether – they were far too busy working for money in factories.

Time for change

By the late 1860s, the government saw that Britain needed more educated people. Engineers and scientists were needed to build and design machines. They had to understand mathematics. Mechanics needed to

read instruction manuals, and secretaries and clerks needed to know how to write letters and calculate prices. Even factory workers had to be able to read notices! So in 1870, the government introduced the Elementary Education Act. This said:

- Schools should be built where there aren't any, paid for by local taxes.

- There should be a school place available for every child aged five to twelve.

- Parents had to pay a small fee, but it was free for the very poor.

Ten years later, in 1880, education from five to ten was made compulsory (required by law). The leaving age rose to 12 in 1889, and in 1891, school became completely free. So what was the new school system like?

Education was designed to equip children for life after school. There was some PE, known as 'drill', and some History and Geography too.

▼ **SOURCE A** This timetable is from a typical day at school in Bristol in 1897. Boys and girls learn different things – the idea then was to prepare boys and girls for what was viewed as their different roles in life.

SCHOOL TIMETABLE

Morning (9am–12 noon)

<u>Boys and Girls together</u>

The three Rs = <u>R</u>eading, <u>W</u>riting and <u>A</u>rithmetic

Afternoon (2pm–5pm)

Boys	Girls
Science, Woodwork and Technical Drawing	Cookery, Needlework and Housework

▼ SOURCE B A photograph of a Victorian schoolroom. Can you see one of the students asleep on the front row?

What were the lessons like?

Students sat at wooden desks in rows, facing a blackboard and a large world map. Some had walked miles to get to the cold, draughty schoolroom. Students copied from the blackboard or repeated things as a whole group. Lessons must have been pretty boring! In Geography, they might list all the countries on the globe or learn the names of railway stations on certain lines.

Teachers were tough – and so were punishments. Leaving school without permission, sulking, answering back, throwing ink and being late were all punishable offences. Hitting students (usually with a long stick, called a cane) was a common punishment. So was wearing a 'dunce's hat' – a pointed hat with the letter D on it that was given to students who couldn't remember things or got poor marks.

What equipment did they use?

Younger children learned to write on slates, using slate pencils. Paper was expensive but slate could be used again and again – students just rubbed out the letters when they'd finished. Older students used paper 'copybooks' and wrote in them with a metal-nibbed wooden pen. They dipped their nibs into ink-pots and scratched the letters onto the page. They had to be careful not to spill any ink!

Later on...

Hitting students with a cane, ruler or slipper as a punishment was eventually banned by the government in 1986.

Key Words

dame school   ragged school

Over to You .ıll

1 Complete the sentences below with an accurate term:
   a A basic school, often run by women in the front room of a house was called a _____ _____.

   b Education for children aged five to ten was made compulsory in _____.

2 Why, in the mid-1800s, did the government feel it was becoming more important to educate children?

3 Compare your timetable with the one from 1897. In what ways are they similar and different?

4 a Look at **Source B**. Make a list of some of the major differences between the classroom in **Source B** and the one you are sitting in.

   b Apart from the classroom, what other major differences are there between Victorian schooling and schooling today? Hint: Think about equipment, punishments and lessons.

Change

1 Why are each of the following dates important in the development of education in Britain?

   | 1833 | 1844 | 1870 |
   | 1880 | 1889 | 1891 |

2 Outline how education changed in Britain during the nineteenth century.

Look at **Source A**. It is a painting from the late 1700s. The patient is in absolute agony – look at his face. He is being held down while the surgeon cuts off his leg. The poor man hasn't been given any painkilling drugs – he is completely awake when the surgeon starts to slice into his skin and saw through his calf. It is highly unlikely that the medical equipment being used has ever been washed either. It will be stained with the dry blood and pus from a previous patient. One well-known surgeon used to sharpen his knives on the sole of his boot before using them. And you know how filthy the streets were! What do you think patients' chances of survival were? Why were conditions so bad? And why have they improved so much since then?

Objectives

- Outline how and why attitudes towards cleanliness changed in the nineteenth century.
- Explain how surgeons won the battle against pain and infection.
- Assess the significance of important surgeons.

▼ **SOURCE A** An English cartoon showing an amputation taking place, by Thomas Rowlandson, published in 1793.

Rowlandson 1793

The enemy within

At the time **Source A** was painted, a patient in a British hospital had two major enemies: the pain during the operation, and infection afterwards. Either could kill you. Only when these two obstacles were dealt with would it be possible to make any real medical progress. In the nineteenth century, doctors started to find the solutions to these problems, and changed the way the sick were cared for forever.

Can I have something for the pain?

For hundreds of years, doctors and surgeons had tried to reduce a patient's pain during surgery. Getting a patient drunk was a common method – and sometimes people inhaled nitrous oxide (or 'laughing gas') to numb the pain a little. But, in 1846, an American dentist called William Morton publicly demonstrated that a patient could be put to sleep for a short time using the fumes from a chemical called **ether**. The patient felt no pain during the operation, and woke up shortly afterwards. This was the first public demonstration of anaesthetics and the idea soon caught on in Britain, among London's surgeons. However, ether irritated patients' eyes, and made them cough and vomit during operations. So, in 1847, a Scottish doctor called James Simpson tried getting patients to inhale the fumes from a chemical named **chloroform** as an alternative. Again, it worked, and had fewer of the nasty side effects of ether. Soon, chloroform became the most common anaesthetic in the country – even Queen Victoria used it in 1853 as a painkiller while giving birth to her son Leopold.

Horrible hospitals

The use of anaesthetic was a great step forward, but it didn't stop people dying from infections after operations. Hospitals were dirty places, where patients were all housed together whether they had a highly contagious fever or a broken arm. The operating theatres were no better. The only thing that was ever cleaned out was the sand box under the operating table, which was used to catch blood during surgery. Doctors and surgeons didn't understand the need for cleanliness because they didn't know that germs caused disease. It would take a few more famous people to solve this problem!

Meanwhile... 1861

Japan's first modern hospital was built in Nagasaki in 1861 by a Dutch navy surgeon, Pompe van Meerdervoort. From the 1600s to mid-1800s, the Dutch had exclusive trading connections with Japan. Books on medical sciences from the West were obtained from the Dutch, then translated into Japanese.

Key Words
ether   chloroform

Earlier on... 1123

The word 'hospital' comes from the Latin word 'hospitale', meaning 'a place for guests'. St Bartholomew's, founded in 1123, is Britain's oldest hospital. Hospitals were originally places for the sick to rest and pray, but by the 1700s, the idea of hospitals using modern methods to cure patients began. Rich people with a desire to do good things donated money to help open such new hospitals, including Guy's in London (1724), Bristol Royal Infirmary (1735) and York County Hospital (1740).

Fact

In the 1840s, a famous London surgeon named Robert Liston amputated a patient's leg in just two and a half minutes. Unfortunately, he worked so fast that he accidentally cut off the patient's testicles!

Over to You

1 a Write a short description of the scene in **Source A**. Use no more than 75 words.

   b Make a list of things in **Source A** that would not happen during an operation today.

2 In your own words, using names and dates, explain how the problem of pain during operations was dealt with in the 1800s.

Source Analysis

1 Explain why the development of anaesthetics did not completely change medical treatment in the 1800s.

2 How useful is **Source A** to a historian studying the development of medical treatment in the 1800s?

The fight against infection

By the end of the 1850s, surgeons were able to perform much safer operations. They could spend longer working on the patients because they were 'under anaesthetic' – there was no danger of them waking up and dying of pain and shock. However, people still died of blood poisoning and nasty infections because surgeons did not understand the importance of keeping things clean. Read **Interpretation B** carefully.

▼ **INTERPRETATION B** Adapted from a book by John Leeson called *Lister as I Knew Him* (1927). Leeson worked with the famous doctor Joseph Lister, and this passage is about a patient who was admitted to the hospital in the 1850s.

'A strong, young farmer came into the hospital and told the surgeon that his girlfriend had made comments about his nose – it was too much to one side; could it be straightened? He had heard of the wonderful things that were done in London hospitals. He was admitted; the septum (bone between the nostrils) was straightened and in five days he was dead. He died of hospital **sepsis**.'

Germ Theory

'Sepsis' is from the Greek word for 'rotten'. At this time, it was common for wounds to go 'rotten', resulting in patients dying of blood poisoning. In fact, the number of patients dying after operations in the 1850s was astonishing – as many as six out of ten. Then, in the 1860s, the French scientist Louis Pasteur made a major breakthrough. Through careful experimentation Pasteur showed that germs caused disease, in his idea called 'Germ Theory'. He went on to say that many of these germs could be killed by heat – and proved it in his laboratory. We still use **pasteurisation** – the heating of food and drink (check your milk carton!) – to kill certain germs today.

Acids and antiseptics

Joseph Lister was one of several British doctors who had been influenced by Pasteur's theories. In 1865, Lister decided to take the theories a step further. He thought that it might be germs that caused so many of his patients to die from sepsis. Lister decided to try to kill these germs with an antiseptic ('anti' means 'against'), in the hope that more of his patients would survive. Lister chose carbolic acid as his antiseptic. Using a pump, a bit like an aerosol can, he sprayed anything that might possibly come into contact with the wound during an operation. Spraying everything, he hoped, would make all the germs die, resulting in fewer patients dying of infection. He was right (see **C**).

▼ **C** The percentage of Lister's patients living and dying before and after the use of antiseptics.

Before antiseptics were used

Date	Number of patients	% that lived	% that died
1864–1866	35	58%	42%

After antiseptics were used

Date	Number of patients	% that lived	% that died
1867–1870	40	84%	16%

▼ **SOURCE D** Lister demonstrating his antiseptic spray in the 1880s. Note the doctor on the left putting the patient 'to sleep' with an anaesthetic.

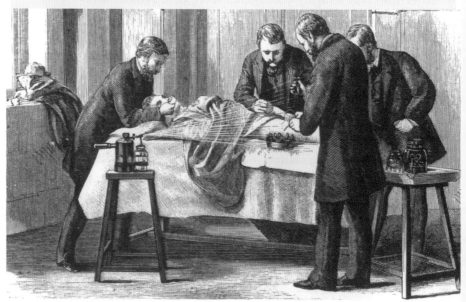

Lister's impact

Lister's (and Pasteur's) findings weren't immediately accepted. These ideas about germs were new – and some people couldn't accept that tiny germs could kill a person. But by the 1880s, doctors and surgeons all over the country were trying antiseptic sprays and other cleaner ways to work. Hospitals waged a war against germs. Walls were scrubbed clean, floors were swept and equipment was **sterilised**. Surgeons started to wear rubber gloves, surgical gowns and face masks during operations (see **E**).

Other key developments

Other important medical developments were taking place around this time. For example, Edward Jenner discovered a way of preventing smallpox, one of Britain's biggest killers, in 1796. His method, known as vaccination, proved so successful that eventually, in 1853, the government made it compulsory for all babies to be vaccinated against smallpox. As a result, there was a huge fall in the death rate due to smallpox. In addition to this, Florence Nightingale campaigned to improve hospital hygiene, and helped to raise standards of nursing by setting up a professional nurse training school in 1860.

Over to You

1 Write a sentence or two to explain the following words:
   a sepsis
   b pasteurisation
   c sterilise
   d vaccination.

2 a Explain how Jenner, Pasteur, Lister and Nightingale improved people's health. Make sure you include key words like 'germs', 'vaccination' and 'antiseptic'.

   b Was one of these people more important than the others or were they equally important? Give reasons for your answer.

3 Look at **Source A** on page 228 and **Source E** below.

   a Draw two spider diagrams, one describing the main features of an operation in the late 1700s and the other describing the main features in 1900.

   b Compare the two diagrams and write a paragraph explaining how operations changed between the late 1700s and 1900.

▼ **SOURCE E** An operation from around 1900. Look for all the different ways in which this surgeon tries to keep a cleaner operating room.

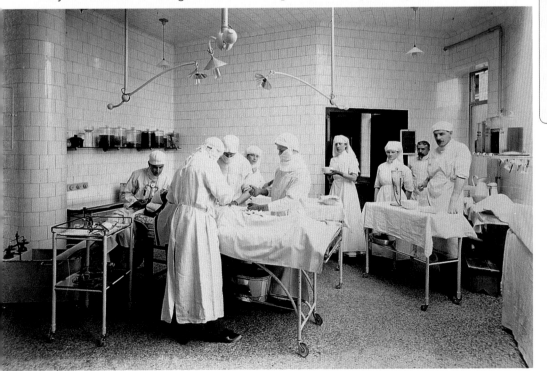

Significance

1 Define 'antiseptic'.
2 Explain the significance of antiseptics in the development of surgery in the nineteenth century.

12.5A How did people have fun during Victorian times?

Where did you spend your holidays this year? Did you stay at home? Go to the seaside? What activities did you do in your free time? Now imagine you live in Victorian times. Do you have any leisure time? If so, what activities do you do? Are they completely different from today's activities?

Objectives

- Identify at least five ways in which people spent their leisure time (or free time) in the 1800s.
- Explain why the amount of leisure time increased in this period.

Spare time

The idea of families being able to 'go on holiday' is quite a new one. In 1800, few ordinary people had holidays. Sunday was most people's only day off, so the majority rested after they had been to church. Workers were given a day off for religious festivals (Christmas Day, Easter Sunday and so on) but these 'holy days' only amounted to a few days each year.

By the mid-1800s, things had started to change because new laws were making an impact. The Factory Act of 1833, for example, banned children under nine from working in factories, and limited children aged nine to thirteen from working more than nine hours. Other laws stopped women or children under ten working in mines, and limited them to ten-hour days. Many factories found that without women and children, they could not keep open – so the men got time off too. As a result of these shorter working hours, people found themselves at home earlier in the evenings, and off work on Saturday afternoons. All of a sudden, ordinary workers had enough leisure time to enjoy new sports and other pastimes, or even go away for short holidays to the seaside.

In 1871, Parliament introduced bank holidays, giving most workers a few more days off throughout the year on the days when banks and offices closed. Many people found themselves asking a question that they had never asked before: 'What am I going to do with my leisure time?'

Let's go to the theatre

There were no televisions, cinemas, internet streaming channels or games consoles to keep people amused and provide entertainment. Richer people would go to large, elegant, expensive concert halls or theatres to watch classical music concerts, operas and plays.

For poorer people, there were music halls, which were cheaper than trips to the opera or theatre. A music hall was a large building where the audience would pay to see a wide variety of acts including singers, comedians, acrobats and magicians. The audience sang along with songs they recognised and shouted rude comments at performers they didn't like.

▼ SOURCE A An audience and actors at what was sometimes called a 'penny gaff' around 1870, a music hall to which the admission was a penny.

By 1880, there were over 500 music halls in Britain and some performers became the superstar celebrities of their day. Singer Marie Lloyd, for example, was mobbed when she appeared in public. She is most famous for singing 'My Old Man (Said Follow the Van)' and 'A Little of What You Fancy Does You Good'. Travelling circuses were also popular at this time, and Britain was visited by some of the most famous circuses of all time from America, including the Barnum & Bailey Circus, which attracted audiences of around 10,000 per show.

Melodramas were also popular among ordinary people. Melodramas were plays with highly dramatic plots and lots of songs. Like pantomimes, which were also popular at the time, the audience were encouraged to boo and hiss at the villain and cheer for the hero.

Shall we go to the pub?

When ordinary workers had any time off work, many of them went to their local pub and drank heavily, in much the same way as they did in medieval, Tudor, Stuart and Georgian times. In London, one house in every 77 was a pub and in parts of Newcastle there was one pub for every 22 families. As you can imagine, pubs were lively places where people would sing, chat with friends or play games such as dominoes or cards.

Meanwhile...

As well as having more free time, many people began to have spare money to spend on treats. Chocolate was a very popular treat – first as drinking chocolate from 1824, and then as solid bars of chocolate from 1847. In 1879, the world-famous Bourneville chocolate factory, owned by the Cadbury brothers, opened in Birmingham.

Over to You

1 a Explain the following terms:
   * music hall
   * melodrama.

  b Describe the different types of entertainment enjoyed by rich and poor at this time.

2 a What is 'leisure time'?

  b Why did the amount of leisure time enjoyed by many people start to increase in the 1800s?

▼ **SOURCE B** An illustration of the inside of a pub, from a series of eight illustrations titled *The Drunkard's Children* (1848) by George Cruickshank. Note the small child drinking too, which was legal at the time.

New crazes

Photography, reading comic books, cycling, cross-stitching (a type of embroidery), roller skating, having a 'shampoo' and head massage in a bath house, and listening to musicians in a bandstand at the local park were all popular in the 1800s. Reading books became more common too, as more people learned to read at school and at home. Novels by authors such as Charles Dickens (who wrote *Oliver Twist*), Jane Austen (*Pride and Prejudice*), Robert Louis Stevenson (*Treasure Island*), Lewis Carroll (*Alice's Adventures in Wonderland*) and Mary Shelley (*Frankenstein*) sold thousands of copies.

▼ **SOURCE C** A copy of one of the most famous novels of all time, George Eliot's *Middlemarch* (1871–1872). George Eliot was, in fact, an Englishwoman called Marian Evans. She used a man's name because she felt people would take her books more seriously. At this time, there was a belief that women rarely wrote 'serious' novels, only light-hearted romance novels.

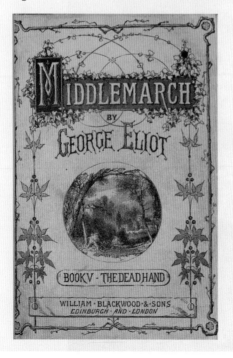

New sports

For hundreds of years, people had been playing many of the sports we play today, but without any proper rules. And there were different versions of the same game in different parts of Britain. But with more leisure time, and with trains able to take players and spectators around the country, the sports had to become more organised. Players formed organisations to create standard rules and set up leagues and competitions. And soon watching sports was as popular as playing them.

Football Association (FA) formed 1863. The first women's international game between Scotland and England took place in 1881 – just seven years after the first men's football international (also between Scotland and England).

FA Cup began 1871.

First official County Championship for cricket 1890.

Captain Webb swims English Channel 1875 – huge boost to swimming.

Rover Safety cycle invented 1885 – great boost to cycling.

Snooker invented by British Army officers in 1875.

Lawn Tennis invented 1873. First Wimbledon 1877.

Amateur Athletic Association founded 1880.

Football League set up 1888.

Rugby Football Union set up 1871.

Rules for golf established 1888. The Ladies' Golf Union (association for women's golf) was founded in St Andrews, Scotland, 1893.

Blood sports

Blood sports are activities that involve hunting for animals, wounding or killing them, or betting on fighting animals. Many blood sports had been popular for centuries but some began to die out in the 1800s. The RSPCA was set up in 1824, and bear baiting and cockfighting had both been banned by 1849.

A day at the seaside

The growth of the railways meant that ordinary people were able to travel away from home. They would save up all year so they could go to coastal towns like Blackpool, Brighton, Southend or Margate. Hotels, amusement arcades, piers and promenades were built to entertain the thousands of 'day trippers' who travelled to these seaside towns in search of fun.

▼ **SOURCE D** Ramsgate beach in July 1887. Can you see the following?
  - the pier
  - the Punch and Judy show – a puppet show performed in a small booth with the audience sitting outside
  - the ice-cream seller
  - the seafront hotels
  - the 'bathing booths' (portable changing rooms that swimmers wheeled into the sea)
  - the railway station, which brought visitors right up to the sea front.

Leisure time for the wealthy

During the late seventeenth century up to the Victorian period, it was common for the children of rich families to spend six months or more doing a 'Grand Tour' of Europe after they left school. As well as a way of spending leisure time, the tours were also a way for an upper-class young adult to finish off their education by seeing arts and culture across Europe.

In the late 1800s, other new leisure trends for the wealthy included the rise of health resorts and the development of skiing. Many health and ski resorts were set up in the Alps, a mountain range that covers parts of France, Austria, Germany, Italy and Switzerland. Fresh mountain air was seen as good for a person's health.

Over to You

1 Describe the different types of entertainment enjoyed by rich and poor at this time.

2 a What are 'blood sports'?
  b Why do you think some of these 'sports' gradually began to disappear?

3 Look at **Source D**.
  a Write a short description of this scene.
  b In what ways was Ramsgate beach in 1887 different from a typical British beach today?

Change and continuity

1 Make a list of what you enjoy doing in your spare time.
2 Explain two ways in which how people spend their spare time today is different from how people spent their spare time in the 1800s.
3 Compare how people spend their leisure time today with how they spent their leisure time in the 1800s. Describe two similarities and two differences.

The high street

By 1901, about 80 per cent of the population lived in towns or cities… and they all needed a place to shop! It wasn't long before 'high-street shopping' became common. The painting below is of Eastgate Street in Chester in the late 1800s. It is a great example of what a Victorian city high street would have looked like. The labels below this painting will help you to understand what's going on.

Objectives

- Understand what a typical Victorian high street might have looked like.
- Examine where some of our most famous high-street shops began.

▼ **SOURCE A** Painting by Louise Rayner of a high street in Chester around 1892. Rayner lived in Chester for several years and painted many of the city's streets. Look out for the following:

1 Pavements: From the mid-1800s, many high-street pavements were improved. By 1860, the first street cleaners had been employed.

2 Tramlines: Horse-drawn tramcars ran on fixed rails along the cobblestone streets. By 1890, electric trams replaced the horse-drawn ones. By 1901, motor cars had been invented, but they were only for the very rich because they were so expensive.

3 Street traders: As well as the shops, people could buy from street traders who carried goods around on their backs or sold them from carts. Can you see the street traders?

4 Shops: All sorts of goods could be bought in town and city centres. What sort of shops and goods can you see for sale?

5 Street lights: An 1835 law set up a system of town councils that used local taxes to fund improvements to street lighting, as well as roads, water supply and sewage systems.

6 Rich and poor: A wide variety of people visited the high street. Can you see the upper-class men having a chat? What about the poor children (one looking bored; the other staring through a shop window)?

New high-street shops

Up until the 1800s, goods were mainly sold in separate shops. You'd go to one shop for your shoes (the shoe shop), another for a hat (the hat shop), another for a coat (the coat shop) and so on. But by the middle of the century, a few shops began to grow into what we now call department stores, selling many different types of goods under one roof. Some, like John Lewis, still exist today.

The 1800s saw the birth of many of our familiar high-street shops. WHSmith (in London in 1828), Boots (Nottingham, 1849), Sainsbury's (London, 1869), and Marks and Spencer (Leeds, 1884) all started trading at this time.

▼ **SOURCE B** An early Sainsbury's store, c.1900. When the original Sainsbury's store first opened in 1869, the shop only sold three items: milk, eggs and butter.

Meanwhile... 1880

By 1880, the invention of refrigeration meant that meat could be shipped from Australia and New Zealand without going mouldy. 'Fridges' inside shops meant that meat, milk and fish could be stored easily.

New ideas on the high street

In 1844, 28 workers from Rochdale, Lancashire, each saved up to buy a stock of food and open a shop of their own. Workers sold their goods at fair prices and shared the profits out among their customers. Their co-operation with each other gave its name to their first shop – The Co-operative. Today, 'Co-ops' exist all around the country.

Fact ✓

In 1875, the Sale of Food and Drugs Act allowed local councils to check the quality of food. The first inspectors found devious tricks of the trade being used to fool customers (like mixing river water with milk or putting sawdust into flour!). Gradually, food quality improved.

Earlier on... 1400s

In Istanbul, a large shopping area called the Grand Bazaar was built in the 1400s. Today, it is one of the world's largest covered shopping centres, and has more than 58 streets and 4,000 shops.

Over to You

1 List some of the well-known shops that appeared in Victorian high streets in the 1800s.

2 How did The Co-operative chain of stores get its name?

3 a How did the 1875 Sale of Food and Drugs Act make things safer for customers?

  b How did the invention of refrigeration help:
  • shop owners?
  • customers?

4 Prepare an information panel for the gallery in which Louise Rayner's painting hangs. The panel, which will be displayed next to the painting, should:
  • start with a basic description
  • explain what the painting tells the viewer about life in Victorian Britain – use details from the scene to help you
  • explain why it is important to look after and preserve paintings like this.

Source Analysis

1 How useful is **Source A** to a historian studying Victorian town centres?

In 2009, the Bank of England released a new £2 coin. The Queen was on one side and on the reverse was a picture of a man named Charles Darwin... and he was facing a chimpanzee! Darwin also appeared on a £10 note between 2000 and 2018. So who is he, and why is he facing a chimpanzee? And why are his achievements still remembered today?

Objectives

- Describe Darwin's theory of **evolution**.
- Examine why Darwin's theory caused so much controversy.

Charles Darwin was born in 1809, the son of a doctor from Shrewsbury. At this time, most people in Britain were Christian Protestants – they believed that God had created all living things at the same time – and all these creatures, including humans, had been the same for all time, and that's how they would stay. This is known as the 'creation story', which is described in the Bible. When Darwin was growing up, very few people would disagree with this. But in 1859, he published a book that gave a different explanation, which shocked the world.

▼ **SOURCE A** The Darwin £2 coin, and part of the £10 note that featured his face.

1 In 1831, Darwin got a job as a scientist on board a research ship named HMS *Beagle*. The crew's mission was to travel the world to find out about far-off lands.

Darwin collected all sorts of plants, animals, insects and rocks. The voyage took him all around the world.

2 In 1835, the ship arrived at a small group of islands called the Galapagos Islands in the Pacific Ocean.

3 While there, Darwin noticed that some birds, cut off from each other on different islands, were identical... apart from their beaks!

ISLAND A   ISLAND B

This got Darwin thinking.

4 Darwin investigated the islands more and looked at the food the different-looking birds were eating.

Darwin thought that the type of beak the bird had depended on the food available on their island. So the bird that had only seeds available developed a big, strong beak for cracking seeds... and the bird on another island developed a long curved beak for reaching into cactus flowers.

5 Darwin arrived home after nearly five years at sea. He spent the next few years thinking about the bird beaks, and then wrote a book.

In 1859, Darwin's *On the Origin of Species* was published. In it, he proposed a new theory about how life develops. He suggested that all living things had evolved (kept changing ever so slightly) over millions and millions of years, and only those best suited to their environments survived and reproduced (had offspring).

6 To use giraffes as an example, Darwin said that Giraffe B, which can reach tall trees, will be more likely to survive than Giraffe A, which will starve and die.

Can't reach leaves... dies out

Eats & lives to reproduce

Giraffe B would survive because it can feed itself and reproduce. It would probably mate with another tall giraffe (who had also survived), so their baby giraffe would have a long neck too... and over millions of years, all giraffes would have long necks!

7 Darwin's theory shocked the world.

According to Darwin, animals had not been created at the beginning of time in the way that people had always thought. They were changing (or evolving) all the time!

8 Darwin's next book caused even more controversy.

In 1871, Darwin published *The Descent of Man*. In it, he claimed that man evolved gradually from apes over millions of years.

Key Words

evolution   fossil   naturalist

▼ **SOURCE B** A portrait of Mary Anning by B. J. M. Donne, painted a few years after her death in 1847.

Controversy and acceptance

The Descent of Man suggested that humans weren't created by God – they were actually just advanced apes. Up to this point, God was the only explanation for human existence. Darwin had come up with a new theory – one that explained human existence through science.

Darwin's theories are still controversial, and many people completely disagree with him. But his ideas are now widely accepted, and taught in Science classes all over the world today.

When Darwin died in 1882 he was buried in Westminster Abbey alongside great minds such as Isaac Newton and Charles Dickens. And on the 200th anniversary of his birth his image was put onto a £2 coin – next to an ape!

Challenges to old ways of thinking

Other Victorian scientists and **naturalists** brought new ideas to the public at this time – and revolutionised the way some people thought about their place in the history of the world:

- Mary Anning was a famous **fossil** hunter. In the early 1800s, she identified many prehistoric fossils from the time of the dinosaurs. Some scientists argue that fossils recovered by Anning may have contributed to Darwin's theories.

- Richard Owen was another fossil hunter who is credited with first using the word 'dinosaur' (which means 'terrible lizard' in Greek). He campaigned for a museum to house objects from the natural world – resulting in the creation of the now world-famous Natural History Museum in London in 1881.

Significance

1 Explain the significance of Charles Darwin and his theory of evolution for changing how people thought about the human race and its place in the world.

Over to You

1 a Why do you think Darwin's theories were so controversial at the time?

  b Suggest reasons why they are still controversial today.

2 Why do you think Darwin was chosen to go on a £10 note and a £2 coin?

3 Who was Mary Anning?

4 In what ways do you think Mary Anning and Richard Owen changed the way some people felt about the human race and its place in the history of the world?

Between 1845 and 1849, a famine struck the people of Ireland, which was then ruled by Britain. Around one million people starved to death, and a similar number chose to leave Ireland to start a new life in America. But what caused this famine, and how did the government respond? How do people today view this tragedy?

Objectives

- Outline the causes of the Great Hunger.
- Judge whether the British government did enough to help.

The British in Ireland

In 1840, more than eight million people lived in Ireland. Over half were poor peasants who rented tiny farms from landowners. A large number of these landowners were English, from families that had taken the land from the Irish many years before. Now the Irish had to rent land that had once belonged to them! Most of these peasants lived on nothing but the potatoes they grew in their fields. They couldn't even afford bread.

Since 1801, Britain had ruled Ireland from London. The British Parliament made all the decisions relating to Ireland, yet British laws meant that Catholics couldn't vote. As most of the Irish peasants were Catholics, this gave them no say in the running of their country.

Fact ✓

Although Ireland had long been under English control, the Act of Union in 1801 formally united Great Britain (England, Wales and Scotland) with Ireland, creating the United Kingdom of Great Britain and Ireland.

Famine

In September 1845, a disease called **blight** started to destroy the potato crop. Millions were left without their main source of food. The same thing happened over the next few years. By 1849, nearly a million people had died of starvation. Another million left Ireland altogether for a new life in America.

As you can imagine, the Great Hunger, as this famine was known, is a significant event in Irish history. Some people believe that the British government acted terribly and didn't do anything to help. Others say that the British government did a bit to help, but not enough. Some have even argued that the British deliberately left the Irish people to starve. What do you think? Read through the following evidence.

▼ **INTERPRETATION A** Part of Tony Blair's statement, in which he apologised for the Great Hunger on behalf of the British government, while visiting Ireland in June 1997. Blair was the British Prime Minister at the time.

'One million people died in what was then part of the richest and most powerful nation in the world. This still causes pain today. Those who governed in London at the time failed their people through standing by while a crop failure turned into a massive human tragedy...'

▼ **INTERPRETATION B** Written by historian Duncan Gunn in *The Little Book of British History* (1999).

'One of the greatest natural disasters to strike the Western World in modern times, the potato famine that hit Ireland... resulted in more than one million deaths and the forced migration of a million more. Its effects would not have been a tenth as bad if the British Government of the time had made the slightest effort to relieve the starvation.'

▼ **SOURCE C** Written by a British government official in 1847. The man was actually in charge of the Famine Relief Association.

'It is my opinion that too much has been done for the Irish people. Under such treatment the people have grown worse instead of better... it is not the job of Government to give people food.'

▼ **INTERPRETATION D** Adapted from text written by historian Bea Stimpson in *The World of Empire, Industry and Trade* (2000).

'The British prime minister, Robert Peel, ordered Indian corn to be bought and handed out to the starving Irish. He started public work schemes so that poor labourers could earn money. He started public works programmes but the schemes couldn't cope with the numbers, so were abandoned.'

▼ **INTERPRETATION E** Written by historian Andrew Langley in *Victorian Britain* (1994).

'The British Government was slow to give help. Worse still, it gave no protection to peasant farmers who were too poor to pay rents on their land. Many were evicted [thrown out] from their homes by the landowners, most of whom lived in England.'

▼ **INTERPRETATION F** Adapted from a speech made by John Connor, an Irish politician, talking in the Irish Parliament during a debate on the 150th anniversary of the famine in 1995.

'I do not think the English Government tried to kill the Irish. There were famines in England at this time and the Government ignored them too, and left the people to die. This is what they were like in those days. They thought it was not the Government's job to feed people.'

Ireland and Home Rule

After the famine, many Irish people felt that the British government hadn't done enough to help. Some Irish politicians started the **Home Rule Movement**, a campaign for Ireland to have its own parliament in Dublin, while still remaining part of the UK. This idea became popular in Ireland, where many wanted to be free of British rule. One British Prime Minister, William Gladstone, supported this movement and twice tried to get Parliament to agree to Irish Home Rule. However, both times the politicians in London voted against it, and a united Ireland remained part of the UK until 1922.

Key Words   blight   Home Rule Movement

▼ **SOURCE G** An 1848 illustration of an Irish family being evicted from their home for not paying their rent.

Over to You

1 Define the 'Great Hunger'.

2 What was the impact of the famine? Write down the sources and interpretations that help you with your answer.

3 a Choose a source or interpretation that is critical of the British government. Explain the way it criticises the British government.

   b Choose a source or interpretation that supports the British government. Explain the way it supports the British government.

4 Hold a class debate. Your debate should focus on two areas:
   • Did the British deliberately leave the Irish people to starve?
   • Was Tony Blair right to apologise for the famine?
   Your teacher will help you to organise and structure your preparation and discussions.

Interpretation Analysis

1 Study **Interpretations B** and **D**. They give different views on the government's role in the famine. What is the main difference between the views?

This book covers the years 1558 to 1901 – when some amazing and lasting changes took place. By 1901, most people were healthier, more likely to live in towns and cities, and more educated than anyone could have imagined in 1558. Shops contained goods from all over the world, transported in trains and steamships. This section highlights some of the key changes and innovations that took place during this time.

Objectives

- Examine the extent to which Britain changed between 1558 and 1901 in key areas such as population, politics and science.

The relationship between the monarch and Parliament

1558 Monarch (Queen Elizabeth) in control, but takes advice from Parliament, which gets taxes for the monarch

1901 There is still a monarch (Queen Victoria died that year; King Edward VII took over) – but Parliament creates the laws and controls the country

How many people?

1558 England = 3.5 million. Ireland, Scotland and Wales made up a further 1.5 million of Britain's overall population. Total = 5 million

1901 England and Wales = 32.5 million, Scotland = 4.5 million, Ireland = 4.3 million. The British Empire contained around a further 400 million people

How did people communicate?

1558 Mainly word of mouth – printed books were available, but still quite expensive.

1901 Printed books and newspapers were widely available. The telephone had been invented (1876) but this new method of communication had not caught on yet.

Society

1558 Monarch and the ruling classes (such as landowners) were very powerful – and made all the laws. Peasants were still very poor, but the feudal system of the Middle Ages had disappeared

1901 The country was still very divided between rich (and the better-off middle classes) and poor. Approximately two in three men now had the vote – but no women could vote

How united was the United Kingdom?

1558 Two monarchs, one for England, one for Scotland. The English monarch controlled Wales and large parts of Ireland too

1901 One monarch, one Parliament for England, Scotland, Wales and Ireland. The Act of Union in 1707 united Scotland, England and Wales, and a further one in 1801 officially included Ireland, creating the 'United Kingdom of Great Britain and Ireland'

Who lived where?

1558 Nine out of ten people lived and worked in the countryside, mainly in farming. London's population was about 100,000, and Manchester's was about 4000

1901 Around eight out of ten people now lived in towns and cities. Factories were a common sight. London's population was about 6.5 million, and Manchester's was about 540,000

How big was the British Empire?

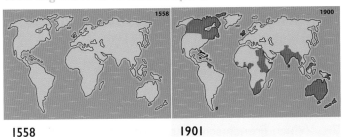

1558   1901

How did people get around?

1558 Richer men and women travelled by horse and carriage, while the poor walked

1901 Travel was much faster. The train was a common mode of transport. Roads were better too – and motor cars had been invented, but they were only for the very rich because they were so expensive

Popular entertainment

1558 Hunting still very popular for the rich. Blood sports and mob football were popular for the poor, as was drinking at the local tavern

1901 The rich still went hunting, and to concerts or fancy parties. Poorer people went to pubs or music halls. Some also took short holidays at the seaside. Some blood sports were banned, while other sports like football and golf became more organised

Eating and drinking

1558 Beer, wine, cheese, meat, bread, vegetables, salad, tobacco. Knives and spoons used. New foods brought back from the Crusades and by explorers were becoming more common – such as lemons, melons, apricots, sugar, syrup and spices like nutmeg and cinnamon

1901 All the same foods were available – but frozen meat and fish, a wider variety of fruit from newly explored places, and tinned and packet food had been introduced

Law and order

1558 Trial by jury introduced. Older, savage forms of punishment still used. Torture commonly used to get confessions. No police force

1901 A professional police force now existed and the death penalty used only for very serious crimes. Prisons had been reformed

Education

1558 Most children did not go to school. Education was not compulsory

1901 School was compulsory for all 5–12-year-olds

Science and medicine

1558 More understanding of Earth's place in the universe than ever before. Better knowledge of the human body due to more accurate drawings, but no knowledge that germs caused disease. Life expectancy was around 35 years. Treatment of wounds improved, but operations were still very dangerous

1901 Knowledge that germs caused disease. Inventions such as vaccinations, antiseptics and anaesthetics meant that life expectancy was around 50 years, but no antibiotics yet

Over to You

Alice   Robert

1 Imagine Alice lived in Britain in 1558, and Robert lived in 1901.

   a List five changes that took place that would make Alice and Robert have different experiences of life in Britain.

   b Of all the changes that took place for them, which do you think was the most important? Give reasons for your choice. See if other people in the class agree with you.

Change and continuity

1 Copy one of the sentences below that best describes Britain in 1901:
   • Britain had changed completely between 1558 and 1901.
   • Britain had changed a lot by 1901 but some things had not changed.
   • Britain had not changed much at all between 1558 and 1901.

2 Explain why you have made your choice.

3 Write a clear and organised summary that analyses how Britain changed between 1558 and 1901.

Quick Knowledge Quiz

Choose the correct answer from the three options:

1 What were workers in the north who went into factories and smashed up new machinery in the early 1800s known as?

   a Luddites
   b Chartists
   c Swing Rioters

2 Which of the following was **not** a Chartist demand?

   a Every man of 21 years of age or over should be allowed to vote
   b Voting should be done in secret
   c Education should be free for all

3 Who became the first woman in Britain to qualify as a doctor?

   a Dorothea Beale
   b Elizabeth Garrett Anderson
   c Caroline Norton

4 The workers in which factory famously went on strike over pay and working conditions in 1888?

   a the Cadbury factory
   b the Bryant & May factory
   c Watt and Boulton's Soho Foundry

5 What was the name of a type of school run by a local woman in her front room, where a child might learn to count and say the alphabet for a small fee?

   a ragged school
   b dame school
   c grammar school

6 Which anaesthetic became popular after Queen Victoria used it in 1853 as a painkiller while giving birth to her son?

   a ether
   b nitrous oxide
   c chloroform

7 Which French scientist demonstrated that germs could cause disease, in an idea called 'Germ Theory'?

   a Robert Liston
   b Louis Pasteur
   c Edward Jenner

8 Popular among poorer people in Victorian Britain, what type of entertainment showed a variety of acts including singers, comedians, acrobats and magicians?

   a cinema
   b opera
   c music hall

9 Which famous high street supermarket began in Rochdale in 1844?

   a Sainsbury's
   b The Co-op
   c Asda

10 Who, in 1859, wrote *On the Origin of Species*, a book that proposed a new theory about how life develops?

   a James Simpson
   b Florence Nightingale
   c Charles Darwin

 **Literacy Focus**

Reading for meaning

When you read historical sources or interpretations, you have to carefully extract the meaning from what you are reading. The task below asks you to read three different accounts of one event – see if you can work out what actually happened on 16 August 1819 at St Peter's Field in Manchester. Read pages 218–219 to recap the events of that day.

▼ **INTERPRETATION A** Adapted from an 1841 book by Samuel Bamford, who helped to arrange the meeting. He was found guilty of 'assembling with unlawful banners at an unlawful meeting for the purpose of inciting discontent'.,

'I saw the cavalry come, swords in hand. They dashed forward and began cutting the people. "Stand steady," I said, "they are riding upon us." The cavalry could not get through the mass of human beings; and their swords were used to cut a way through held-up hands and defenceless heads. "Shame!" was shouted, then "Break! Break! They are killing them in front, and they cannot get away."

On the breaking of the crowd the cavalry dashed whenever there was an opening, pressing and wounding. Women and youths were randomly cut down or trampled.

In ten minutes the field was almost deserted. The dead remained where they had fallen.'

▼ **SOURCE B** Adapted from William Hulton, a magistrate who ordered the soldiers to move into the crowds, describing his actions at the 1820 trial of Henry Hunt (one of the reformers who led the meeting).

'The number of persons assembled was estimated at 50,000; the meeting did undoubtedly inspire terror. Many gentlemen stated to me they were greatly alarmed and my opinion was that the town was in great danger. The cavalry waved their swords and advanced slowly. I saw none of the cavalry galloping. The space which the cavalry made in their approach was immediately filled up by the people, I think for the purpose of cutting them off. The impression made on my mind was that the people were going to injure the cavalry. I saw bricks and stones flying at the cavalry and I saw them attacked. I told Colonel L'Estrange [leading the troops] to clear the crowd. Many of the people did not move and it was only when the cavalry rode against them that they took flight.'

▼ **INTERPRETATION C** Adapted from Lieutenant Jolliffe, one of the leading soldiers, who was interviewed about the events. His account appeared in an 1847 book by George Pellow.

'The cavalry were trapped in by the mob and powerless either to make an impression or to escape. They were entirely at the mercy of the people, on all sides, pressed upon and surrounded. It only required a glance to discover their helpless position.

The soldiers drove the people forward with the flats of their swords, but sometimes the edge was used. I think it is down to the compassion of the soldiers, when you consider the size of the crowd, that more wounds were not inflicted; beyond all doubt most injuries were caused by the pressure of the hostile crowd.'

1 Read the source and interpretations carefully – note who the writers are.

2 Make brief notes on each account. What do the writers say happened?

3 Which two accounts seem to agree with each other?

4 Make a list of the differences between the two that agree and the other one.

5 Suggest reasons why the accounts disagree.

6 Does the fact that two of the accounts agree mean that they are right?

During any period in history, there are usually things that are changing and things that are staying the same (known as 'continuities'). Sometimes there can be dramatic changes in one area of life, but very little change in another.

Historians sometimes don't agree with each other about which areas of life experienced the biggest changes in a historical period. However, whatever your opinion might be, it is important to try to argue your point in a structured and detailed way, and back up your views with evidence and facts!

> **TIP:** For example, if you were an ordinary worker in Tudor times, then your working life would most likely be spent in the countryside, working on a farm. But by the end of the Victorian era, most ordinary workers were employed in factories in the large towns and cities that had grown up around Britain – this is a dramatic change for many people in this historical period!

Responding to questions about change

One way of thinking about a question on change is:

1 **Plan:** Study the question. Do you agree or disagree with it? What do you know about that area of change in this period of history? Also, make some notes about *other* changes in this period. There will likely be different areas of changes, but some may be bigger (made more impact on people, or affected more people) than others. You could make a mind-map to help you.

2 **Judge:** Once you have thought about the different changes, you need to decide: which do you think was the largest or most important change? List in bullet points the reasons for your choice.

3 **Answer:** Remember to focus on the question asked. So, after steps 1 and 2, decide how far you agree with the statement given in the question.

> **TIP:** Do you strongly agree with it? Do you not agree with the statement at all? Or do you only slightly agree? There is no right answer for this, it is all down to what you think!

4 **Explain and conclude:** You now need to add details and reasons to support your decision and explain why you are taking this view. Use your plan to help you add detail. Try to refer to other areas of change when answering this question.

> **TIP:** You will need to use examples in your answer. Don't simply say 'The population grew' – why not say 'the population of Britain changed greatly. It went from around 3.5 million in Tudor times to over 40 million by 1901 – and the British Empire contained around a further 400 million people.'

> **TIP:** To explain your judgement and your reasons, you can use phrases like:
> * This was a change because...
> * This had not been seen before...
> * This can be seen in both periods through...

Now that you have reached the end of this book, you can consider the changes in the period you have been studying – from 1558 (the Tudor period) to 1901 (the Victorian period).

Assessment: Change

Your challenge is to answer this question:

> How far do you agree that science and medicine saw the largest change between 1558 and 1901 in Britain? Give reasons for your answer.　　　　　　　　　　　　　　(20)

The steps and sentence starters below show you one way to structure an answer to this question.

1　Plan: Study the question. Do you agree with the statement? What do you know about science and medicine in this period?

There may be other areas of change in this period that are important too. Create a mind-map and add details to it to help you.

2　Judge: Look at your mind-map. Which of the changes do you think was the *most* important? List in bullet points why you think one area of change was more important than the others.

3　Answer: Now that you've made your judgement, **answer the question directly.** Remember that the question asks you *how far* you agree with it.

> I... that science and medicine saw the largest change between 1558 and 1901 in Britain...

4　Explain and conclude: Finally, add some **details and reasons** to support *why* you think what you think. Try to refer to other areas of change.

> In the Tudor period, science and medicine was...
>
> By the end of the Victorian period...
>
> So, the key changes in science and medicine were...　　　　(5)

> There were other changes that were important too. Another area of change was...　　　　　　　　　　　　　　　　　(5)

> Yet another area of change was ...　　　　　　　　　　　(5)

> In conclusion, I (strongly agree/agree to a certain extent/disagree) that science and medicine experienced the largest change between 1558 and 1901, because...　　　　　　　　　　　　　　　　　(5)

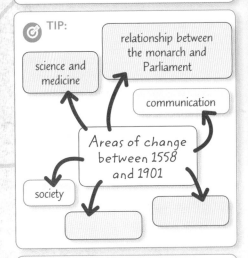

TIP: Look at the diagram on pages 242–243, and at pages 8–9 which outlines what the country was like in 1558. There are also sections that focus on science and medicine – for example, pages 152–155 and 228–231.

TIP:

- relationship between the monarch and Parliament
- science and medicine
- communication
- *Areas of change between 1558 and 1901*
- society

TIP: Remember, you are being asked to judge whether science and medicine changed more than any other areas – so make sure you compare it with other changes.

TIP: You could pick one of the phrases below that fits best with your judgement:

strongly agree...

don't agree very much...

agree to a certain extent...

TIP: Don't just write what changed – try to explain the *impact* of the change too. For example, if you write that very little was known about the human body in 1558, but by 1901 there was a greater understanding of the human body and how to prevent certain illnesses and infection, you should explain *how* this affected science and medicine.

TIP: Remember to conclude your answer. Explain *how far* you agree.

Glossary

abdicate to give up power

abolish to bring to an end; for example, the slave trade

Act official law that should be followed

Act of Settlement an Act passed by Parliament stating that after Queen Anne's death the throne would pass to the nearest Protestant heir

Act of Union an Act passed by Parliament to unite England, Scotland and Wales under the control of one Parliament, based in London

ally a group on the same side as another in battle

American Indian any member of any of the first groups of people to live in North or South America, before the Europeans arrived; most commonly used in the USA

anaesthetic a drug or gas that is given to someone before an operation to stop them feeling pain

antiseptic a substance that is applied to the skin to reduce the possibility of infection

anti-slavery against the idea of slavery

apprentice someone who is learning a trade or craft

architect a designer of buildings

armada a fleet of warships

artillery large guns, such as cannons, used in warfare on land

auction a public sale in which goods are sold to the person who offers the highest price

back-to-back housing rows of houses built very close together without room for a garden

bankrupt when a person (or business) does not have enough money to pay their debts

baroque a style of art and architecture which came from Italy in the late sixteenth century – baroque buildings usually have central towers or domes and are highly decorated, often using dramatic lighting or colour

beacon fire set in a high place as a warning or signal

belladonna a chemical used by Tudor women to make their eyes shine and sparkle

bid an offer (of a certain price) for something

Bill of Mortality a weekly list of the causes of death in a particular place

Bill of Rights the agreements made between William and Mary and Parliament in 1689

birch a bundle of twigs tied together and used to hit children as a punishment; a cane was a single piece of wood

blight a type of disease that infects and destroys crops, for example potatoes

blood sport a sport that involves the wounding or killing of animals

Board of Health a group set up in some towns to investigate how the disease cholera spread and how it could be prevented

Bow Street Runners the forerunners of the police force; a group of men who were paid to capture as many criminals as possible

branded permanently marked, using a hot metal instrument to burn the skin; used to show who owned slaves

British Empire the collection of countries and colonies (areas) that Britain ruled over; at its height, Britain ruled over 50 colonies around the world

bubonic plague a type of plague that causes huge, round boils or 'buboes'; carried by fleas

canal a long, narrow, man-made channel of water

canting a secretive street language used by sturdy beggars

capital crime a crime for which the punishment is execution

cast iron iron that has been heated into a liquid and placed in a mould to make a shape

cause the reason why something happens

Cavalier nickname for a soldier who fought for the king during the English Civil War

cavalry soldiers on horseback

Chartist member of a campaign group of ordinary working people who wanted to bring about changes to the voting system; they issued the 'People's Charter' in 1838

chloroform a strong smelling liquid used as an anaesthetic when the fumes are inhaled

cholera a deadly disease caused by a germ that lives in contaminated water

citizen a person who lives in a town; in Tudor times this referred to a wealthy town person

civil war a war between two groups of people in the same country

class a group of people with roughly the same economic or social status

cochineal a red dye or colouring obtained from insects

colony an area of land controlled by another country

con artist a person who cheats or tricks someone by gaining their trust and persuading them to believe something that is untrue

consequence the impact or results of something that has happened

constable a man in charge of a group of watchmen

constipation a health condition in which the sufferer has difficulty going to the toilet, usually because of hardened faeces

constitution the set of political ideas, laws, rules and principles by which a country is governed, especially in relation to the rights of the people it governs

constitutional monarchy a form of monarchy in which the king or queen rules in accordance with a set of rules and laws

contaminate to make something impure by infecting it with an unclean or dangerous substance

crescent a curved, moon-like shape

cudgels a game for two people; each person has a heavy stick and they take it in turns to hit each other; the person left standing is the winner

dame school a basic school run by women, often in the front room of their house; students paid a few pennies to attend

death warrant a piece of paper ordering someone's execution

Declaration of the Rights of Man a list made during the French Revolution that stated 'rights' that every man should have

deformed part of the body that does not have the expected shape

Divine Right of Kings the belief that kings and queens could do as they wished because they were appointed by God

domestic system the system where people worked in their homes or small workshops rather than in factories

economist an expert in economics: the study of how money is made and used, and how businesses run

empire a collection of communities, regions or areas of land (or whole countries) that are ruled over and controlled by one leading or 'mother' country

Enlightenment also known as the 'Age of Reason', the period during the 1600s and 1700s when people began to explore the world more and make new discoveries

enquiry an investigation or an interesting historical question that you are studying

enslaved made a slave

entrepreneur a business person who takes risks, often with their own money, in order to make a profit

epidemic rapid spread of a disease

ether a colourless liquid that was used as an anaesthetic when the fumes were inhaled

evidence facts or information about a particular event, person or place that historians use to help them understand the past; this could be written evidence

evolution the way in which living things change and develop over millions of years

excommunicate to officially exclude someone from the Christian Church

execution the process of killing or beheading an enemy or convicted criminal

exiled expelled from your home country

extremist a person with very strict views or a supporter of extreme measures (often political or religious); extreme measures are considered by most people to be unreasonable and unacceptable

factory system the system where people worked in factories to produce goods in large numbers; replaced the domestic system

faeces human waste and animal waste

familiar a 'demon' or creature, in the form of an animal, that accompanies a witch

fossil the remains or impression of a prehistoric plant or animal embedded in rock

found to start something up, such as a school or business

French Revolution a period of rebellion in France, starting in 1789, whereby poor French people rebelled against the king and his rich followers

galleon a large warship

gallery a place to sit in a theatre

gallows a wooden frame used for hanging criminals

gentleman a man of wealth and influence in society, a landowner

grammar school a school that taught mainly Latin and Greek grammar

guillotine a machine with a blade, used to cut off a person's head

Home Rule Movement an organisation or group that campaigns for greater (or complete) independence from the ruling 'mother country'

hornbook a flat, double-sided paddle, shaped like a table-tennis bat; used to help students read and write

House of Correction criminals and people who refused to work were sent here; they were forced to make things that were later sold

independence existing separately from other people or things; an independent nation is not controlled by another country

indigenous people the first people to live in a land

Industrial Revolution a dramatic change in the way things were made; a time when factories replaced farming as the main form of business in Britain; sometimes used to describe the changes in population, transport, cities and so on in the period between around 1750 and 1900

industry the work and methods involved in making things in factories

infantry soldiers on foot

infer to work something out from the evidence given to you, that isn't actually said or shown. Inference means 'reading between the lines' of a source and working out what a source is suggesting or making you think

interpretation historical evidence created much later than the period studied, produced by people with a particular opinion about an event in the past

Interregnum the period from the execution of Charles I in 1649 to when Charles II became king; when Oliver Cromwell ruled as Lord Protector

iron ore the raw material (rock or earth) from which iron can be obtained

Justice of the Peace someone who investigated crime, gathered information and held trials; sometimes called a 'magistrate'

labourer a person who does manual work such as working in the fields

locomotive a steam engine that moved wheels along a set of rails or track – often called 'trains'

Lord Protector the title of the head of state in England between 1653 and 1659, a position first held by Oliver Cromwell

Major-General a man appointed by Oliver Cromwell to run one of the 11 districts in England

malaria a disease spread by mosquitoes

martyr a person who is killed because of their religious or other beliefs

mechanised done by machine

melodrama a musical play with a very dramatic plot and exaggerated emotions

merchant a person whose job is to buy and sell goods in order to make a profit

Metropolitan Police a force of mainly ex-soldiers and men, set up in 1829, to enforce law and order on the streets of London

miasma name given to what people thought was an 'infectious mist' given off by rotting animals, rubbish and human waste; many believed it caused illness and disease

mine a system of holes in the ground where substances such as coal, metal and salt are extracted

miner a worker who digs coal and other materials out of the ground

music hall a venue that puts on a wide variety of entertainment acts; cheaper to visit than a theatre

musket a type of long gun

musketeer a soldier who carried a musket

mutiny the act of refusing to follow the orders of a person in authority

naturalist a person who studies plants and animals

New Model Army the army established during the Civil War by the Parliamentarians

Parliament controls the country and is made up of the monarch, the House of Lords and the House of Commons

Parliamentarian a supporter of Parliament during the English Civil War

pasteurisation heating of food and drink, for example milk, to kill germs

pauper someone with no job who relies on charity

pauper apprentice orphan who worked in a factory in return for food and a bed

petition a document signed by a large number of people asking for some action from the government or another authority

pike a long pole, tipped with a steel spike, used as a weapon

pikeman a soldier who used a pike

pirates a person who attacks and robs ships at sea

pistol a small hand-held gun

pit the standing area nearest the stage in a theatre

plague an infectious deadly disease

plantation a huge farm that grows cotton, sugar, tobacco and so on; a plantation owner normally used slaves to do the work

playwright someone who writes plays

plot a plan, usually made in secret, by a group of people to do something illegal or harmful

Poor Law a law passed in 1601 that placed paupers into four categories; each group was treated differently

population the number of people in a particular town, area or country

privateers a person allowed by a government to attack and steal from ships at sea

protest an event organised by people who would like to officially state their unhappiness about a particular issue, usually against the government; protests can be peaceful, but can also become violent

public ordinary people in general, rather than a particular group of people

public health the general state of health and cleanliness of the whole population

Puritan a strict Protestant who believed in simple church services and lifestyles; Puritans protested against the practices of the Catholic Church

quack a person pretending to have medical knowledge or cures

quill pen a pen made from a feather; dipped in ink to write

racist a person who believes that some races of people are better than others and treats people unfairly because of this

ragged school a charity school that was free to attend for very poor children

raw material natural substance such as coal, iron, ore, gold, oil, clay and so on

recusant a Catholic who refused to accept the authority of the Church of England

reformer a person who campaigns for change

regicide the official word for killing a king or queen, or for someone who kills a king or queen

Reign of Terror a time in the 1790s, after the French Revolution, when many of those who had opposed the French Revolution were executed

Religious Settlement a course of action followed by Elizabeth in order to keep the peace between Catholics and Protestants

Renaissance a rebirth in learning that began around 1400

republic a country without a king or a queen

Restoration the return of a monarch to the throne of England when Charles II became king in 1660

revolution a revolution can be a complete change in the way a country is ruled (this is a political revolution), but it can also mean a different kind of change, for example an important change in the way that people do things

riot an occasion when a large number of people behave in a noisy and violent way in public, often as a protest

Roundhead nickname for Parliament's soldiers during the English Civil War

routine an established pattern of behaviour that people follow most of the time

Royalist a supporter of the king during the English Civil War

sash coloured strip of cloth used to identify soldiers in battle

scapegoat a person who is blamed for wrongdoings or mistakes

scramble a method of buying slaves; a price is agreed before the buyers rush into a cage to grab the 'best' slave they can

Sepoy an Indian soldier serving British authorities

sepsis a serious, sometimes deadly, bacterial infection of the blood

sewage human and animal waste

sewer a drain to remove waste water and other rubbish

shin-hacking a game for two people; each person wears their heaviest boots, they take it in turns to kick each other, and the person left standing is the winner

ship tax a sum of money, introduced by Charles I, paid by people who were living by the sea

significance something (like an individual, event or development) that makes an impact at the time and continues to make an impact many years later; historians are often asked to judge the significance of something

slave trade the capturing, selling and buying of slaves

social pyramid a name given to the structure of society; the richest people are at the very top of the pyramid, with the working class at the very bottom

source historical evidence from the period studied, usually created by someone who was directly involved with an event or an eyewitness to an event; sources provide information historians need to create interpretations

steam engine an engine that uses steam as a means of power

sterilise to clean an object so that it is free from any germs

strike when workers stop doing their work for a period of time, usually in order to try to get better pay or conditions

strolling players travelling actors, musicians and entertainers

sturdy beggar a criminal who used clever tricks to get money

suburb an area of a town or city away from the centre

surgery the treatment of injuries or diseases by cutting open the body and removing or repairing the damaged part

tabloid a newspaper or magazine that has small pages, short articles and lots of photographs; it often focuses on sensational crime stories, gossip, famous people and sports

terrace a row of houses

toll a small fee, paid to use a bridge or road

trade union an organisation of workers in a trade, group of trades or profession, formed to protect their rights and working conditions

traitor a person who betrays someone or something

transportation a punishment; guilty criminals could be sent to a faraway land for a number of years; it also means taking someone or something from one place to another

treason the crime of betraying your country, especially by attempting to kill the monarch or remove the government

trial by jury where a group of people listen to evidence and decide whether someone is innocent or guilty of a crime

tuberculosis (TB) a deadly lung infection

turnpike road a stretch of road run by a group of businesspeople who improved and maintained the road and charged people to use it

typhoid a deadly disease caused by a germ that lives in contaminated water or food

vaccination the administration (usually by injection) of a substance to help the immune system develop protection from a disease

vagabond a wanderer or tramp

viceroy someone who rules in another country or colony on behalf of the monarch

watchman man who patrolled the streets at night

Whitsun the seventh Sunday after Easter, also called Pentecost

wrought iron iron that has been heated up and hammered into shape; more flexible than cast iron

yeoman in Tudor times, a farmer who owned or rented land; most were relatively wealthy although some were quite poor

Index

OXFORD
UNIVERSITY PRESS

Great Clarendon Street, Oxford, OX2 6DP, United Kingdom

Oxford University Press is a department of the University of Oxford.

It furthers the University's objective of excellence in research, scholarship, and education by publishing worldwide. Oxford is a registered trade mark of Oxford University Press in the UK and in certain other countries

British Library Cataloguing in Publication Data
Data available

978-0-19-849465-2
10 9 8 7

Paper used in the production of this book is a natural, recyclable product made from wood grown in sustainable forests.

The manufacturing process conforms to the environmental regulations of the country of origin.

Printed in Great Britain by Bell and Bain Ltd. Glasgow.

Acknowledgements

We are grateful for permission to reprint from the following copyright texts:

Clement Atlee: speech from Hansard is © Parliamentary copyright and is used under the Open Parliament Licence v3.0; **J F Aylett:** *In Search of History 1714–1900* (Hodder & Stoughton, 1985), copyright © J F Aylett 1985, and *The Suffragettes and After* (Hodder & Stoughton, 1987), copyright © J F Aylett 1987, reprinted by permission of Hodder Education; **BBC:** BBC Bitesize revision guide, 'Attitudes on Empire', reprinted by permission of the BBC; **Peter Beech:** 'Much ado about nothing much', *theguardian.com*, 14 Apr 2009, copyright © Guardian News and Media Ltd 2009, reprinted by permission of GNM Ltd; **Brunel 200:** on Brunel from www.brunel200.com, 2006, reprinted by permission of the Bristol Brunel 200 project; **Michael Bush:** letter to the Guardian in 'A fitting memorial to the Peterloo massacre', *theguardian.com*, 15 Aug 2007, copyright © Guardian News and Media Ltd 2007, reprinted by permission of GNM Ltd; **G C:** 'The Economist explains – Why the first world war wasn't really', *The Economist*, 2 Jul 2014, copyright © 2014, reprinted by permission of The Economist Group Ltd via Copyright Clearance Center, Inc; **Susan Doran:** *Elizabeth I and her Circle* (OUP, 2015), reprinted by permission of Oxford University Press via PLSclear; **Stephen Ember:** 'The Making of a nation – American history', Voice of America, 2012, from www.learningenglish.voanews.com, reprinted by permission of VOA News; **Niall Ferguson:** 'Why we ruled the world', 1 May 2003, www.niallferguson.com/journalism, reprinted by permission of the author; **Bob Fowke:** *Who? What? When? Victorians* (Hodder Childrens' Books, 2003), reprinted by permission of Hodder Children's Books, an imprint of Hachette Children's Group, London; **Walter Holland and Susie Stewart:** 'Public Health: The Vision and the Challenge', 1 Oct 1998, www.nuffieldtrust.org.uk, reprinted by permission of Nuffield Trust; **Ike Ijeh:** 'How the Great Fire shaped modern London', *Building*, 6 Sept 2016, reprinted by permission of the author and Building, Assemble Media Group. **Terry McEwen:** on Ada Lovelace, www.historic-uk.com, reprinted by permission of Historic UK; **Eric McLamb:** 'The Ecological Impact of the Industrial Revolution', syndicated by *Environment News Service (ENS)*, 2 Apr 2018, copyright © Ecology Prime Media Inc, 2018, reprinted by permission of the author and Environment News Service; **Mary Murtagh:** 'Story of Britain's past is written in stone', *Liverpool Echo*, 14 Aug 2007, reprinted by permission of The Liverpool Echo/Reach plc; **John H Lienhard:** No 587 on Alexander Graham Bell from *Engines of our Ingenuity*, at www.uh.edu, reprinted by permission of the author; **Jan Morris:** *Pax Britannica* (Faber, 1968), copyright © James Morris 1968, reprinted by permission of United Agents (www.unitedagents.co.uk) on behalf of the author; **Royal Society of Chemistry:** 'Celebrating the legacy of Michael Faraday', from www.rsc.org/news-events/ articles/2016/sep/michael-faraday, reprinted by permission of The Royal Society of Chemistry; **Fiona Shaw:** on *Greatest Britons: William Shakespeare*, BBC, Nov 2002, reprinted by permission of Fiona Shaw via Independent Talent, and of the BBC; **David L Smith:** post on the Cromwell Association website at www.olivercromwell.org, reprinted by permission of the author; **Shashi Tharoor:** '"But what about the railways...?" The Myth of Britain's Gifts to India', *theguardian.com*, 8 Mar 2017, copyright © Guardian News and Media Ltd 2017, reprinted by permission of GNM Ltd.

The Oxford Impact Framework is a systematic approach to evaluating the impact of Oxford University Press products and services. It was developed through a unique collaboration with the National Foundation for Educational Research (NFER) and is supported by the Oxford University Department of Education.

OXFORD IMPACT FRAMEWORK
EVALUATING EDUCATIONAL PRODUCTS AND SERVICES FROM OXFORD UNIVERSITY PRESS

CREATED WITH  Evidence for Excellence in Education   SUPPORTED BY  Department of Education University of Oxford

The publishers would like to thank the following for permissions to use their photographs:

Cover: Matthew Hollings

Artworks: Martin Sanders, Moreno Chiacchiera, Rudolf Farkas, QBS Learning

Photos: p11, p26: GL Archive/Alamy Stock Photo; **p13:** with kind permisison from Harvingston Hall; **p15:** Pictorial Press Ltd/Alamy Stock Photo; **p16:** Stan Pritchard/Alamy Stock Photo; **p20:** English explorer and adventurer Sir Humphrey Gilbert cutting the first sod of Newfoundland, claiming the land for England, 1583 (colour litho), English School, (20th century)/Private Collection/© Look and Learn/Bridgeman Images; **p22 (BL)** Heritage Image Partnership Ltd/Alamy Stock Photo; **p23 (B):** IanDagnall Computing/Alamy Stock Photo; **p23 (T):** Niday Picture Library/Alamy Stock Library; **p22 (TL):** Pictorial Press Ltd/Alamy; **p22 (R), p28:** ClassicStock / Alamy Stock Photo; **p31 (M):** ©Charles Drake/Wikpedia; **p31 (B):** Peter Jordan_NE/Alamy Stock Photo; **p30:** George Brice/Alamy Stock Photo; **p31 (T):** Albert Knapp/Alamy Stock Photo; **p32 (B):** North Wind Picture Archives/Alamy Stock Photo; **p32 (TR):** The Print Collector/Alamy Stock Photo; **p32 (TL):** Portrait Elizabeth Vernon, Countess of Southampton (oil on panel), English School, (16th century) Boughton House, Northamptonshire, UK/The Buccleuch Collections/Bridgeman Images; **p32 (M):** The Print Collector/Alamy Stock Photo; **p33:** The Picture Art Collection/Alamy Stock Photo; **p37:** Chronicle/Alamy Photo Library; **p38:** Timewatch Images/Alamy Stock Photo; **p39:** Portrait of William Shakespeare (1564–1616) c.1610 (oil on canvas), Taylor, John (d.1651) (attr. to)/National Portrait Gallery, London, UK/Bridgeman Images; **p45:** Bridgeman Images/TopFoto; **p54:** Mary Evans Picture Library; **p56:** Lebrecht Music & Arts/Alamy Stock Photo; **p57, p69:** FALKENSTEINFOTO/Alamy Stock Photo; **p59:** Pictorial Press Ltd/Alamy Stock Photo; **p58:** Look and Learn/Robert Embleton; **p60:** Mary Evans Picture Library; **p61 (L):** Granger Historical Picture Archive/Alamy Stock Photo; **p61 (R):** Chronicle/Alamy Stock Photo; **p65:** Daboost/Shutterstock; **p70:** Chronicle/Alamy Stock Photo; **p81:** Granger Historical Picture Archive/Alamy Stock Photo; **p82:** Niday Picture LibraryAlamy Picture Library; **p83:** Everett – Art/Shutterstock; **p84:** PhotoEdit / Alamy Stock Photo; **p87:** National Archives; **p92:** Coronation Procession of Charles II to Westminster from the Tower of London, 22nd April 1661, 1662 (oil on canvas), Stoop, Dirck (c.1614–c.83)/Museum of London, UK/Bridgeman Images; **p93:** Mary Evans Picture Library; **p94:** GL Archive / Alamy Stock Photo; **p96:** Heritage Image Partnership Ltd / Alamy Stock Photo; **p101 (L):** Heritage Image Partnership Ltd / Alamy Stock Photo; **p101 (R):** OUP DAM/Ratikova/Shutterstock; **p106:** © The British Library Board/BRIDGEMAN ART LIBRARY; **p109:** GL Archive/Alamy Stock Photo; **p110:** eye35.pix; **p111:** Artokoloro Quint Lox Limited/Alamy Stock Photo; **p112:** Lebrecht Music & Arts/Alamy Stock Photo; **p113:** ACTIVE MUSEUM/Alamy Stock Photo; **p115:** World History Archive/Alamy Stock Photo; **p128:** ImagesEurope/Alamy Stock Photo; **p129:** North Wind Picture Archives/Alamy Stock Photo; **p132:** Chronicle/Alamy Stock Photo; **p135:** James Barrett/Alamy Stock Photo; **p138:** Malcolm Haines/Alamy Stock Photo; **p139 (T):** Michael Seleznev/Alamy Stock Photo; **p139 (B):** Chris Dorney/Alamy Stock Photo; **p140 (T):** Alamy Stock Photo; **p140 (B):** The Royal Mint; p141 (T): Alamy Stock Photo; **p141 (B):** The Granger Collection/Alamy Stock Photo; **p145 (T):** Chronicle/Alamy Stock Photo; **p145 (B):** World History Archive/Alamy Stock Photo; **p148:** Chronicle/Alamy Stock Photo; **p152:** Pictorial Press Ltd/Alamy Stock Photo; **p153:** Hulton Deutsch/Getty Images; **p154:** Pictorial Press Ltd/Alamy Stock Photo; **p155 (T):** Otto Herschan Collection/Getty Images; **p155 (B):** Colport/Alamy Stock Photo; **p159:** The Idle 'Prentice Executed at Tyburn, plate XI of 'Industry and Idleness', illustration from 'Hogarth Restored: The Whole Works of the celebrated William Hogarth, re-engraved by Thomas Cook', pub. 1812 (hand-coloured engraving), Hogarth, William (1697–1764)/Private Collection/The Stapleton Collection/Bridgeman Images; **p161:** Chronicle/Alamy Stock Photo; **p163:** Ben Molyneux/Alamy Stock Photo; **p165:** Lordprice Collection/Alamy Stock Photo; **p166:** Historical Images Archive/Alamy Stock Photo; **p171:** Art Directors & TRIP/Alamy Stock Photo; **p172:** Everett Collection Historical/Alamy Stock Photo; **p174:** Lebrecht Music & Arts/Alamy Stock Photo; **p175:** Mr Standfast/Alamy Stock Photo; **p176:** incamerastock/Alamy Stock